D0176476

ANGELS IN OUR LIVES

Everything You've Always Wanted to Know
About Angels and How They Affect Your Life

by
Marie Chapian

© Copyright 2006 – Marie Chapian

All rights reserved. This book is protected by the copyright laws of the United States of America. This book may not be copied or reprinted for commercial gain or profit. The use of short quotations or occasional page copying for personal or group study is permitted and encouraged. Permission will be granted upon request. Unless otherwise identified, Scripture quotations are from the New King James Version. Copyright © 1982 by Thomas Nelson, Inc. Used by permission. All rights reserved. Scripture quotations marked AMP are taken from the Amplified Bible, Copyright © 1987 by the Zondervan Corporation and The Lockman Foundation. All rights reserved. All emphasis within Scripture is the Author's own. Please note that Destiny Image's publishing style capitalizes certain pronouns in Scripture that refer to the Father, Son, and Holy Spirit, and may differ from some publishers' styles. Take note that the name satan and related names are not capitalized. We choose not to acknowledge him, even to the point of violating grammatical rules.

Destiny Image® Publishers, Inc.
P.O. Box 310
Shippensburg, PA 17257-0310

"Speaking to the Purposes of God for this Generation
and for the Generations to Come."

For Worldwide Distribution, Printed in the U.S.A.

ISBN 10: 0-7684-2370-8
ISBN 13: 978-0-7684-2370-9

This book and all other Destiny Image, Revival Press, MercyPlace, Fresh Bread, Destiny Image Fiction, and Treasure House books are available at Christian bookstores and distributors worldwide.

4 5 6 7 8 9 10 11 / 09 08 07

For a U.S. bookstore nearest you, call
1-800-722-6774.

For more information on foreign distributors, call
717-532-3040.

Or reach us on the Internet:
www.destinyimage.com

CONTENTS

For Sam

ENDORSEMENTS

My attention was fully captured as I read Marie Chapian's book, *Angels in Our Lives*. Yours will be too. Her refreshing writing style and the obvious revelation she carries on the subject draws your heart to question, to explore and to embrace these wonderful Kingdom realities. Read...and then expect...angels in your life!

—Patricia King
Author, *Light Belongs in the Darkness*
Founder, Extreme Prophetic

Marie Chapian's *Angels in Our Lives* is a powerful book that will challenge you to pursue a deeper, faith-filled relationship with the living God. Through her inspiring personal accounts with angels and her extensive knowledge of the Word, her book catapults faith in the supernatural and gives deep insight into the realities of the heavenly realm.

—Ché Ahn
Senior Pastor
Harvest Rock Church

INTRODUCTION

ANGELS were at God's side cheering and praising Him at the creation of the world. Angels were there when Adam fled the Garden, when Noah built the ark, when Moses walked into the court of Pharaoh and demanded that he should let God's people go. Angels have seen every birth, every marriage, and every death. They know all about cult religions and tribal battles. There isn't a fight or a bloody dispute they haven't seen. Angels are at christenings, baptisms, deathbeds, treaty signings, and wars. They are our heavenly co-workers and friends who serve the Lord day and night, century upon century, eon upon eon. Over 5,000 years old, they've seen it all. They never tire and they never give up. They are our guides, protectors, Heaven's news reporters, and our friends.

When I talk about angels, I discover the majority of people have the impression that angels are creatures on the order of invisible elves who are going about performing miracles whenever they feel like it. Angels are credited for everything from finding a good parking space and a five-dollar bill in the weeds to saving a child from drowning. We also hear of these invisible beings in reports of near-death experiences when they appear as winged creatures in shining white robes.

Much speculation has been made about the world of the supernatural, and particularly about angels, but today the Lord is preparing us for a time when much more will be required of us than our human theories and conjectures. In order to know the created world, both visible and invisible, we must know the Creator of those worlds. The Bible tells us that we must not focus our attention on the things which are seen but on the things which are not seen, because the things which are seen are temporary but the things which are not seen are eternal. (See 2 Corinthians 4:18.) God wants the eyes of our spirit to be open to see beyond the natural realm into the realm of *His* Spirit. He wants us to see the ministry of angels and to cooperate with what they're doing on the earth today. He wants us to partner with His heavenly host in bringing His will to pass on the earth and in Heaven.

Our guide is the Word of God, which saves us from speculation. Grounded on what God Himself tells us about Himself and His heavenly host, the Bible gives us solid footing for our journey. God is reaching out to us, and He is eager to bless us every mile of the way. Supernatural wonders are taking place, and His Holy Spirit is being unleashed around the globe in a fresh, new wave of power and glory. God is calling us to partake of and participate in all He is doing today.

"I am a fellow servant of yours," the angel told John on the Isle of Patmos. In other words, the angel said, "I am here to co-labor with you and with your brothers and sisters, the prophets, and all those who do the words of this book." The is time for us to join forces with Heaven's host and learn of God as He presents Himself in His Word.

I know you want more of God. You want supernatural manifestations of the love and splendor of God in your personal life, your family, your work, and your ministry. You want it all. I write this book to encourage you to take this miracle path God is opening up before you. As you read, you'll follow a Scripture path to understand the nature and acts of angels and the heavenly host. I'll share some very humble experiences of my own and some inspiring experiences of others who live in the dimension of the supernatural. I pray that your heart and mind will open up to a revelatory understanding of the angelic realm and of its Captain and Master, the Lord Jesus Christ. I know you want Heaven to open in your life. Please allow this little book to help expose this to you by showing you the way.

PROLOGUE

IN the Presence of the Lord we find ourselves wordless. We're overcome. A magnitude of incomprehensible beauty surrounds us as all
portals of Heaven resound with a brightness that reverberates with the
magnificence of:

Perfect love.

Perfect peace.

Perfect beauty.

Perfect perfection.

Perfect ecstasy.

Glory is now a word that speaks of mystery, for in God's Presence
we're groaning with the bliss of seeing the unknowable, of caressing the
breath of the unutterable.

"Jesus?" we whisper. "Jesus?"

"Here am I."

We're shocked silly at the sound of His voice. We feel ourselves disintegrate in the radiance of such a sound. His eyes are explosions rip-
ping into our faces. Our heads become small torches. Our bodies jerk,
stunned, singed by fire. We cower, we shiver, and we want to cry for
help. But to whom do we cry?

Our ears have turned to trumpets.

Our hands to lighted cities.

Our feet to ships lost at sea.
"Did you not call?"

I am certain my ears will snap off my head. I don't know if I'm standing or hanging in the air. Angels cry out in voices of thunder.

I am on my knees now. Every unconfessed sin I've committed flies before my nose like a flock of black crows. I'm emptying out fast. I'm dying of spirit-hunger.

Is the glory of God killing me?
In His Presence is fullness of joy, say the Scriptures.
(See Psalm 16:11.)
But...
In the cities of our darkness we once cried into the palms of our hands, "Where are you, God?"
We cried and cried.

And now He answers. Not with death, but with life, with a pledge and seal to keep us forever in the fire of His eye, as angels cover sky and earth.

I shrink beneath the canopy of their eyes.
He answers!
He answers, and opening the heavens to us, calls out,
"Enter!"
The angels, shining in His light, reach out their hands for ours.
God calls once more and I have found my eternity.
"Enter."

chapter 1

LISTEN

A hundred million angels accompany me as I journey through the years of my life. It's a distinctive joy to the angels when each of God's children follows their urging to visit the heavenly realm in our human state. There, in the heavenly realm, *I meet with and walk with* the Lord Jesus. I experience the glory and purpose of God, the Father, beyond my finite understanding.

Christians pray for heavenly visitations; we pray for miracles, deliverance, healings, signs, and wonders—and will God answer our prayers? We know from His Word that He wants to answer our prayers. Is there a catch? A secret? When our prayers are to a god (with a small g) whom we can understand and control, a god (or genie) we can order around to do our bidding and bring to fruition all our hopes and dreams, we are continually disappointed. Confronted face- to-face with the power of the living God, we discover that He answers only that which glorifies Him.

God must be glorified. Period. My life must glorify Him. Period.

How can I glorify Him if I don't know Him? God longs for us to *know Him.* Knowing Him, I cannot help but love Him. When I enter His Presence, I enter the very essence of His nature; I enter His heart's nucleus of perfected love. In His Presence, encased in so unspeakable a privilege, my spirit takes wing to join His Holy Spirit and in a miraculous fusion, I become one with the love that calls His own to abide in that marvelous place forever.

God wants us to love His Presence.

I think of the biblical account of the Israelites in the wilderness who couldn't tolerate the Presence of God when He came to them in His glory on Mount Sinai. (See Exodus 20:18-19.) The Israelites cried out in terror to Moses, "No! You speak with us, and we will hear; but let not God speak with us directly, lest we die!"

The Presence of God nearly did them in. But why did the Presence nearly do them in? Why not Moses? Why could Moses bask in the Presence of God and not be fried to a crisp? Why is it that Moses could talk with God directly as a *friend*? What was the secret?

I believe the answer is that Moses *loved* the Presence of God. He *welcomed* God's Presence, he *lived* for His Presence. God wants us to love His Presence, and He wants us to ache for, live for, adore, and passionately love His presence.

Think of it. Moses was a man totally uninitiated in the ways of the living God, Yahweh, who spoke to him first from a burning bush. In spite of his lack of knowing the living God, Moses *listened*. I wonder how many other people God had spoken to who wouldn't listen—or, rather, couldn't hear?

Maybe the soulish mind of reason impeded these people's spiritual ability to hear God's voice. ("But a bush can't speak. I must be dreaming."—"Water from a rock? Ha!"—"Manna from heaven? Never."—"God can talk to *me* face to face, personally? That's ridiculous.") Think of the countless ways we halt the hand of God from touching or moving us upward in levels of faith that supersede reason and decorum. What keeps us from levels of faith so dynamic that nothing of this earth can diminish, tarnish, or discourage us again?

Our angels, God's special messenger agents, are at our side ready to usher us into deeper revelation, wisdom, and experience, as well as to help us to gain understanding and power in the Holy Spirit. The Lord has so much more to tell us, to show us. He has so much more for us to learn and experience, and for us to give and *be*. *God loves to give.*

The supernatural realm of God's giving heart is waiting for us to enter. Study Scripture and you will see that what is called holy on earth always refers to a *divine relationship*. His heart is open for us to enter. He wants to become one with us. When we are fused into His heart, His love utterly saturates us. We are no longer tugging along in life on our own. We are no longer fussing about what's what and how-to and what-for on our own. We're *transformed*. Call it being born again. We're saved from ourselves and our tiny, pinched picture of the Big Picture. In Christ Jesus:

> At last I find my real self.
> At last I find my real intelligence.
> At last I find my real talents.
> At last I find my real beauty.
> At last I live my holy destiny.

What God calls holy on earth has purpose and destiny that begin with His will and my obedience. The fragrance of His holiness carries me through every pitfall and hardship because I know Him and live in Him. And still, there is more. I am but a babe in the school of the Holy Spirit.

The messenger angels we read of in the Bible arrive with the words, "Be not afraid…" and, as I enter into the Presence of God with my soul and spirit yielded to Him, His Holy Spirit fills me and I, unafraid, am ready, hungry, and willing to receive all He has for me.

chapter 2

WHO ARE THE ANGELS?

T HE universe throbs with life. The cosmos is brimming with legions (myriads) of angelic beings of various ranks and species. The God of the universe who wants me to know Him and love His Presence, has created a universe teeming with life both seen and unseen. Before He allows me to be ushered into visions, insights, and revelations of the invisible, He wants me to pursue His Presence above all else.

In the past many of us may have pursued His blessings more than Him. We may have wanted the *benefits* and blessings He lavishes on us more than the ecstasy of simply knowing Him. We may have wanted wisdom above Him, but in particular, and I say this with tears, we wanted *power*. Power, as we wrongly believed, to make His name known and bring Him glory.

Here's the thing: God wants to take us to a higher place beyond ourselves and our *limited* vision of life and the world and what we think of as power. He wants us to know His power as never before. *His power is His Presence*.

First, love Him.

Introducing the Invisible

God loves to show you His heart and mind. *"For by Him all things were created that are in heaven and that are on earth, visible and invisible, whether thrones or dominions or principalities or powers. All things were created through Him and for Him"* (Col. 1:16). And He is not keeping secrets from you. He loves it when you hunger for Him and you hunger to know Him.

He is taking us into the heavenly realm where our spirit is built up, our inner person is strengthened, our mind is rejuvenated, and our heart is made new.

The information you'll gain from reading this book can be stored in your mind merely as good Bible information with some biblically-based experiences in the angelic realm, *or* you can receive into your spirit an illumination of His Spirit to catapult you toward a more magnificent relationship with your Savior. I pray you'll choose the latter.

The Bible explains that God formed His creation on two levels: physical and spiritual. All energy, power, and life in the physical world emanate from the invisible spiritual world as its source. Without God's sustaining power the atoms would rip apart and our universe would go up in smoke. Poof!

> ...[God] *has appointed* [Jesus] *heir of all things, through whom also He made the worlds; who being the brightness of His glory and the express image of His person,* **and upholding all things** *by the word of His power...* (Heb. 1:1-4).

The physical world is but a part of God's creation. We must remember that the invisible portion of God's creation is actually more permanent and real than the physical world because the material world has no lasting attributes. Here on earth a tree grows, a tree blooms, a tree dies. Here on earth cities are built and thrive as great centers of power, such as ancient Rome or Athens or Babylon, and in time their power is destroyed. Poof! Our life spans on earth are short.

We were created for eternity. We were created to love God and partner with our angels and all of Heaven to live in the beauty of His Presence here as well as in eternity.

Angels are referred to over 300 times in the Bible. These references are found in at least 34 books, from Genesis to Revelation. Angels were present when God created the world. God asks Job, *"Where were you when I laid the foundations of the earth? ...To what were its foundations fastened? Or who laid its cornerstone, when the morning stars sang* *together and **all the sons of God** [bene elohim: the angels] **shouted for joy?**"* (Job 38:4-7).

The angels are created beings belonging essentially to the invisible realm. In order to see the angelic host and walk with them, we must see and walk *in the spirit.*

Thrones, dominions, principalities, and powers refer to the categories of angels whom Christ rules over. This hierarchy among spirit beings was established before He created the world. We can be assured and comforted in the knowledge that Christ is Ruler over His holy angels as well as the fallen angels. He has immeasurable superiority over every created thing in the universe. *All things were created through Him and for Him.* This means we can trust God, really trust Him! No demon in hell has more power than God. The truth is that satan himself is under the holy thumb of God.

ANGEL DEFINITION

Here's one definition I like: "An angel is the name given in the Bible to those super beings whose home is heaven and who function as the unseen agents in the carrying out of the will of God."[1] God's angels are supernatural, celestial beings of *pure* spirit, superior to humans in power, goodness, beauty, intelligence, and abilities, and they serve God in countless ways by doing His bidding and His bidding only. Angels are messengers and attendant spirits, perfectly obedient to God. They exist solely to do His will, which includes the care and protection of humans as God directs. When an angel keeps that rock from falling on your sweet head or when he turns your car out of the way of an oncoming 18-wheeler, it's because your Savior told him to do so.

Angels are called "holy ones" in the Book of Daniel:

I saw in the visions of my head while on my bed, and there was a watcher, a holy one, coming down from heaven…(Daniel 4:13).

WHAT DO ANGELS LOOK LIKE?

Angels could be standing right next to you this minute! Hebrews 13:2 makes the point that angels can be moving in our midst, looking like regular people and we don't even know it! *"Do not forget to entertain strangers, for by so doing some have unwittingly entertained angels"* (Heb. 13:2). They are invisible until the Lord permits them to reveal themselves, and then, *wow!* There they are. When the angels in Genesis 19 arrived in the city of Sodom, the people thought they were simply ordinary men. They looked like regular guys.

What do angels look like? They take on many appearances—God is incredibly creative. Angels can be the blaze of a crackling brush fire or the flame of a slim wax candle; angels can be the wind rattling against the windows or the gust of a winter storm; angels can be flashes of dancing color, a snake in the apple tree, or the stranger next to you on the train.

Angels can be quite frightening, and we know this because most of the time when angels appeared to humans in the Bible they began their dialogue with, "Don't be afraid." Take the brave Daniel for example. Here was a man who was afraid of nothing. He didn't give two hoots if he was tortured for praying to the true and living God; he went right ahead and prayed. He was intimate with God. He was faithful. He was in love with God's Presence. What happened to him as a result of this relationship with God? He was thrown into a stinky den of desperate wild beasts. Imagine. There you are, loving God and living your life as a good person, and you're thrown to the lions for it. Daniel spent an entire night in a pit with starving lions, and we don't read that he had an ounce of fear in him.

But then *later*—what happens when an *angel* appears to him? How does he react when he sees an angel? One look at the angel and he *faints dead away!* He describes his experience: *"I had no strength left, my face turned deathly pale and I was helpless"* (Dan. 10:8 NIV).

Imagine Michael, God's glorious archangel, appearing to you in person. What would you do? Would you just roll over and drop dead?

Would you gasp, "Hold it!" and run for your Bible to find a scriptural precedence for such an unusual occurrence? How did other people in the Bible react to the presence of angels? Read the accounts of the appearances of angels to humans in the Bible. (See Angel References section of the book for Scripture passages.) How many of these people were immediately thrilled and delighted to be confronted by an angel? *Not one.* Not one person cheered, "An angel of God! Yippee! Pull up a chair! To think God, my Savior, sent you!" No, each one of them cowered in horror and/or disbelief and/or argued with them. "Naw, this can't be real," they told themselves.

Take Sarah, Abraham's wife. Sarah burst out laughing at the words of the angel who told her she would bear a child. (See Genesis 21:6.)

And Mary *protested*, "Who me? Bear a child? Physically speaking, that's impossible!" (See Luke 1:34.)

Zacharias *argued* with the angel, and so his voice was taken away from him until his son, John the Baptist, was born. (See Luke 1:20.)

Jacob actually got down and wrestled with the angel and the fight concluded with a permanent injury, a dislocated hip, rendering Jacob with a limp for the rest of his life. (See Genesis 32:24.)

Lot had no idea he was acting as a host to angels until their words of warning not to look back came true. Lot's wife didn't listen and did as she pleased; as a result of looking back, she turned into a pillar of salt during the sulphur shower that rained down from the heavens. (See Genesis 19:26.)

Paul was knocked silly when Jesus appeared to Him on the Damascus road. Paul was nearly fried to a sizzle in the Lord's Presence. Blinded and dazed out of his mind, he stumbled on to Damascus. The Lord Jesus Himself appeared to Paul, and we can see by this miracle how our bodies react in the presence of holiness, and how the Presence, the nearness of God, acts as an alarm to every cell of our being and changes the very atmosphere in which we stand. (See Acts 3:3-9.)

The Lord is calling us to develop spiritually, to be conformed to His image, to *walk in the Spirit.* (See Galatians 5:16.) As Paul learned to live in the Spirit, he was visited many times by the Lord; he worked signs and wonders, and was taken up in the spirit to the third heaven. His mind, body, soul, and spirit became *accustomed* to God's Presence.

WHERE ARE ANGELS TODAY?

The answer is *everywhere*. *"The earth is the Lord's and all its fullness, the world and those who dwell therein"* Psalm 24:1 tells us. If the earth, its fullness, and the whole world are God's property and possession, then all that is in the earth is hovered over by the Spirit of God.

Let's take this further. If everything is the Lord's, then everything on earth is known by Him. His Spirit hovers over all things—rocks, trees, plants, all things within the entire God-glorifying, visible universe are touched by the invisible Spirit of God. Jesus said, *"I will never leave you, nor forsake you,"* (Heb. 13:5), and no entity is ever by itself on this earth. His angels, who do His bidding, are dispatched to every parcel of land, every kernel of dirt, every drop of dew, every morsel of matter, and us. Why? *Because the earth is the Lord's.*

The angelic host fills the heavens and they love and live in God's Presence 24/7. They love as God loves. They love us because God loves us. *"For God so loved the world..."* (John 3:16). We are the collective "whosoever" of this verse. We possess the promise that God doesn't want one of us to perish without Him. (See Matthew 18:14.) We can be assured that we are surrounded by angels on our spiritual journey through life. (See Hebrews 1:14.) They are lovingly innumerable.

Psalm 148:1-3 has all of God's creation praising Him:

> *Praise the LORD from the heavens;*
> *Praise Him in the heights!*
> ***Praise Him, all His angels;***
> ***Praise Him, all His hosts!***
> *Praise Him, sun and moon;*
> ***Praise Him, all you stars of light!***
> *Praise Him, you heavens of heavens,*
> *And you waters above the heavens!*

I praise Jesus *"For by Him all things were created that are in heaven and that are on earth, visible and invisible, whether* **thrones** *or* **dominions** *or* **principalities** *or* **powers.** *All things were created through Him and for Him"* (Col. 1:16). I praise Jesus because He is *"the image of the invisible God,"* the firstborn over all creation, as it says in Colossians 1:15-16. This is amazing to contemplate.

The Greek word that is translated as "image" in the above verse is *eikón,* which means *"likeness."* Jesus is exactly like God in His very form and essence, and always has been and will be thus through all eternity. In Genesis, God says, "Let *us* make man in *our* image, according to Our likeness" (Gen. 1:26). Jesus couldn't be created and Creator at the same time. (God is a triune God—Father, Son, and Holy Spirit.) And the angels? The angels were there, too!

Thrones, dominions, principalities, and powers refer to the categories of angels whom Christ rules over. This hierarchy among spirit beings was established before He created the world. Christ is ruler over His holy angels as well as the fallen angels. He has immeasurable superiority over every created thing in the universe. *"All things were created through Him and for Him"* (Col. 1:16).

Powers and principalities of satan's domain rule over nations and cities as well as villages and households. The definition of "powers" (as seen in Ephesians 3:10) is "angelic beings," which are demonic angelic beings, not God's angelic beings. Daniel waited three weeks for answered prayer while Michael, the archangel, had a wrestling match with the prince who was ruling over Persia. (See Daniel 10:13.) These "princes" are ferocious and powerful spirits. Satan's design is to deceive the nations, but all heavenly beings are governed by the authority structures established by God. (There is more on this subject in Chapter 11, The Order of Angels.)

We are God's children and we are His *prize creation. "The Angel of the Lord encamps around those [of us] who fear Him [who revere and worship Him with awe] and each of them He delivers"* (Ps. 34:7 AMP).

The Lord preserves all those who love Him; He takes care of me.... (See Psalm 145:20.)

He gives His angels charge over us to protect us. (See Psalm 91:11-12.) We are never alone.

How Many Angels Are There?

By biblical accounts, there exist untold trillions of these heavenly beings. Daniel wrote: *"I beheld till the thrones were cast down, and the Ancient of days did sit, whose garment was white as snow, and the hair of his head like the pure wool: his throne was like the fiery flame, and his wheels as burning fire. A fiery stream issued and came forth from before him: **thousand thousands ministered unto him, and ten thousand times then thousand stood before him:** the judgment was set, and the books were opened"* (Dan. 7:9-10 KJV).

Over a thousand years later, John on Patmos concurred, *"And I beheld, and I heard the voice of many angels round about the throne ...**and the number of them was ten thousand times ten thousand, and thousands of thousands**"* (Rev. 5:11 KJV).

God's angels are on *our side*, and they far outnumber the demons, principalities, and powers of the devil. The influence of satan and his principalities and powers will meet their end when they are consigned to the lake of fire that God has prepared for them. (See Matthew 25:41 and Revelation 20:10.)

Be encouraged by the number of angels God has working for Him. Be encouraged by the number of angels who love you and want God's glory-best for you. Be encouraged by the number of angels God has who are eager to assist you as you fulfill your divine destiny on this earth.

Angels and God's Pleasure

Angels love to do God's pleasure because that is what they are created for. (See Psalm 103:21.) They fight with enormous power and authority for the cause of Christ and operate in the material, earthly realm as well as the invisible heavenly realm. (See Revelation 12:7.)

Who are the angels?

They are amazed at God's divine plan as they help to execute it. (See 1 Peter 1:12.)

You and I were created to bring God pleasure. The angels bring Him pleasure continually. They bring Him pleasure because they are completely happy to love, know, and trust Him. If an angel complains about God, he's a demon. Granted, God's holy angels are not human. Granted, they don't have our limitations. Granted, they don't get colds or toothaches, and they don't get married or divorced, but one crucial similarity we share with angels is found in our DNA. Do you know what that is? I'll tell you if you haven't already guessed. You and I have within us one certain capability like the angels—and that is *choice*. We have the power of choice.

A third of God's angels *chose* to plunge out of glory and everything beautiful and happy. They shot out of heaven with satan to their everlasting doom. Those angels *chose*. I know, it sounds crazy. Why would an *angel* choose to leave God? It's just ludicrous, isn't it? But you and I have that same choice. His angels love to bring Him pleasure, and you and I must purpose and choose to do the same.

What Form Do Angels Take?

Let's look at the biblical accounts. The Bible tells us how angels appear as shining figures bathed in light and dressed in white. (See Revelation 4:4.) Often they appear as fierce warriors. Sometimes they show up as ordinary men. Angels take on many different appearances in the Word of God such as:

Serpent: Satan appeared to Eve in the Garden of Eden as a serpent. (See Genesis 3.)

As men: Three angels appeared as men to Abraham (one of them, most Bible scholars agree, being a theophany, or Christ Himself). (See Genesis 18:2.) Two angels of the Lord appeared as ordinary men to Lot in the city of Sodom. (See Genesis19:1-12.)

Flames in a burning bush: The angel of the Lord/the Lord Himself appeared to Moses as flames in a burning bush. (See Acts 7:30.)

31

Wind or flames of fire: (See Hebrews 1:7.)

Horses and chariots of fire: (See 2 Kings 6:17.)

Angels unawares: These are angels in any form whatsoever.

WHAT DO ANGELS DO?

1. They drive spirit horses. (See 2 Kings 2:12; 6:13-17; Zechariah 1:7-11; 6:1-6.)

2. They guard gates. (See Revelation 21:12; cf. Genesis 3:24.)

3. They wage war in actual bodily combat. (See Revelation 12:7-9 ; 2 Thessalonians 1:7-10.)

4. Angels execute judgments. (See Genesis 19; 2 Samuel 24; 2 Kings 19:35; 2 Chronicles 32:21; Psalm 78:49; Matthew 13:41-42; Acts 12:23; Revelation 8:1-9,12; Revelation 15:1-16:2.)

5. They minister to saints. (See 1 Kings 19:5-7; Daniel 6:22; Matthew 4:11; Acts 10; Hebrews 1:14.)

6. They rule nations. (See Daniel 10:13-21; 12:1.)

7. They watch over children. (See Matthew 18:10.)

8. They sing, praise, and worship God. (See Luke 2:13; Psalm 103:20; 148:2; Revelation 5:11.)

9. They strengthen us as we go through trials. (See Matthew 4:11; Luke 22:43.)

10. They lead sinners to Gospel workers. (See Acts 10:3.)

11. They guide ministers. (See Acts 8:26.)

12. They appear in dreams. (See Matthew 1:20-24; 2:13-19.)

13. They minister before God. (See Revelation 8:2; 14:15-19.)

14. They bind satan and guard his abyss. (See Revelation 9:1; 20-1-3.)

15. They re-gather Israel. (See Matthew 24:31.)

16. They protect saints. (See Psalm 34:7; 91:11; Acts 12:7-10.)

17. They separate the good from the bad. (See Matthew 13:19-41.)
18. They accompany Christ to the earth. (See Matthew 16:27; 25:31; 2 Thessalonians 1:7-10.)
19. They witness confessions. (See Luke 15:7.)
20. They receive departed spirits. (See Luke 16:22.)
21. They give laws and revelations. (See Acts 7:30-33; Hebrews 2:2; 2 Kings 1:15; Daniel 8:15-19; 9:21-23; 10:10-20.)
22. They impart God's will. (See Acts 5:19-20; 10:1-6.)
23. They bring answers to prayer. (See Daniel 9:21-23; 10:12-13; Acts 10.)
24. They are present in the Church. (See 1 Corinthians 11:10; Ephesians 3:10; 1 Timothy 5:21.)[2]

Angels are near you to bring you closer to God. They are messengers called *"malak"* in the Old Testament, a word which occurs 108 times. *Angellos* is the Greek word that translates as "angel," and this word occurs 186 times in the New Testament. Both words are also translated as "messenger." Luke 7:24 tells us that men can be messengers also (referring to the messengers of John), but they are separate from the holy angelic messengers of God.

Hebrews 1:14 (NIV) says, "Are not all angels ministering spirits sent to serve those who will inherit salvation?"

For years nobody paid much attention to the ministry of angels. Now, thanks to misled New Age devotees, there are over a million Websites pertaining to angels on the Internet, but most of them have nothing to do with the truth of God's angelic realm. A Harris interactive poll that was conducted in 2005 found that seven in ten Americans believe in the existence of angels. A Gallup report stated that 72 percent of Americans believe in angels.[3] On the other hand, we have certain church folk who consider angels as having nothing to do with the earth today. These people are afraid of the supernatural. They're like the Sadducees in Jesus' time who with their materialistic dogma, rejected the reality of the spirit realm in the world. These people regard angels as mere theological *symbols*. That's so sad, isn't it? Why? Because the presence of angels surges throughout the entire Bible, and this attests to their importance in the Kingdom of God, and therefore, to us humans today! *"Jesus Christ, the same yesterday, and today, and forever"* (Heb.13:8 KJV).

The Lord's preeminence is permanent; His leadership is forever. He who walked the paths of Galilee, who turned the water into wine, who hugged babies, and admonished, *"Let the little children come to Me, and do not forbid them; for of such is the kingdom of heaven"* (Matt. 19:14), and He who *created the world* is the same Savior *today*, right now, as you read this. His mind, heart, and will are still preserved and upheld in eternal love—love for the world, love for *you*.

God has not changed. Nowhere in the Bible does it say that angels were around *back then*, but they've gone bye-bye now. In fact, Hebrews 12:18-22 talks about Moses arriving at Mount Sinai in a blast of supernatural wonder (and terror) and you and I arriving at Mount Zion, the city of the living God, the heavenly Jerusalem, to *"an innumerable company of angels."* Angels were with Moses when God gave him the Ten Commandments and angels are with us now.

Angels were with Jesus every minute of His life on earth. They were active in every second of His life on earth in both seen and unseen forms. Jesus was never out of their sight because He was never out of the sight of the Father. Angels were a vital presence in the earthly life of Jesus, and they attended to Him through each stage of His sojourn here. Later we'll examine how angels were His constant spiritual companions, but first let's look at the different ranks of angels and their classifications in order to learn how angels want to play a part in *our* lives today.

Open my heart, Lord.
Create in me a hungry spirit so I might find You.
Draw me! I will run after you!

Your name is like perfume poured out.
O love, draw me.

ENDNOTES

1. Herbert Lockyear, *All The Doctrines of the Bible.* (Grand Rapids, MI: Zondervan Publishing House, 1964).

2. Ibid.

3. *Readers Digest,* April 2006.

chapter 3

WHEN ANGELS FIRST APPEARED

THE first mention of angelic visitations in the Bible took place with an Egyptian slave girl named Hagar. Hagar was pregnant, but this was not of her own choosing. She had been given as a concubine to 86-year-old Abraham by his wife, Sarai (which was Sarah's name before God changed it to Sarah). Later when Hagar became pregnant by Abraham she began to taunt Sarai. Hagar's patronizing, arrogant attitude drove Sarai into a jealous tizzy. She began making life intolerable for the pregnant slave girl. Finally, in desperation, Hagar packed her things and took off in the dead of night in hopes of finding her way back to Egypt. There in the wilderness by the spring of water on the road to Shur, *the angel of the Lord found her*. He asked her where she came from and where she was going.

What a way to open a conversation in the middle of the desert! Hagar knew this was no human being talking to her, of course. His question shows us the compassion and decorum of the Lord. By asking her the question, "Where are you going?" Hagar could vent the anguish she felt inside. Naturally, the Lord already knew where she was heading, just as He knew where Adam was when He called out in the Garden, "Adam, where are you?"

Here's Hagar, alone and lost in the middle of the desert and she now has someone to complain to. The angel could have announced right off, "Hagar, drink your water and go back to Abraham's camp," but the Lord in His exceptional kindness, acknowledged that her feelings were important, that she wasn't just chattel. He listened to what she had to say.

Sometimes we get the idea that the Lord doesn't care how we feel if what we feel is negative and droopy. And sometimes we get the idea that one person's feelings are more important than another person's. This portion of Scripture utterly destroys every notion of discrimination. Hagar was not of the tribe of Abraham, God's chosen. But God was with her. He was with her to help her and to give her an opportunity to use her power of *choice*.

"Go back," He told her tenderly. *"Go back to Abraham's camp."*

He gave her a promise that her descendants would be multiplied *"...so that they shall not be counted for multitude"* (Gen. 16:10).

He told her she would bear a son and call his name Ishmael, *"...because the LORD has heard your affliction. He shall be a wild man; his hand shall be against every man, and every man's hand against him. And he shall dwell in the presence of all his brethren"* (Gen. 16:11b-12).

About 17 years later, Hagar again was found in the desert, not as a runaway this time, but as an outcast. Banished from Abraham's camp because of her ongoing jealous conflicts with Sarah, she traveled on foot through the scorching desert with her son, Ishmael. Desperate and alone, she finally ran out of water and had no recourse but to put her son under a bush to die.

As she sat there weeping with death on her shoulder, the angel of the Lord came to her once more. He called out to her and told her not to be afraid.

Twice the angel of the Lord appeared to this Egyptian slave girl. She was not a person of distinction, not a religious hero, a famous lecturer, a well-known TV personality, or even a nice pastor's wife. She wasn't even a *Hebrew*.

✛ ◈ ✛ ◈ ✛ ◈ ✛ ◈ ✛ ◈ ✛

Don't ever be surprised at things God does or the people God chooses.

✛ ◈ ✛ ◈ ✛ ◈ ✛ ◈ ✛ ◈ ✛

Can you imagine Hagar's reaction?

We should be able to relate to that moment in their lives. I know I can. It was a moment when all looked hopeless and it seemed that nothing would ever work out. They must have thought, "Let's just sit down and wait for the sun to eat us up." But when we belong to the Lord, we are *His*; we are not our own. Our life is hid in *Him*.

All at once, with the sound of the Voice from Heaven, Hagar realized things would be OK and that her son would not die. Let me repeat. Hagar was not one of God's chosen. She was from a pagan culture. Yet God saw and knew all. He was there from the moment Sarah gave the order for her to pack her bags and leave for good. He saw. He heard.

The Bible says that God heard the voice of the lad. Hagar sat stunned. God created a miracle of water for Hagar and her son.

Then God opened her eyes, and she saw a well of water. And she went and filled the skin with water, and gave the lad to drink. So God was with the lad... (Genesis 21:19-20a).

He sees. He hears.

In this emotional and dramatic story of Hagar we are introduced to the first appearances of angels in Bible history.

ANGELS OF DESTRUCTION

Another dramatic account of angelic appearances in the Book of Genesis is when the angels of the Lord came to visit Abraham, informing him that he'd have a son. Abraham's excitement turned to worry later, for as the angels of the Lord were leaving, the Lord told Abraham that the wickedness of Sodom and Gomorrah had become too great, and He was about to destroy the two cities. Abraham was startled at this news. He argued with God, reasoning and pleading with Him to spare Sodom if 50 righteous people lived there. God told Abraham He would not destroy the city if there were 50 such people. Then Abraham asked if He would spare them for the sake of 45 righteous people. God agreed. Abraham didn't stop there. He asked God if 30 righteous people were found, would He spare them? Again, God agreed. And again Abraham asked. Would He spare them for 20?

Yes.

For 10?

God agreed to withhold judgment if as few as ten righteous people could be found in Sodom. But sadly, He didn't find ten such people.

Abraham's nephew, Lot, lived in Sodom and the two angels came to his home to check out the spiritual condition of the city. What they found was such deplorable depravity that when the Sodomite men tried to seize them to molest them physically, the angels struck them all with blindness. The angels ordered Lot to flee out of town with his wife and two unmarried daughters. (See Genesis 18:1-19:26.) In this fateful account we see God's holy ones, His angel messengers, as messengers of deliverance as well as destruction.

We also see that when God gives us difficult instructions, He gives them for our good, not our harm. (*"I know the thoughts that I think toward you, says the LORD, thoughts of peace and not of evil, to give you a future and a hope"* Jer. 29:11.) The angel told Lot and his family not to look back. The flaming sulfuric ash encased Lot's disobedient wife and the Bible says she turned to a pillar of salt. (See Genesis 19:26.) Lot's wife didn't understand that obedience was her place of safety. Had she taken the word of God's messenger seriously, she would have never looked back, no matter how upsetting and treacherous their escape was, and no matter how much she wanted to hang on to her old life.

It's significant to note that Lot was far from being a model of holy propriety. Lot was a man of poor judgment. He had chosen to live in a sinful environment, to do business with and create alliances with profane people in order to reap certain comforts and benefits. *Yet God came to him and spared his life.*

God is a God of mercy. Lot may have made mistakes and strayed from the godly standards he had learned from his uncle Abraham, but God didn't stray from him.

And He never strays from you.

ABRAHAM AND THE ANGELS

A most intense, agonizing moment in Abraham's life came with his next divine angelic visitation. His miracle son, Isaac, had been born to his 90-year-old wife, Sarah. (As I mentioned before, God had changed her name from Sarai to Sarah.) Now God instructed Abraham (at the age of 100!) to take his beloved boy up to a mountaintop, build an altar, and sacrifice him as a burnt offering. Abraham, stricken with grief, could only obey. Abraham knew of the heathen practice of human sacrifice. He knew that certain pagan rites included the sacrifice of firstborn sons, so his anguish and abhorrence must have been monumental. Nevertheless, he obeyed.

With the knife in midair, ready to plunge into his boy's flesh, he heard, *"Abraham! Abraham!"*

Abraham recognized that voice.

Do not lay your hand on the lad, or do anything to him; for now I know that you fear God, since you have not withheld your son, your only son from Me (Genesis 22:12).

Nowhere along the trek up the mountain nor during the time it took Abraham to make the preparations—gathering the wood, piling up the rocks—did he have an inkling that God wasn't serious. Never while lighting the brazen censer, fanning the coals, or binding his precious son did God give him one tiny indication that He was just testing him.

The same is true for you and me. That fiery trial you're going through is painful and terrible, and what's more, it seems unfair. You may be very upset with the Lord and confused about His hand, which doesn't seem loving at the moment. Yet angels are hovering over you every minute to help you, to encourage you, to bring you *good* news in time if you will but listen and obey. You must listen with the ears of your spirit. It's easy to listen to the natural world around you. We can fall into deception so easily by trusting our own energies and acumen to solve or figure out problems that belong to God.

I hear the Lord continually calling and telling us, like the angel of the Lord told Abraham, *"Blessing, I will bless you!"* (Gen. 22:17). Press on. Press on, for the Lord is about to do great and wonderful things for you. Stop thinking of answered prayer as a cosmic gamble. Stop thinking that maybe He'll answer or maybe He won't.

✤ ⊕ ✤ ⊕ ✤ ⊕ ✤ ⊕ ✤ ⊕ ✤

With the Lord every problem has a purpose. The bigger the problem, the bigger the purpose.

✤ ⊕ ✤ ⊕ ✤ ⊕ ✤ ⊕ ✤ ⊕ ✤

Abraham's problem was huge, and look what happened. God promised him:

> *I will multiply your descendants as the stars of heaven and as the sand which is on the seashore; and your descendants shall possess the gate of their enemies. In your seed all the nations of the earth shall be blessed, because you have obeyed My voice* (Genesis 22:17-19).

You and I are blessed today because father Abraham obeyed the voice of the Lord. The angel of the Lord who called Abraham from heaven was, as many Bible scholars believe, a pre-incarnate revelation of the Son of God, a theophany.

AN ANGEL AS MATCHMAKER

Are you looking for a mate? Or are you praying about a mate for your children? In Genesis 24 our God used an angel as a matchmaker! (Have you ever thought of God's angels as matchmakers? It's time you do.) This is an area the devil loves to get his talons into. He works hard to get us to make wrong choices in mates, enter into bad relationships, marry the wrong people, raise unhappy kids in dysfunctional homes, get divorces, and eventually die broke and sick with grandchildren who don't talk to us. The family and home are huge targets for the devil, as you know. I don't have to give you the statistics. Just look at your own life and the lives of others you know. Maybe you're happily married now with the mate of God's choice, but it hasn't always been a smooth road, has it? And how much havoc does the devil wreak in our households? If there is any place we need God 24 hours a day, it's in our homes.

If the devil and his demons have so much influence on us through wrong motives, unmet needs, loneliness, lust, and whatever other weaknesses he can use to help us destroy ourselves, what about God's angels? What power do they have in matchmaking?

Abraham sent his servant, Eliezer, to Mesopotamia, Abraham's original home, which was approximately 450 miles away, to find a bride for his son, Isaac. Abraham told Eliezer that the Lord God of Heaven had sworn to him to *send His angel before him.* Sure enough, the angel of the Lord led Eliezer *directly* to Rebekkah who consented to the marriage and the beginning of a romantic love story. Rebekkah later give birth to the Bible's famous twins, Jacob and Esau.

God's angel messengers do exactly as God tells them, and when God sends His messengers to supernaturally bring a man and woman together, that bond will be one that pleases Him and one He destines to fulfill Heaven's purpose. As we partake of God's divine character, spending time alone with Him, we enter the intimacy with Him that He so desires and loves. Everything that pertains to us, including our relationships, and especially our relationships, has eternal purpose.

INTIMACY

We were created for intimacy. And our primary intimate relationship is to be with God. From this place of intimacy flows absolutely everything in life that pertains to us. Keeping that relationship of intimacy with the Lord is easy. It's a matter of being alone with Him every day.

How do we expect to be happy and live good lives without intimacy with Jesus? As a Christian psychotherapist, I have been flat-out amazed at how much time and energy is lost through soul-driven misbeliefs. We tend to think being Christians means being *good people.* Or kind people. Or hard-working people. We hold to certain ideas:

Husbands and wives should always get along. Children should never make problems. Hard work should always bring rewards. Love should always make me feel good. These are all misbeliefs. In the ground-breaking book, *Telling Yourself the Truth*, which I wrote with the late Dr. Bill Backus, we detail the many misbeliefs that defeat us in life and then we give a proven method of recovery and victory. More than a million people's lives have been changed through *Telling Yourself the Truth*, not counting the mountains of material written by others following the pioneering publication of this book.

We need to recognize that there is a very real enemy out there whose aim it is to defeat us in every way he and his demons can conjure up.

What Is Your Truth?

The angels spend every second of their existence in the Presence of God. Sinless and wise, they live to do His bidding. What might His bidding be for you today? Maybe it is to wash the windows, change the oil in the car, get up three hours early and pray, make lunch, shop, or get to work on time. Whatever His bidding, you are a partner with the angels in bringing it to pass.

The Holy Spirit nudges your conscience. He is telling you the secret to everything is to *be like Christ*. Your angels are with you to help you.

What is your truth? What is your reality?

Jacob's Visitations

Jacob was no paragon of scruples. He exploited his brother Esau's weakness in order to steal his birthright, he deceived and lied to his blind, dying father by impersonating Esau, and he cheated Esau out of his father's blessing. Moreover, he tricked his uncle Laban out of his possessions, and yet God had His hand on him from the beginning.

During his rather checkered life, Jacob had several encounters with angels. The first was in a dream as he was running from home. His brother, Esau, had threatened to kill him, so Jacob had to run for his life to his uncle Laban's. In his dream Jacob saw *"...a ladder...set up on the earth, and its top reached to heaven; and there the angels of God were ascending and descending on it"* (Gen. 28:12). The Lord God stood above the ladder and announced to Jacob that through him his descendants would be as many as the dust of the earth and in his seed *"...all the families of the earth shall [would] be blessed"* (Gen. 28:14).

What a promise! In this contact of Heaven to earth we see a picture of how the mind and heart of God work. Does He labor and stew over our faults, our sins, and our checkered pasts?

No! He sees our purpose and our destiny!

GOD SEES YOUR PURPOSE AND DESTINY

Jacob was dishonest; in fact, he was a cheat and a conniver. But is that how God saw him? Absolutely not. God saw him as the man he created him to be, a patriarch of Israel. *"Behold, I am with you,"* He told him. *"...I will not leave you until I have done what I have spoken to you"* (Gen. 28:15). What amazing words to a man who was running for his life. If this tells us anything, it tells us God's ways are not our ways. It shows us that no matter how far we've gone from Him and His purposes for our lives, He is right there with us to set us back on our true course as our true selves. *We must learn to see with His eyes.*

The ladder in Jacob's dream was a divine, holy stairway, and this image gives us a most graphic portrayal of the Lord's personal involvement in the matters and affairs of earth. Here is a beautiful illustration of the holy calling of God's vast and powerful angelic-host angels as they are sent to carry out the Lord God's will, plans, and purposes on earth.

This is a message to every human being on earth: God has sent His angels to accomplish great things for heaven, and God's greatest gift at the top of Heaven's stairway is His Son, Jesus Christ, who said to Nathanael, *"You shall see heaven open, and the angels of God ascending and descending on the Son of Man"* (John 1:51). Jesus, who is the Mediator between God and humankind, has become the stairway to an *open Heaven.*

"I will not let You go unless You bless me!" Jacob insisted. He wanted the best from God, and he was not willing to settle for less. *He simply had to get blessed!* (By the way, Jacob was 97 years old when he entered this wrestling match with the angel, so don't be talking about being too old to change!) Jacob refused to let go of the angel in that wrestling match.

Discipline is that kind of fight. We fight against our own flesh. We cry out, "Lord, I am willing to clean up my life, rid myself of every hindering sin and negative thinking pattern, every selfish and self-indulgent act to be able to please you."

Just as Jacob was in no position to earn God's favor, yet God saw his purpose and spoke to him, we can expect supernatural communication from the Son of Man and His angels as Heaven opens to us.

The blood of Jesus does a thorough washing of our souls so that we can live out our perfect destiny in Him without guilt or shame. He forgives! Jacob was pretty shaken after his dream, and he set up a shrine on the spot, made a vow to follow God, and, though He determined to be in a position for God to bless him, the life ahead would not be easy for him. He was to meet with the scheming and selfishness (his own old traits) of his father-in-law, Laban. He was to live with bickering wives, though he loved but one; he was to raise ferocious, fighting sons who through the rape of a daughter, plundered and slaughtered all the males in an entire city.

Later, his favorite son, 17-year-old Joseph, was sold by his brothers as a slave to Midianite traders, and then one day, as an old man of 130 years, in a drought, he was to move his entire tribe to Egypt where he spent his last 17 years. On his deathbed he looked back on his life and spoke of the importance of angels when he exclaimed, *"The God who has fed me all my life long to this day, the **Angel** who has redeemed me from all evil"* (Gen. 48:15).

GOD'S BOOK OF REMEMBRANCE

When God calls you, He sees you as a hero. He sees you as being mighty, strong, and fulfilling His purpose on earth. He sees you walking in an open heaven that proliferates with gifts. He sees you as one who is anointed and blessed.

In your darkest hour, speak to your soul. Command your soul, as David taught us in Psalm 103:1, *"Bless the Lord, O my soul; and all that is within me, bless His holy name!"*

Each time you conquer your emotions and each time you conquer your propensity to give up or to sin, you enter another bright page in God's "Book of Remembrance."

Let me remind you of the words of Malachi 3:16:

Then those who feared the Lord spoke to one another, and the Lord listened and heard them; so a book of remembrance was written before Him for those who fear the Lord and who mediate on His name.

Read Chapter 11 of Hebrews—God's Hall of Faith. Read the recorded acts of bravery and courage that were accomplished by His saints. Read what the Holy Spirit said of Sarah, a hard taskmaster, a complainer, one who mocked and laughed at God and then lied about it! Hebrews 11:11 says: *"By faith Sarah herself also received strength to conceive seed, and she bore a child when she was past the age, because she judged Him faithful."* She's called a woman of faith! Not a complainer or any other negative thing—a woman of faith!

God met with Jacob near the River Jabbok in a wrestling match and Jacob's life was forever changed, and his character made a complete about-face. Jacob the conniver became Israel the Prince: *"He who had power with God and with man"* (Gen. 32:28). Jacob is in God's Hall of Faith also: *"By faith Jacob, when he was dying, blessed each of the sons of Joseph, and worshiped leaning on the top of his staff* (Heb. 11:21). How beautiful. These are our forefathers and mothers whose homeland was only a dream to them for over 500 more years.

When you, like Sarah, Abraham, and Jacob, step out of your natural weaknesses, leaving the confined, pinched ways of a small spirit behind and step into power and a big spirit, Heaven will throw a party.

chapter 4

EMBRACED BY HIS WING

I'M preparing lunch for my children who should be home any minute. I stand at the stove and I hear a noise. It's an other-worldly noise, not from this sphere. Is God trying to tell me something as I stir the carrots into the soup? The sound is that of a distant hum and it causes the kitchen to vibrate. If this were an earthly sound I would dive under the counter.

Then I see it—the wing. A giant wing covers me, the kitchen, and the whole house. I'm covered in the howling hum of a gigantic, hovering wing. I move away from the stove. I walk on my toes as though I'm among the sleeping. I abandon the soup and tiptoe through the rooms of the house with the wing above me. I gaze upward into its trembling feathers and reach out my arms. I climb into the thick roots of the wing. Then I'm squeezed between the succor of these holy feathers.

This is how He comes to us, hiding us in the shadow of His majesty, His protection, His banner. He is Jehovah Nissi, our mighty banner. He is our hovering safety. His banner over us is love in its perfection. He, the Lord Himself, is our Banner, our shining assurance of victory. This is no angel wing. This is the presence of the Lord.

The Lord God Almighty covers us in Himself, in His mighty protecting wing, and under His wing we must trust Him. He keeps us as the apple of His beautiful eye. *"This is my will for you,"* He reveals from the furrows. *"As an eagle stirs up its nest, hovers over its young, spreading out its wings, taking them, up, carrying them on its wings, so will I lead my beloved ones…. I will hide you under the shadow of my wing."*

Later we eat our soup and I tell the children it's ambrosia from Heaven. We are hugged in the Presence of God. Jesus leans down and kisses our noses.

chapter 5

SOUL, BODY, SPIRIT

MOST books about angels on today's market focus on the blessings angels bring to us *outwardly*. We hear about the many miraculous encounters with God's angels who save us from all kinds of harm. We hear how angels help us in situations of danger and peril. I love to hear about and experience these encounters, too, and I talk about them in this book. They are the external, outward experiences. I want to share how to open up the vistas of spiritual experiences in the heavenly realm that take place *inwardly*. By inwardly I mean in our *spirit*.

Each part of our being—soul, body, and spirit—has unique functions. These functions can operate alone as well as simultaneously. Your body, for example, can be busy riding a bicycle while your mind (part of your soul) is busy concentrating on what to have for dinner. The same is true for your spirit. You are praying in the spirit and suddenly you're taken up to heavenly places. Your body doesn't go up with your spirit. Your body stays put. When I walk daily in the woods with the Lord, my body is walking in the woods, but my spirit is in the second and third heaven with the Lord Jesus.

When we live predominantly in the soul realm, we're living in the realm of the personality. We aren't living in the spiritual victory and power we were born for. In this soul realm we find life is a battle for us. In the soul realm we struggle with faith and doubt, worry, fear, temptations, and insecurity and we try to fight the devil in our own power, rather than in the power of the Holy Spirit. Some of us have fought until we have fought ourselves sick. We fight and fuss and remain in a sorry, needy state, always asking questions like, "If God loved me why would He allow such-and-such in my life?" Or, "If God is love, how come He lets bad things happen?" We can live and die in this confused state of the soul. We call ourselves Christians without ever growing beyond babyhood in the spirit. We become people who never learn how to partner with our angels. We never really understand the love and power of God if we live mainly in the realm of the soul.

QUESTIONS FOR GOD

I'm not saying human beings should never question God. Goodness knows, we have all pondered and looked for answers as to why God does or not do this or that. Why does He take so long to answer our prayers?

✣ ❀ ✣ ❀ ✣ ❀ ✣ ❀ ✣ ❀ ✣

Angels don't cringe when we ask faithless questions, but they usually remain quiet.

✣ ❀ ✣ ❀ ✣ ❀ ✣ ❀ ✣ ❀ ✣

These are not bad questions, they are just soul-questions. We humans have a lot of questions for God. Consider the angels, though. They aren't beating their breasts, demanding to know why God allows suffering to continue on earth. The angels in Heaven don't complain about being overworked or under-appreciated. They aren't given to depression. The reason? Angels know the mind of God, and God's mind is all-powerful, all-seeing, all-good, and all-loving.

The closer you are to God and the Word of God, and the more hours and years you spend with Him, the more He imparts His mind and will to you. It's not only how and how much he imparts, but how and how much you're able to receive. God doesn't want us to think of Him as some sort of divine magician in the sky. He wants us to understand and to be at peace with His sovereign will. *He wants us to know Him and love Him.* As we press in closer to Him, submitting to Him, loving Him, emptying our lives in His hands, we begin to accept unequivocally His perfect will. This doesn't mean sitting back and letting the world trample on us. It means becoming like the Lord! (See Ephesians

5:1.) God does not operate according to our human formulas no matter how holy they may appear. Beware of nifty formulas designed to get God to do things your way.

When I was very young I had so many questions I hailed at Heaven's door. Why this? Why that? How come? What for? Why me? Now, because of the power of the Word in my life, I have within me a knowing, a sense of calm. As a warrior and intercessor, I am more equipped with faith that is fixed in obedience and complete submission to Him and His perfect will.

We were born to conquer and overcome the power of evil in our lives, not to succumb to it. Evil exists, period. The Lord Jesus died to empower us to rise above its hold on us. *"Greater is He who is in you than he who is in the world"* (1 John 4:4 NIV). There's some old evil thing or two lurking around every corner, but you and I were born to repel and overcome it all because of the Spirit of God within us. We are not spiritual wimps. We're more than conquerors! We are born of God and we overcome the world and all its evil and strife. (See 1 John 5:4.) We do this with our solid faith and a whole lot of wisdom. This doesn't mean we live with our heads in the sand or in some tra-la-la state of denial. No, no, no! It means we are wise, strong, brave, and beautiful in the Holy Ghost. And we're getting better all the time!

THE SOUL REALM VERSUS THE SPIRIT REALM

Your soul makes up a huge part of you. Your soul includes your mind, passions, desires, dreams, hunger for learning, personal character, attitudes, likes, dislikes, feelings, emotions, drives, fears, and your personality. These are what comprise your character. Living in the soul realm is exhausting and futile. Your soul-self cannot comprehend the mind of God. Oh, you can study the Word of God without the illumination of the Holy Spirit, sure. Lots of people do, and they miss the impact, the majesty, the glory and power, and the *life* of its words.

One of the reasons Jesus said He spoke in parables is because only His own could understand them. *"It has been given to you to know the mysteries of the kingdom of heaven,"* He said, *"but to them* [the spiritually blind] *it has not been given"* (Matt. 13:11).

Your soul needs to be in submission to the Holy Spirit within you. Otherwise, you can pray and try hard to live the Christian life, but if you are soul-dominated you will try to solve your problems by using your wit and intellect, but these aren't enough. Your values can become tainted and you'll begin to make excuses for doing what you know will hurt you and others. God wants us to have a triumphant, glorious life of joy, love, and power in the Holy Spirit. If we stay dominated by the characteristics of our soul-self, our angels are unable to do much more for us other than to keep us from falling off cliffs or finding us a parking place.

This reminds me of a funny story. A man named Joe is late for an important appointment and he is having a hard time finding a parking space. He's pretty desperate so he prays, "Lord, if you'll just give me a good parking spot so I'm not late for this appointment I promise I'll change my life. I'll quit swearing and I'll quit drinking and smoking— if you'll just help me out and give me a good parking space." Suddenly a parking space opens up right before his eyes in front of the building." Joe is overjoyed. "Never mind, God," he exclaims, "I just found one!"

BORN AGAIN AND YOUR SOUL-SELF

When you gave your life to God by asking Jesus Christ to be your Lord and Savior, your *spirit* was born again. Your body and soul weren't born again. Your *spirit* was born again. Your spirit-self became alive with the nature and character of Jesus Christ at that moment. You were given everything that pertains to life and godliness. (See 2 Peter 1:2-4.) This happened when your human spirit became fused with God's spirit. I like the illustration that is provided by someone having a cup of tea. You pour yourself a nice cup of tea. Then you add milk and a little sugar. You stir the tea with a spoon, and then it's impossible to separate the tea from the milk or the milk from the tea. You have a brand-new drink. When you receive the Spirit of Christ into your life, your human spirit is reborn and you have a brand-new spirit. Your spirit, now alive with the Spirit of God, that same Spirit that raised Christ from the dead, is to align your soul and body with the power of the Holy Spirit.

The heavenly visitations, visions, and dreams I write of in this book happen in the *spirit*. They don't happen in the imagination, nor does the body leave this earth. We enter heavenly places *in the spirit*. Our human spirits, filled and reborn with the Spirit of God, will bring new life and beauty to every aspect of our souls as we pursue following God and His will. Our souls have a will, and that means we can choose to be led by the Holy Spirit in our actions, behaviors, thoughts, goals, dreams, wants, interests, and relationships—in everything. Our souls need training by the Holy Spirit.

"Whatever things are true, whatever things are noble, whatever things are just, whatever things are pure, whatever things are lovely, whatever things are of good report, if there is any virtue and if there is anything praiseworthy— meditate on these things" (Phil. 4:8). These are soul-training words.

Here are more soul-training words:

"Be anxious for nothing, but in everything by prayer and supplication, with thanksgiving, let your requests be made known to God; and the peace of God, which surpasses all understanding, will guard your **hearts and minds** *through Christ Jesus"* (Phil. 4:6-7).

Your heart and mind are parts of your soul. Bring your heart and soul into alignment, and you will be able to enter portals of glory that you never dreamed possible. God wants to reveal Himself to you in such a way that your soul will rejoice as never before.

David prayed, *"Bless the LORD, O my soul; and all that is within me, bless His holy name!"* (Ps. 103:1). By praying, *"Bless the Lord, O my soul,"* he was training his soul to obey his spirit. He was decreeing to his soul, "Listen, soul, you bless God!"

You commune with your angels in the spirit, not within your soul. Angels are not soul-creatures; we are. Angels have emotions and wills, but the emotions and wills of angels are not soulish; they're divine. Angels will make themselves known without distinction. They will show up as God commands to the redeemed, the unredeemed, and even to animals. A good example of the latter category is when the angel of the Lord appeared to Balaam's donkey in Numbers 22. (More about this amazing event later.)

YOUR SPIRIT-SELF

Your spirit is where God's spirit connects with you and where you connect with Him. It's the place in you that is ignited by Heaven and all Heaven's beauty and glory and power. Your spirit, when you were born again in Christ Jesus, created a huge event in Heaven, one the angels cheered about.

It makes so much sense, doesn't it? Your soul must be aligned with your spirit. In that way you open yourself to God's touch in even the most subtle ways.

The Lord showed me that angels appear in many forms, even as shafts and pillars of light, which only the *spiritual* eye can see. We must learn to see with the eyes of our spirit.

SUPERNATURAL JOURNEY

On one of my journeys with the Lord, He took me over the land of Israel. He showed me a dark cloud over the land and pinpricks of light were piercing through the dark cloud. These pinpricks of light were the prayers of those who were interceding for the nation of Israel. They were the prayers of those who loved Him as the Messiah. I then saw a greater light come down through the cloud and touch the pinpricks of light, magnifying them into great shining shafts of light that pierced through the dark cloud. These shafts of light were carried up to God's throne by thousands of angels, and as they were, more light was shot down over the land.

ALIGN YOUR SPIRIT

Talk to your spirit. Align your soul with your spirit. Notice that I use the word "align" when I'm talking about positioning our soul and our spirit. We don't want to try to wipe out the existence of the soul realm—that would be denying our humanity like some ascetics who put themselves through awful tortures in their futile efforts to purge themselves of the natural human condition. You are spirit, but you also have a soul and a body. Your soul becomes beautified by your spirit's cooperation with the Holy Spirit within you. How does this happen? By feeding your spirit on richer food than what you use to feed your soul. Jesus said, *"I am the bread of life. He who comes to Me shall never hunger"* (John 6:35).

How do we know the difference between feeding our soul and feeding our spirit? When we vegetate before our TV screen night after night, are we growing closer to God or are we being influenced by the negative culture of the world? Will a diet of entertaining ourselves and seeking personal fulfillment give us the power we need to overcome the trials of this life?

You and I, together with the angelic host, are to meld together and bring Heaven to earth, and that means our spirit-self will have to transcend the lower, base nature of our souls. Instead of giving into our soul-driven demands, we must ask God questions that are more on the order of, "What is your will concerning this or that?"

"What does this or that trial mean, and how am I to grow from this experience?"

"How can I best deal with this trial through your Holy Spirit? How can I soak in your will, bring your will to pass, and overcome and triumph in order to honor you?"

"What Scripture portions will guide me toward strengthening my spirit to understand and love your mind?"

"How can I love you more and love my neighbor as myself?"

You'll see amazing things happen in your life if you do this.

Your Angels Help You Have Faith for Trials

As we face our trials, we need faith. We need faith more than we need solutions. When I have a huge financial need, one that is bigger than the means available, I need faith. In addition to committing myself to giving more money than I actually earn, I find that financial demands fly at me like rockets.

I'm hit with bills, demands, and needs left and right. (Sound familiar?) I could easily become overwhelmed, crawl into bed, pull the covers over my head, and sleep till noon. My prayer life can become the stormiest event of the day. In a dramatic way I ask, "What am I supposed to do, Lord? What do you want me to do?" These are questions emanating from the turbulent emotions within my soul.

Then it dawns on me. It hits me. This experience is actually a *gift* from God. I must receive this gift graciously. But aren't gifts supposed to be nice things, something that we want, you may ask? This is not always the case. Sometimes difficulties may be gifts as well.

God is a *spirit*. Those who worship Him must worship Him in Spirit and in truth. (See John 4:24.) The situation I faced was this: a spiritual gift manifested itself to me (internally) so that I could *tangibly conquer* what the Lord had already conquered by dying on the Cross for me. I can't handle the problem by my own means, and if I could handle the problem by my own means He would have to send me a worse problem until I finally surrendered to His authority in solving life's problems.

ANGELS AND SURRENDERING TO GOD'S AUTHORITY

What do I mean by surrendering to God's authority? Does surrendering to His authority have something to do with angels?

Number one: Angels are completely surrendered to the authority of the Father. They do nothing that God does not ask them to do. If you and I are created in the image of God and filled with His Spirit, we, too, must exercise our free wills by choosing to do exactly as He tells us. Angels do exactly as the Lord tells them down to the minutest details. Where in the Word of God do we read that God wants His children to be miserable and overwhelmed by fear, worry, loss, and sorrow?

Number Two: Angels live in God's Presence, which means night and day they are saturated in the breath of His omnipotent love. Angels are utterly confident of being loved, of being formed in, steeped in, and alive forever in His love. Angels behold the face of God and everything angels think and do is predicated on God's perfect, non-changing love. You and I can have the confidence of angels because we are no less embraced by love than they are.

The eyes of my understanding are opened and I see trials as gifts from God. Now my love for Him takes a giant leap forward. When I realize that I am to handle the hard times with grace, my whole life does an about-face. My prayer life jumps up several notches. I praise God for the opportunity to overcome, because He has *already conquered every defeating enemy*. I praise Him for His ability to pierce through the trials to solutions that are meant to glorify Him. I know the solutions are only to be found through the power of the Holy Spirit.

Thank you, Jesus, I live in the Spirit realm. It's my home. I live in the grace of your greatness.

Let's recap. By my reaching into Heaven through faith—through solid, strong, unshakable faith, I enter the "secret place of the most high," which is *His Presence*. And nothing can hurt me when I'm in His presence. (See Psalm 91.)

When I was a young girl, I used to think I should enter a convent because then I'd be *really* spiritual. I'd live such a disciplined life of prayer that I'd be on top of everything. I'd be so spiritual that my troubles would diminish like dust in the wind. As I grew older, however, I realized that these words—*"Do not be conformed to this world"* (Rom. 12:2) and *"You are in the world but not of the world"*—were for every Christian who ever lived and walked on this earth and for every Christian who will ever walk the earth. Then I realized that this included me. I needed to live a holy life with the knowledge that I was set apart whether I was in or out of the convent. I could be a Galatians 2:20 person, one who is *strong* and *brave*, one who is *totally alive*. Though I didn't have a nun's vocation, I was crucified with Christ, nevertheless I lived, but the life I now lived I lived through the power of the son of God. (See Galatians 2:20.)

In order to love Him, I must trust Him. I can't truly love anyone without truly trusting that person. Realizing this, I press into the heart of the words of Job, *"Though He slay me, yet will I trust Him..."* (Job 13:15).

God gives me gifts I don't like. Sure I would never run to His storehouse of blessings and call out, "Just give me one of your biggest unmanageable problems!" But by His Spirit I will use *all* that comes to me to glorify Him. That's what is meant by *"...all things work together for good to those who love God, to those who are the called according to His purpose"* (Rom. 8:28). The Lord wants a mighty army of faith-empowered believers, and not a blubbery, spoiled lot of Christian toddlers.

I repent of my worries, Lord.
I come against the lies of the enemy:
Devil, leave me and my beautiful mind and thoughts.
I have the mind of Christ who empowers me with wisdom.
I resist the devil and he flees from me!
The Lord is my glory and the lifter of my head,
He is a shield for me and makes me more than I am!

WHAT ABOUT YOUR BEAUTIFUL BODY?

Decide to triumph in Christ Jesus as a non-negotiable fact. Decide not to allow your earth-bound soul-self to beat down your spirit-self and play havoc with your body. You want a large spirit to enlarge your life! You want a spirit that connects with the mind and heart of God with ease! You don't want a raggedy, needy soul that makes your spirit path full of rips and tears. Your body needs a healthy soul and spirit.

I'm like a renter in this body—that is, I take care of it, I furnish it, I even pamper my body with treats like exercise, nutritional supplements, great healthy food, lots of water, plenty of rest, etc. I try to be good to my body while I have it.

If I live where there isn't enough food, where I sleep in dirt and have never seen a vitamin pill or a doctor, I am the renter of my body and I *receive all* my strength and life from God. I am no less responsible to bless my body while I am starving than while I am fed and fat.

What happens if my rental body gets sick? Do I pray for healing? You bet I do. Of course I pray for healing. Praying for healing is elementary. I can't imagine a Christian who doesn't pray for healing when he or she is sick.

I'm talking about prayer. We have to realize that Romans 12:1-2, which tells us that our bodies are to be living sacrifices—our reasonable service—is another basic spiritual kindergarten activity. Our bodies are *His*, not ours. Our bodies are the temples of the Holy Spirit. *"Do you not know that your body is the temple of the Holy Spirit who is in you, whom you have from God, and you are not your own?"* (1 Cor. 6:19). In light of these truths, we pull our bodies into alignment with our souls and spirits, and we drench our bodies from the *inside out* with the power of the Holy Spirit. We pray *in* the spirit.

TRIUMPH WITH THE ANGELS

Our problem is that we spend our lives praying from the *outside in*. Angels guide us from the outside in, and we know this from the words of Psalm 91: *"He shall give His angels charge over you. to keep you in all your ways…"* but He also gives us angels to give us an *inner* poke. We must do our body-soul-spirit work from the *insideout*, with the Spirit doing the teaching and leading.

✛ ⊕ ✛ ⊕ ✛ ⊕ ✛ ⊕ ✛ ⊕ ✛

Angels speak to your *spirit*.

✛ ⊕ ✛ ⊕ ✛ ⊕ ✛ ⊕ ✛ ⊕ ✛

Learn to listen. Quiet your soul and listen.

If my body is ailing, I rush to get hands laid on me for healing, and this is scriptural. It's good to ask people to pray for me. How could there be anything bad about asking another Christian to pray for me? However, receiving prayer from my brothers and sisters is not the beginning, middle, and end of my healing. I will have to do some serious body-spirit activity on my own.

In my meetings people are healed. I pray for people all the time to get healed and they're healed instantaneously. I mean, it's fabulous! I see healing as *natural* when the Holy Spirit is in our midst.

If you are miraculously healed by a single prayer or at a meeting (mine or someone else's) I rejoice with you. I celebrate. I light candles. *But* the chances are that down the road some other ailment or problem will hit you head-on and you will have to do the serious body-spirit work yourself. If you don't, you'll be one of the spiritually impoverished persons I write about at the beginning of this chapter.

What do I mean by body-spirit work? I mean taking *spiritual charge* over your body. Remember, you are spirit, soul, and body. Angels are only spirit, except when they show up on earth in human form for the express purpose of helping us and doing God's will.

TAKING SPIRITUAL CHARGE OF YOUR BODY

One way to take spiritual charge over your body is to *speak* to your body: *"Body, I now address you in the love of the Lord Jesus. Body, I am speaking healing and wholeness and vitality to you."*

Do this by naming the part of your body that needs healing and putting your hands on that part of your body, as in the example below:

"Back, arm, stomach, or other body part, I speak peace and perfect working order to you. I speak healing to you in the name of Jesus Christ of Nazareth."

"(Body part) _____ , you belong to God. God formed you in His great wisdom. He formed you with love and with His perfect will so that you would function well."

"(Body part) _____ , I dedicate you to God and His purposes. Be at peace, body. Be healed. Be whole. Be restored to perfect health. You are safe in the protection of the Lord God Almighty."

When I lay hands on people as I pray for their healing I can actually feel alarm and fear in the tissues of their bodies. I can almost hear the cells in their bodies crying in fear and wonder at what's happening to them. The first thing I do is pray for peace to enter that body. I talk to that person's body to reassure it. I talk to that body almost like it's a child who needs comfort. "It's all right," I say. "Calm, be calm. God is with you. You are loved and you are safe serving this soul and spirit. Be at peace. It's OK now, it's OK. The Holy Spirit of God is now moving upon you to heal you...." And then, after a while, I can feel that body actually relax under my hands, as a quieting takes place.

Awhile ago I prayed for a lady's swollen arthritic knees. I started out by talking to her knees: "What a sweet little knee," I cooed to one, and then did the same with the other. (Imagine the woman's reaction.) "You're a good little knee," I went on. "God loved you enough to give you to this dear lady to bless her," I said. "Be at peace. It's OK. The Holy Spirit is now moving upon you to heal you...." I felt a healing angel hovering near and could sense his touch on her precious knees. The woman felt it too.

I wasn't surprised when the knees responded as I continued to speak healing into them. Psalm 103:1-4 is a passage that is absolutely basic to our divine inheritance as God's children. *"He heals all your diseases"*(NKJV), it says. Remind your body of this truth. It weeps to know this.

This woman had received prayer for healing at least a zillion times. She was the first one to hop forward at every altar call for healing. At prayer meetings she clamored for the chair where she could get healing prayer for her arthritis. She sent in prayer requests to TV evangelists. She made declarations, memorized healing Scripture verses, and she rebuked the arthritis devil. God honored all those prayers because when Jesus, the angel, and I proclaimed her body as lovely and perfect, healing flowed through her body.

However! And there is a "however." She would now have to *partner* with her angel and with God. She would now have to stop eating junk;

she'd have to change her diet and eat in healthy ways, she'd have to exercise regularly, take her supplements, and glorify God with her body.

Here's a postscript to the knee story. I saw the lady recently and she is aglow, not only with healing from without, but with healing from *within*. Her spirit is a big spirit. Her soul is in alignment with her spirit, and she is training her body to serve her well. She is doing everything to keep her body healthy and healed, including exercise.

✤ ⊕ ✤ ⊕ ✤ ⊕ ✤ ⊕ ✤ ⊕ ✤

It's possible to lose our healing by neglect just as we can get sick by neglect

✤ ⊕ ✤ ⊕ ✤ ⊕ ✤ ⊕ ✤ ⊕ ✤

Sometimes we pray for someone's healing and Holy Spirit and the angels will be right there with us, but the healing won't be manifested immediately. My prayer at these times is that we would be like Hannah who trusted God and the Word of God. Remember Hannah in First Samuel 1-2? Do you remember how she rejoiced with hilarious joy at the words of the priest, Eli, that she'd conceive and bear a son? Hannah didn't rejoice any more vigorously when her baby was born than the moment when she received the promise. I love that.

Today, right now, because of your faith, God wants to bring a triple; no, a *quadruple* blessing upon you. He will make you beautiful for Himself and for the world *and* He will heal you from your head to your sweet toes.

Sometimes healings in themselves don't make us beautiful. I know a man who was healed from cancer and he's as nasty-tempered as ever. He acknowledges that his healing is a gift from God, and he says he's grateful, but the personality of his soul is much bigger than the beauty of his spirit.

Talk to your body. Talk to your soul. Take spiritual charge and be the beautiful person God has called you to be.

THE PASSION OF YOUR SOUL

Growing up, I was an actor in the theater and later a visual artist, a psychotherapist, and an author. I wrote my first novel, *I Love You Like a Tomato*, (Forge Books, 2003) under my Italian family name, Marie Giordano. The book celebrates the fictional life of ChiChi Maggiordino, an Italian immigrant who lives her life to heal her dysfunctional family and be the best mime and actor she can be. This goal to be a mime and to dance and act I know about firsthand. I gave my experiences to ChiChi, my fictional character, and she just "took off." It was as if the character had taken my words and ran with them. Readers e-mail me and tell me they love ChiChi as if she were a member of their family. It's a strange, supernatural connection, this one of author and reader—and I feel this connection now with you as I write this book. I can sense your angels' delight and desire to partner with you in God's Kingdom.

ART AND GOD

Now, more than ever, Spirit-filled artists, musicians, dancers, and writers are stepping up to Heaven's plate, and the Holy Spirit is speaking in exciting, fresh, and powerful ways.

I've been to the Vatican Museum in Rome many times and I've stood under the great Michelangelo ceiling of the Sistine Chapel. I am like the countless others who have made this pilgrimage, and I remain an anonymous lover of the Word and will of God that is painted so magnificently on the ceiling and walls of the Sistine Chapel. One is reduced to a speck of dirt in the presence of such bigness, such as this monumental work of art which has lasted for ages.

And yet, Jesus Christ of Nazareth has told us *we* are great. *we* are big. *We're* the best art ever created. That's you and me, the members of the human race. Jesus was brutally beaten until His flesh was like hamburger, His mind was addled, and His body was a mess of blood. This happened so that we could rise up before the God of the universe as His finest work. Jesus was not even recognizable as a human being when they strung Him up as a piece of raw, living meat on the Cross. Other crucifixions, which were common in those days, were never this brutal, this demoralizing. This He did so the sins that uglify our lives will be forgiven and paid for and we can be works of art in the Great Art Gallery of the Kingdom of God. How the angels rejoice over this.

How Incredible Are You?

God loves you and guides you and helps you in your life at all times. If you have a love for art or music or a sport—let's say you're a huge fan of a certain baseball or football team— does this mean you're a worldly, non-spiritual person? Heavens, no. Our likes, dislikes, and passions for the things of the world belong in the soul realm. Spiritual passion, on the other hand, has God at the very center of everything. *"That which is born of the flesh is flesh, and that which is born of the Spirit is spirit"* (John 3:6). You are born again of His Spirit! Wherever you go, you bring God with you. If you are sitting in the stands at a Padres game, God is sitting in the stands at a Padres game with you, because He lives in you by His Spirit. (But that doesn't necessarily mean they'll win—ha ha.)

Although you may hoist up a few emotional prayers during an especially tense game at the stadium or on TV, God is not exactly taking precedence over all, because this experience belongs to the soul realm. Is it OK to have passion for things like sports or art or opera or whatever? The answer is yes. However, it goes without saying that there are passions that are clearly not OK—*"Let everyone who names the name of Christ depart from iniquity,"* Paul says in Second Timothy 2:19. And, Peter says, *"Beloved, I beg you as sojourners and pilgrims, abstain from fleshly lusts **which war against the soul**"* (1 Pet. 2:11).

So how do we handle the passions and interests of our soul? What should the soul do with its passions and interests? The answer is to dedicate all to the Lord! Dress your interests in prayer. Allow Him to bless your interests. God wants to party with you!

To use an example, let's say you are an opera afficionado. You simply love the opera. You have an enormous CD library of operas, you have season tickets to your local opera company's offerings, you own a number of books on opera, you've memorized arias, and your idea of the perfect vacation is an opera a day.

Ask yourself these questions: "Do angels enjoy opera? Do angels fancy baseball? Do angels like deep-sea fishing? Of course they do! If *you* enjoy these things, know in your heart of hearts that your angels are right there with you, and so is the Lord Himself. Jesus told you in Matthew 28:20, *"Lo, I am with you always."* He tells you daily in a million ways, "I am *with* you." He enjoys seeing you enjoying life. Give Him your passions and interests so He can place His seal of blessing upon them. Thank Him for everything you love in life.

✛ ⊕ ✛ ⊕ ✛ ⊕ ✛ ⊕ ✛ ⊕ ✛

God enjoys seeing you enjoying life.

✛ ⊕ ✛ ⊕ ✛ ⊕ ✛ ⊕ ✛ ⊕ ✛

PRAYER

Father, in the name of Jesus Christ, my Savior, I choose to enjoy your presence on earth and in my life.

Search my heart and see if there is any unclean drive or motive in me regarding my work, recreation, play, or relaxation activities.

Father, in the name of Jesus, I will not leave you out of any area of my life, and I ask that your Presence would permeate every interest and activity in my life.

Lord, you know I really enjoy _____ , and I am laying this passion before your throne of grace for you to bless it and enjoy it with me.

I choose to live with integrity and a pure heart in order to bring you honor in all that I am and do and enjoy. Thank you!

Everywhere I step my foot, you go with me. Thank you for the joy of life.

Thank you, Beloved One, thank you.

DECREE TO YOUR SOUL

Make the following declarations to your soul. David spoke to his soul, demanding that his soul would bless the Lord, so let's do the same:

Soul, I now address you and command you to align yourself with the power of the Holy Spirit who dwells in me.

Soul, you will not run my life with vain and stupid passions that lead nowhere. Soul, you will bless the Lord with your passions and interests.

Soul, you will lay down all vanity before the throne of God and you will surrender to His will.

Soul, you will be thankful.

Bless the Lord, O soul of mine. Bless the Lord.

FAITH DECLARATION

I hereby take control of my soul's thoughts and passions.

I wash my mind and heart of all negativity, and all destructive agents with the precious blood of Jesus.

I will live with a pure heart and a pure soul. I *will* be holy. I purpose to be like Jesus, a fun, interesting, wise, strong, good, lovely person who lives in the power of the Holy Spirit.

I command my human spirit to be filled and empowered with the Holy Spirit of God in all matters.

"I have been crucified with Christ; it is no longer I who live, but Christ lives in me; and the life which I now live in the flesh I live by faith in the Son of God, who loved me and gave Himself for me" (Gal. 2:20).

I am loved, and I am beautiful to God. The angels are encamped around me at this very moment.

Thank you, Beloved. Thank you.

What would happen if, for one solid day of the week, we did nothing but thank Him? What would happen if we stayed up all night *tonight* thanking Him? What would happen if prayer groups all over the world praised the Lord for one whole night? Just praised and praised Him? Will you try it?

chapter 6

ACTIVATING FAITH

HOW do we enter the heavenly realm and walk in the fullness of the Lord's Presence? How do we take our spiritual inheritance and move in the spiritual blessings God has blessed us with in heavenly places? How do we receive divine impartations from the King of Glory and walk and talk with angels?

It's the *Word of God* that makes sharp separations between the spirit, the soul, and the body. It's the Word of God that builds our spirit, and as we grow and gain understanding about the spirit realm, we become more spiritually attuned. *"For the word of God is living and powerful, and sharper than any two-edged sword, piercing even to the **division of soul and spirit, and of joints and marrow,** and is a discerner of the thoughts and intents of the heart"* (Heb. 4:12).

Our emotions change and fluctuate and they can easily betray us. (They are found within the soul realm.) Our thoughts can be unruly to the point of self-destruction. Our urges for self-gratification can obscure our ability to hear from God. The Lord is calling us to move out of the grip of the soul realm and live through the sweetness of our spirits. As believers in Christ, our spirits are eternally fused with the Lord and His Kingdom. We can't hear His voice unless we listen with the ears of our spirit.

How do we experience God's Presence? It is by the power of the Holy Spirit in us, and it is by faith. We are able to experience realms of heavenly glory because our spirits are large and our faith is large.

How do we hear from angels? By the power of the Holy Spirit in us and by faith.

How do we visit the throne room of God? By the power of the Holy Spirit and by faith.

"Faith is the substance of things hoped for, the evidence of things not seen" (Heb. 11:1).

If you tell me you'll meet me for dinner at six o'clock at a restaurant and I show up at six to meet you as agreed, that's an act of faith, isn't it? I have faith that you'll show up. At 5:30, as I'm on my way to the restaurant, I am not wondering if we'll have dinner together or not. I'm not in a state of doubt about dinner with you. But where's the proof that we'll have dinner together? Where's the proof that you'll show up? For that matter, where's the proof that I'll get there safely and on time, or that the chef wouldn't have quit his job, or that the restaurant hasn't closed down? There is no proof, is there? No certainty whatsoever in our plans. We exercise faith in countless ways every day in the uncertain natural realm. Faith in the Spirit, however, is sure. It's alive and throbbing with energy and power and life. Faith in God is certain. It's *substance*. It's tangible. It's the proof of what we can't see. Faith is the confirmation, proof, testimony, sign, token, documentation, and attestation of what is unseen. (See Hebrews 11:1.)

DEFINITIONS OF FAITH

✣ ⊕ ✣ ⊕ ✣ ⊕ ✣ ⊕ ✣

Faith sees through God'd eyes and from His perspective.

✣ ⊕ ✣ ⊕ ✣ ⊕ ✣ ⊕ ✣

If you can remember the above sentence, I believe you will experience excellent spiritual growth in a short amount of time. It sounds so simple, yet it is truly profound, and every day I prostrate myself before this truth. Every day it is new and fresh to me. *Faith sees through God's eyes and from His perspective.* We train our spirit in this knowledge. Our spiritual training happens through the written Word of

God. We systematically study, meditate, and act upon the Word of God. We learn to see through God's eyes by studying the Word of God; in this way we are able to "hear" and discern His mind. We begin to speak the truths we are learning, and our prayer life grows stronger as our faith grows. We speak and pray according to what we believe. *"Out of the abundance of the heart the mouth speaks,"* Jesus said. (See Matthew 12:34.)

Speaking Faith Into Ourselves and the World

One day the Lord spoke to me as I was driving my car to the woods to walk with Him. He said, *"Whatever you bless I will bless."*

"Whatever you bless I will bless."

I pulled over to the side of the road.

I was blown away, unraveled.

I began to cry as I thought of all there was to bless and how much I had not blessed. What I understood Him to mean by "bless" was "to touch with His Spirit." I knew there was much more to what He meant—and He would show me step by step beyond the dictionary or the Greek/Hebrew or Amplified definition of "bless." At that moment I was lifted right up out of my car into the holy place where the angels were dancing around light-hearted and happy, and the blessing of God fell as kisses on the entire universe.

I've not been the same since that experience. You might say I am one busy girl as I go around blessing everything I see, hear, and get my hands on. (You may consider yourself blessed, too, because I am blessing and praying for you as you read this book. I may not know your name, but God does.)

Faith sees through God's eyes and from His perspective.

We speak forth faith. We speak forth blessing.

One day, as the Prophet Isaiah was in the Temple, he saw the Lord high and lifted up, and His train filled the Temple. Isaiah saw the six-winged seraphim who were crying out praises to the Lord, *"Holy, holy, holy is the Lord of Hosts; the whole earth is full of His glory!"* (Isa. 6:1-3.)

Isaiah managed to remain upright and watch this holy and heavenly manifestation take place. The Bible says the very posts of the Temple shook with the voice of the seraphim. The Presence of God was very thick, and the place was filled with holy smoke. This same smoke, or glory cloud, had guided the Israelites in the desert and had also filled Solomon's temple at its dedication. We often see that glory cloud now, the sweet, thick smoke of God's Presence.

Isaiah immediately became aware of his mortal state. *"Woe is me, for I am undone," he cried out, "...I am a man of unclean lips"* (Isa. 6:5).

Lips. *Lips?*

Notice that Isaiah didn't say, "I am a man of unclean desires" or "I am a man of unclean work habits." He said *lips.*

Isaiah knew that God knew if the lips are unclean, the heart is unclean. Jesus said, *"...out of the abundance of the **heart** the **mouth** speaks"* (Matt. 12:34).

We bless others and the world around us with our mouths by speaking as the Holy Spirit within us speaks. We speak with our hearts. Jesus said, *"**I speak** what I have seen with My Father"* (John 8:38).

The Lord gives wisdom, and *from His mouth* come knowledge and understanding. (See Proverbs 2:6). He breathes into us that which He is. The angel (one of the seraphim) touched a live coal from the altar onto Isaiah's lips and pronounced that his sins were purged. This visitation and purging of Isaiah, the priest, was the divine ordination of Isaiah, the prophet.[1]

The ordination ceremony was officiated over by angels.

OUR FIVE SENSES

Our five senses are spiritual antennas. You need to be able to discern the Presence of God and the presence of evil. You need to have spiritual eyes and ears of discernment. How do we do this? We train our senses by *exercise.* Know when someone is speaking and behaving out of their soul-self. Hebrews 5:14 tells us that *"solid food belongs to those who are of full age,"* that is, those who are wise and experienced in walking in the power of the Holy Spirit, those who *"by reason of use have their senses **exercised** to discern both good and evil."*

TRAIN YOUR SENSES

Train your senses and your spirit to become spiritual antennas to be used to receive God's signals. The problem is that we often think we're OK even when we're on the wrong frequency. We're picking up a lot of input that sounds good, but it isn't from the heart of God. We need to be on God's frequency. This is why continual daily study of the Word of God is so vital in our lives.

If you do not have your nose in God's Word every day, you're starving yourself. I know that when I don't study and meditate on Scripture on a daily basis, I'm a person living an almost-life. I'm like a face without eyes. I'm like a loaf of bread with a huge chunk taken out of it. I'm simply not all there.

I can't train myself in the spiritual gifts without God's Word as my foundation. I'm so hungry and so passionate to know the Lord that I simply must connect with His Word. I must eat the Word, devour the Word, ingest the Word, and allow its nutrients to permeate every cell in my body and mind. My spirit craves His Spirit. The Scriptures also pin me to the wall regarding sin, negligence, and anything that is not of God.

I love David's words in the King James Version, *"Thy word have I hid in mine heart, that I might not sin against thee"* (Ps. 119:11). We train our senses and our souls to not sin against God. We hide His Word or bury it deeply within us so it becomes a part of us. I am no longer an almost-self when His Word is alive and thriving in me. Angels respond to the Word of God because the Word of God *is* God. (See John 1:1.) Go deeper into the Word of God and multiply your hours of Bible study each day, and watch the angels become activated around you.

As you train your senses and practice using your spiritual gifts, you will multiply their use. *"The word [of faith] is near you, in your mouth and in your heart"* (Rom. 10:8). There it is again, your *mouth.*

The Lord's angels are continually nudging me to step out with more faith in ministering to others. So I practice the gift of knowledge. I consider it all practice, actually. So I might say (faith being in my mouth) to a lady I've never seen before, "Who is Marvin?"

"Marvin is my husband," she says, surprised.

From there I look into the Spirit to see how the Lord would lead me to pray for Marvin. (I pray with faith in my mouth.)

I keep on practicing, practicing. Sometimes I'll see angels and one will be holding a coat or some other thing, and I'll say to the person near me, "You're asking God for a new coat and He wants you to know He has one for you."

The person is amazed. "How did you know?" she asks.

Of course I didn't know. God knew.

I'll say to another, "When you were a little girl, you loved to climb trees, especially a certain apple tree...."

This lady looks startled.

"The Lord wants you to know you're the apple of His eye...."

Tears and prayer and beautiful restoration take place right there in the mall or the street or train station or church ladies' room—anywhere.

God's Spirit moves across the whole earth, moving, moving, moving—waiting to be activated through His children by their faith. And who is standing by to help? Right! A great host of His angels!.

Read about the spiritual gifts in First Corinthians 12:4-10. One spiritual gift alone is good, but it's even better when more than one gift is in operation at the same time. For example, when the great Kathryn Kuhlman moved in her gift of healing, she also moved with her gift of spiritual knowledge and her gift of wisdom. She would point to a person in the audience and tell them, "God is healing you right now." When she did so, three gifts of the Spirit were in operation in a single act: the gift of knowledge, the gift of wisdom, and the gift of healing. The person she pointed out would then rise up healed of some awful disease. Ms. Kuhlman's spiritual *gift of knowledge* told her what God wanted to do and *wisdom* told her when and how to release her gift of *healing*.

If you desire to walk with angels, ask the Holy Spirit to fill your spirit with the ability to see into the heavenly realm. Then hold onto the promise of God in His Word through *faith*. Ephesians 2:6 says that you "sit together." Where? "In *heavenly places* in Christ Jesus!" This doesn't mean you'll sit together with Christ Jesus only after you're dead and gone; it means you can also sit with Him here and now. And it also doesn't mean you'll sit around doing nothing, twiddling your precious thumbs all day. "On earth as it is in heaven," we pray. Heaven is a busy place!

God waits for us with His creative miracles, and angels are encamped around you at this moment to partner with you to *do* God's will on earth.

But before I practice *doing*, I must practice *being*. The angels partner with me as I choose the Lord's mind, thoughts, and actions over my own.

Choosing the Lord's mind, thoughts, and actions over my own is elementary. The Bible says, *"The fear of the Lord is the beginning of knowledge"* (Prov. 1:7). The fear of the Lord is the state of mind where our attitudes, will, feelings, deeds, and goals are exchanged for God's. This is as elementary as speaking in tongues. It's a *beginning*.

PETER IN PRISON

Look at this miracle in Acts 12:5-17. Peter is captured and thrown in jail and four squads of soldiers are assigned to guard him. Each squad consists of four soldiers, so at all times two guards are chained with two chains to Peter's hands in his cell while two other brutes stand guard outside the cell door. It's an ugly situation, wouldn't you agree? Here's Peter chained to two of Herod's soldiers in a dank, stinking cement hole of a jail. James, the brother of John, had just been cruelly murdered by the sword as a heretic, and Peter must have been horrified and grieved at his friend's murder, the first of the apostles to be martyred.

All of a sudden the cell lights up like a bright, sunshiny afternoon and an angel of the Lord is positioned out of nowhere right next to Peter. He gives Peter a loving jab in the ribs and pulls him to his feet, "Get up quickly!" he tells him.

Was Peter dreaming? The angel tells him to put on his shoes and his cloak and follow him. Now when an angel tells you to get up and get dressed when you're chained up in prison with two soldiers on either side of you and two more at the door, you'd do as the angel told you, right? Because you'd think you were dreaming.

They trotted past the first and the second guard posts of the prison, then went on through the night until they arrived at the barred and locked iron gates guarding the city. There was no natural way out. They were locked in. Maybe Peter wondered if he had said his proper farewells to his family. He stood there helpless as the angel of God moved toward the locked iron gates and approached them, the barred gate "opened to them of its own accord." Off they went, Peter and his angel, through the gates and down the darkened street until the angel departed from him.

In a daze, in a stupor, Peter came to himself and at once understood the miracle that had just taken place and what had happened to him. An angel of the Lord had delivered him from prison chains.

But here's where the story gets good. (I love this part.) Peter hurries to the house of Mary, John's mother, where everyone has gathered for a prayer meeting (to pray for Peter). He pounds at the door of the gate and when the servant girl sees him, she runs inside, excited and thrilled to tell the others that Peter himself is outside at the gate.

Guess how the praying friends respond. They protest, arguing with the servant girl and telling her, "No, it can't be Peter. It's his angel" (Acts 12:15). Just his angel.

Just his angel?

Were these praying folk so accustomed to seeing angels that an angel showing up at the door was commonplace? *Just his angel?* Jews believed in guardian angels, true. They believed our guardian angels could take the form of the person they guarded, but I can't help wonder exactly how common this occurrence of angels showing up actually was.

Just his angel?

Is that how you'd react if you saw an angel standing at your door? "Oh golly, it's *just an angel.*" Who on earth might you have been expecting? King Kong? Joan of Arc? The Avon lady?

Peter was hustled into the house with much awe and astonishment, and in the meantime, Herod had the soldiers who were supposed to guard him put to death. The point of my retelling you this story is to emphasize to you the seemingly impossible things angels can do for us. *Angels are God's obedient miracle workers who perform God's miracles for us all for the purpose of bringing God glory.* The Lord summoned and sent that angel to help Peter. The angel did not act on his own accord. Again, look at Hebrews 1:14: Angels are all ministering spirits sent to protect and to serve us, God's children. The function of angels is to do God's bidding, as it is also our function to do God's bidding. Sometimes we're just so busy trying to work things out on our own that we don't realize our angels are right beside us ready and waiting to help us.

The spiritual world is far more vast and real than the natural world. Our problem is that we are too attached to the natural, physical world and we lose the reality of the vastness of the spiritual world. (We can be so earthly minded that we're no heavenly good.)

THE TASK OF ANGELS

Angels are God's holy diplomatic envoy. They never meddle where they are not called. They never play roles as our private secret agents or as our hired hands or "Mr./Ms. Fix-its." Angels are our helpers in responding to God's divine truth and they expect us to play our parts in His will. I know I keep repeating this, but it's because when we think of angels we need to remember this truth: *angels respond solely to God's voice and God's will.* They do not act of their own accord. They always and only do God's biddings and we human beings cannot order them around. The angels only obey God. And together we make a powerful team in the service of God.

CREATED TO LIVE IN THE SPIRIT REALM

God created me to live in the spiritual realm. I will live in that realm throughout all eternity.

While we do not look at the things which are seen, but at the things which are not seen. For the things which are seen are temporary, but the things which are not seen are eternal (2 Corinthians 4:18).

I know a couple, Christian parents, whose son was so unruly they were ready to give up hope on him. The son, who was in his 20s, stole from his parents, lied to them, cursed them to their faces, lied about them to others, derided them, insulted them, and borrowed money for a car, telephone, and apartment deposit he had no intention of ever repaying. This son moved back into his parents' house whenever he ran out of money, only to steal from them, lie, throw tantrums, curse, fight, argue, and in general, make life miserable for everyone. The parents were desperate. Living with their son was opening their home to demonic spiritual forces that exhausted them.

Now let's look at Second Corinthians 4:18 again:

While we do not look at the things which are seen, but at the things which are not seen. For the things which are seen are temporary, but the things which are not seen are eternal.

This couple needed the mind of God. They needed to look at the things which are not seen. They needed to understand the things which are seen are temporary, but the things which are not seen are eternal. They had no idea what God thought about their son. It had never occurred to them to ask what God saw when He looked at their son.

The parents had prayed and prayed for their son's help and deliverance. They had sent his name to every major ministry's prayer line, they had come against generational curses, they had followed teachings and praised, thanked, worshiped, fasted, tithed, anointed with oil, cast out, decreed, taken authority, and tough-loved; they'd done it all, and their son's behavior was worse than ever. The demons were having a heyday with that family.

Often there are no easy answers to life's problems, and as a therapist I know this well. There are no quick formulas that magically produce instant answers. Deliverance from demons can be instantaneous, and then there follows the process of rebuilding (which is a wonderful process, but it's still not magic).

The Bible refers to the casting out of demons as healing. Isn't that interesting? *"He who had been demon-possessed was **healed**"* (Luke 8:36). The Greek word for "healed" here is *sozo*, which means saved, delivered, protected, preserved, and made whole.

"Then one was brought to Him who was demon-possessed, blind and mute; and He healed him..." (Matt. 12:22a). Here the Greek word is *therapeuo*, meaning to relieve of disease, cure, and heal. Deliverance from demons and physical healing served to authenticate Jesus as the promised Messiah, but Jesus didn't want people coming to Him for miracles alone because His primary purpose was spiritual healing. Jesus wants us whole—body, soul, and spirit.

In the account in Matthew 15:21-28, a Gentile woman comes to Jesus with a demon-possessed daughter. She begs the Lord to have mercy on her, and after a little play on words demonstrating that He came for Israel before the Gentiles, Jesus answers, *"O woman, great is your faith! Let it be to you as you desire."* The Bible says, *"And her daughter was **healed** from that very hour"* (v. 28). Her demon-possessed daughter was *healed*. In other words, she was made whole.

Taking the truth of God into our lives is a process of becoming whole. I prayed with this Christian couple and asked the Lord to show them His mind about their son. I asked Him to send ministering angels to help them. It was a simple prayer, really. I wasn't led to pray a prayer of deliverance. I didn't do any warfare with them at all. It was just a simple prayer, asking our heavenly Father to show them His mind about their son. They repeated my prayer and I felt something release in the Spirit, something very subtle, like the sound you'd hear if you stepped on dry grass. Just a tiny, cracking sound in the Spirit. At that moment I knew the devil was defeated. The couple had strange expressions on their faces, as though they were listening and were surprised at what they heard.

About three days later I received a call from them. God spoke to them all right about their son, and they told me that He showed them that He saw their son as a beautiful young man, full of the Holy Spirit and *healed*.

When you do (keep) God's Word tucked inside your heart, angels are released on your behalf as your fellow-servants. (See Revelation 22:9.) The parents began to treat their son as the man God saw him as, and not only did this son receive healing, his parents received much needed healing, too. They and their relationship began the journey toward wholeness, which took a matter of some months. The son became open to receive ministry, and he began to change. Their home became a healed home and a happy one. Two years have now passed and the family is continuing to learn and grow in the power of the Holy Spirit without the constant demonic battle that besieged them for so many years.

✤ ⊕ ✤ ⊕ ✤ ⊕ ✤ ⊕ ✤ ⊕ ✤

See as God sees. Love as God loves.
Be wise as God is wise. Be strong as God is strong.
Greater is He who is in you than he who is in the world.

✤ ⊕ ✤ ⊕ ✤ ⊕ ✤ ⊕ ✤ ⊕ ✤

God wants the eyes of our spirits opened. We can handle our problems with the natural, shaky skills that belong in the soul realm or we can approach problems with the mind of the Holy Spirit. We can ask the Lord to send angels to help us overcome the afflictions that assail us, or we can try to fix them ourselves.

Right now set your mind and the eyes of your spirit on the things which are not seen with your natural eyes! Set your mind and heart and all of your attention and energy on the Holy Spirit. Soak in the Word of God and in the holy Presence of the Lord Jesus, and God, the Father.

He wants you to see into the heavenly realm and partner with the ministry of angels.

Partnering With Angels

"I am a fellow servant of yours," the angel told John on Patmos. "[I am here to co-labor with you], and of your brethren, the prophets, and of *those who do the Words of this book."*

That's *us*.

We have crossed over the threshold of an entirely new millennium and the dawning of a new day for the Church at large. Hebrews 2:4 (NAS) reads, *"God also bearing witness with them, both by **signs and wonders** and by **various miracles** and by **gifts of the Holy Spirit** according to His own will..."*. This tells us that Heaven desires to cooperate with us to open deeper supernatural dimensions to us. Let's press forth in *our* desire to bring Heaven to earth and see His Kingdom unfold! This only requires faith on our part—to believe God's promises—which absolutely, utterly cannot be broken.

When you *do* God's Word, you do His will, and the angels of the Lord are released on your behalf to work *with* you. You become partners in God's Kingdom. It's an amazing and glorious partnership, one that is birthed now and extends throughout eternity.

Though "the outward man is perishing," your "inward man is being renewed day by day" (2 Cor. 4:16). Look beyond the natural realm into the realm of the spirit to see and understand the heart and intention of God. See yourself as one who is called to bring Heaven to earth in this day and to partner with your angels in bringing the will of God to pass.

The Difficulty in Describing Glory

It was on the Isle of Patmos where John had a vision of the eternal city of God, which he tries to describe in Revelation 21. This is the city of great glory that Jesus spoke of when He told the disciples, *"In My Father's house are many mansions* [rooms, chambers], *if it were not so, I would have told you. I am going there to prepare a place for you. And if I go and prepare a place for you, I will come again and receive you to Myself; that where I am, there you may be also"* (John 14:2-3).

Here is such an awe-inspiring scene of transcendent splendor that we may never be able to take it in. It is a scene of ecstatic, joyous fellowship with God's beautiful angels and His redeemed and glorified people.

The Lord has given me divine fellowship with His angels, the angelic realm, and heavenly visitations and manifestations, and in my own small way I can understand John's dilemma in trying to describe what he sees. He tries to find words and images that speak of that which is stunning, glorious, and valuable. The best he can come up with is to use precious stones as images, such as jasper stone, clear as crystal, and pure gold-like clear glass. He speaks of the walls as being adorned with jasper, sapphire, chalcedony (a sky-blue agate stone with translucent colored stripes), emerald, beryl, topaz, an apple-green variety of quartz, jacinth, amethyst, pearls, more gold, and more pure glass. John was overwhelmed at what he saw. Who on earth could find vocabulary to describe such glory—to describe the glorious City of God?

John's dilemma was to find human words to tell of the supernatural, the divine, and Heaven itself. He explains that the City of God has no need of the sun or of the moon because the glory of God illuminates it. The Lamb is the light of Heaven. And the nations of those who are saved shall walk in heaven's light. Then verse 24 says the kings of the earth will bring their glory and honor to it. That's *you*! You bring to Him the glory He gives us, and from every nation and ethnic group, His children will live in heaven's light. There will be no more divisions, barriers, exclusions, battles, discord, anger, fear, sickness, or hatred. Here we are free at last—alive in the vivid, blinding Light emanating from God.

ENDNOTE

1. Isaiah 6:1-13.

chapter 7

ANGELS IN PRAISE AND WORSHIP

SEEING THE LIGHT

MANY of the heavenly visitations Christians are experiencing today propel them into blinding light. Many times I think I will surely be sizzled to cinders in the blaze of such light, but happily, I survive. Two days ago I saw before me a red-hot ball of light. This was a real-time vision, like a picture on the wall. I thought I was looking directly into the sun, which is not good for the eyes, and I automatically blinked and turned my head. But I was indoors and it was evening. I turned and looked directly at the light and it was fiery like the sun, a great globe of a sun. I stared at it until tears fell from my burning eyes.

The Word of God often speaks of God's Presence as a *fire*. First Thessalonians 5:19 tells us not to put out the Spirit's fire. John on Patmos described the eyes of God as *blazing fire* (see Rev. 1:14). There is a heat to the Presence of the Holy Spirit. His holy heat prepares our hearts and minds to hear His voice. In the fire of this heat I become very still. I become still, breathlessly still, in order to hear His voice. I wait for Him to speak, and it's in the quiet chambers of my human spirit He speaks. I've never heard an audible blast of a bass baritone call from the clouds: "Hello, it's Me, God!"

The Presence of God lives in me as I press into Him, hungry for intimacy with Him. Not only is He *within* me by His Holy Spirit, His Presence *surrounds* me. I can hear His beautiful voice in the stillness. The Lord manifests a measure of His glory to me as I wait and expect His Presence to fill and surround me. Wonder of wonders, I can experience a measure of His Glory! I am not imagining things. The fiery light of His Presence fills every molecule around me. It's real. *He's* real. Not only does He possess my heart, soul, and mind, but He possesses the very air I breathe.

"For the earth will be filled with the knowledge of the glory of the Lord, as the waters cover the sea," (Hab. 2:14). The glory of God fills Heaven. In Revelation 21, the description of the eternal city of God is a city of great glory, a place of such transcendent splendor that we can't begin to imagine it with our human minds. Sometimes when I hike upon the mountains on my prayer hikes I am completely blown away by the beauty around me. At such times I tell the Lord, "I have never even imagined such beauty as what you're sharing with me in these mountains!" Then I realize if I haven't imagined *earthly* beauty, how much more incredible and unimaginable is *heaven's* beauty? Here is the thing He wants us to know: Heaven and the City of Glory are His dwelling place. The beauty of Heaven is God Himself.

Heaven Lives Inside the Christian

Heaven is also within me. The Presence of God lives in me as I press into Him, hungry for intimacy with the Creator of All There Is. It's unlike any other relationship in life.

The God-empowered life is completely supernatural—and then His power and Presence generate within and become completely natural. In other words, living completely surrendered to His Spirit is our norm. All else is unnatural.

Heaven on earth is knowing God, loving God, allowing Him to shine within us, and experiencing His power and Presence in all we think and do. Supernatural signs and wonders that we cannot ever produce in our own ability will follow. The apostle Paul admonished us to be imitators of God as dear children, to walk in love and as children of light. (See Ephesians 5:1,8.) How beautiful! Our citizenship and personhood belong to Heaven (see Phil. 3:20), and this Heaven is not just in the sweet by-and-by; it's here now. Heaven lives in us.

Meeting an Angel

I was on my prayer walk with the Lord in the woods one drizzly afternoon in autumn and He said to me that He had someone He wanted me to meet. I knew in my spirit He meant He wanted me to meet one of His angels. I was intimidated by this idea and with my old skepticism coming to the fore, I looked for a biblical reference for this. Are we allowed to talk with angels?

The only angels I ever had addressed were demons. (We certainly do talk to demons, don't we? We're always exposing and howling away at bad spirits—why, then, can't we carry on a civil conversation with the beautiful angels of God who are on our side?) I wanted to know if it was biblically permissible for angels to talk to *us*. This was all new to me. I talked to Jesus all the time, sure, but angels? I thought of the angels who appeared to Mary, Joseph, Daniel, Abraham, Jacob, John, and Jesus Himself. I remembered the angel who came to Paul and Silas in prison and told them to get up and make a fast exit. I thought of Peter's angel who unlocked his chains in prison. I thought of John on Patmos, as the angels talked to him and gave him the Book of the Revelation. I thought of Joshua, Daniel, and Zechariah. The list went on.

For every cosmic event, angels have always been there. How about the miraculous event when God came to earth as a man? At Jesus' birth, the angels were there. How about when He was tempted in the wilderness? His angels were there. How about during His earthly ministry? The angels were there. How about in the Garden of Gesthemene? The angels were there. How about at His death, burial, and resurrection? The angels were there. And did it not begin with the archangel Gabriel appearing to and *talking* with a peasant girl from Galilee named Mary?

Throughout the Bible God's angels made themselves known to God's people, revealing to them the very things God wanted them to know. Supernatural visions, revelations, and angelic manifestations are foundation stones upon which the Church was established and upon which it stands.[1]

"The true church only continues to exist today because supernatural manifestations just like these [of today] were a natural part of its life from its very beginning and indeed were the reason for its vigorous growth."[2]

Then it hit me. I remembered the verse, *"Though I speak with the tongues of men and of angels…"* (1 Cor. 13:1). How could I speak with the tongues of angels if I had no idea how they spoke? Chuckling at my reasoning, I repeated Paul's words: *"**Though** I speak with the tongues of angels…"* as if this were something ordinary, just as speaking a human language is ordinary. I know how to speak human languages because I live in a world of humans. Was it possible that I could learn to speak the language of angels because I also live in a spiritual world?

These are the things I pondered that drizzly autumn afternoon in the woods long ago while walking with Jesus. Then He said to me, *"Marie, look ahead."* I looked and before me stood a tall, handsome creature dressed in white. He was lovely, not in the same way we think of as being physically lovely—his *being* was lovely. That is to say, his presence, his essence were lovely. His face had the kindest expression, and I instantly felt at peace. I felt a sense of confidence, a warm, good feeling of OKness. The first words out of my mouth were, "Oh, you're so kind…."

He answered immediately and said, "Because *He* is kind."

He said he exists to do the Lord's will and that I must do the same. He said he is kind as I must be kind because the Lord is kind. The Lord is merciful and I must be as well, he said. He said we are to be like the Lord. Even though his words were not earth-shaking or new to my ears, I found them to be utterly revelatory. It was much better than hearing Handel's *Messiah* for the first time.

I asked the Lord if I could ask questions of the angel. He said, *"You've been asking Me for wisdom, and wisdom asks questions. Go ahead. Ask."*

The angel told me we are co-workers. He told me we were a team to glorify the Lord. I asked him how we could be a team to glorify the Lord.

He said, "Know God and love God." He said that we humans are called to live this life unto the Lord and bring Him glory in this realm as well as the heavenly realm, on earth as it is in heaven, until the day we are finished here.

At that time in my spiritual walk I was operating in "flesh alert." By "flesh alert" I mean I questioned spiritual phenomena. I "tested the spirits." I asked, "Is this of the Lord?" "Is this Bible-tested?" "Am I in the flesh or in the spirit?" "Am I just imagining things?" Most of the teaching I had received was in the form of warnings to be very leery of anything outside the norm. It was OK to speak in tongues and prophesy, but uh-oh, Missy, what's this about *angels* and *heavenly visitations?* Have I gone and dropped off the deep end?

For three years I walked in Heaven's courts, traveled with the angelic host, spending days and months with Jesus personally, wrapped up in the Holy Spirit's Presence and the Father's love without human guidance. I knew nothing of a "church movement," other than what God told me in private. (I knew about global revival because the Holy Spirit showed me before I personally experienced any of the great move of God to the nations today.) It's so thrilling to me now to hear of others' experiences, even those experiences of a hundred years ago, which are exactly like what the Lord has shown me and my own experiences with Him in the heavenly realm.

That blessed afternoon, while meeting my personal angel (Scripture doesn't use the expression "guardian angel"), I was stunned out of my wits. I never even dreamed of such a thing. Meeting my personal angel? Excuse me? I'm an educated person. I'm supposed to be somewhat rational.

God's angel told me he had been with me since birth. God's angel explained to me that he had been assigned to me for life. God's angel told me he is a warrior. He said all angels are warriors. He said he appeared to me in a human-like form because I could understand and relate to the human form. He said that angels take on many forms in the spirit, as does the Lord Himself. (The Lord is a lion, a lamb, etc.) He said I must always speak in the name of Jesus in the spirit realm.

I told him that I figured there must be a lot fewer demons around since the time of the Fall, because we've been casting them out and sending them into outer darkness for these thousands of years. I said, "You'd think we would have had the demonic forces pretty well cleaned up by now," and I laughed, thinking I was making a joke. But angels don't joke about demons. (They conquer them, as we're supposed to do.)

Then, as we were talking, we were at once no longer in the woods and it was no longer a drizzly autumn afternoon. I felt myself being lifted up, up, up, and then we were up in the heavenlies, far above the earth realm and I was standing before an enormous brass double door. I stood there staring at the door. Just staring at it.

The angel said, "Open the door." And I did.

The huge doors swung apart, revealing before us countless angelic beings dressed in white and singing praises to God. Their faces shone as they sang. They weren't of any particular race or color and seemed to be all races and colors put together. I started to sing along with them, but the sound of my human voice was harsh compared to theirs.

Then the angel showed me another huge brass double door, which opened without my touching it and I saw countless angelic beings playing instruments as part of a monumental orchestra. I didn't recognize the instruments and the music was strange to my ears, but sweet enough to eat.

Door upon door opened and I saw millions of angels engaged in various tasks from building enormous machines in a glorious, factory-like atmosphere to sewing banners.

One door opened and I saw a long, golden room. Along its walls were flecks of sparkling colors. The room was gyrating with the force of a powerful tornado-like wind roaring up and down the walls, the ceiling, and the floor. The Lord told me this was the room of answered prayer.

The sky then was filled with angels who shone as brightly as millions of white, blinding suns.

To say I was flabbergasted is an understatement. I asked the Lord Jesus why I was allowed to open the doors and see into the heavenly realm and watch His angels at work. Me, of all people. Why was *I* permitted to talk personally with my private angel? Who was I, after all, to deserve such an honor?

"Why are you giving *me* this great honor, Lord?"

He answered simply, "Because I want to."

I fell to my knees. He didn't give me a lofty mandate.

He said simply, *"Because I want to."*

ANGELS IN PRAISE AND WORSHIP

And I looked and heard the voice of many angels, around the throne and the living creatures and the elders; and the number of them was myriads of myriads, and thousands of thousands, saying with a loud voice, "Worthy is the Lamb that was slain to receive power and riches and wisdom and might and honor and glory and blessing." And every created thing which is in heaven and on the earth and under the earth and on the sea, and all things in them, I heard saying, "To Him who sits on the throne, and to the Lamb, be blessing and honor and glory and dominion forever and ever." And the four living creatures kept saying, "Amen." And the elders fell down and worshiped (Revelation 5:11-14 NAS).

Worship and praise are the language and essence of Heaven. When we worship and praise the Lord, whether corporately in a great hall or alone in our room, we can be assured there are angels singing right along with us. The angel told John on Patmos, *"I am your fellow servant among your brethren the prophets, and of those who are mindful and practice* *the truths contained in the messages of this book. **Worship God!**" (Rev. 22:9 AMP).*

Whenever I am lifted into the Presence of the heavenly host or even sense the angels surrounding us in our earthly realm, I can't help but praise the Lord. I just begin carrying on and praising Him. I especially love walking in the woods at night because there I can praise the Lord as loudly as I want to, and I can dance and pray with nobody around except the wind, the shadows, and the trees. I can hear the angels singing in the marvel of an empty sky and I see their faces and their uplifted arms as clear as day. I am part of a monumental choir. I am part of a universal dance concert. I am joined with Heaven and every created being who has ever cried out, "Holy is the Lamb!"

EXPLOSIONS OF LIGHT IN THE SKY

I drive to the dried-up lagoon and head into the brush in the dark. I walk along under the nighttime sky and praise the Lord full blast. What could be more exhilarating? I am alone out here in the wild, without a single heron or duck on the baked mud of the abandoned lagoon. As I praise the Lord, I feel a strangeness in the air. A quarter moon leans out of a starless sky like an anorexic banana. I can hear the traffic of the distant freeway and I can see the muted lights of the houses on the far canyon ridge ahead. I call on the angelic host and praise the Lord some more. The air around me is thick and still; not a breeze stirs. No stars above. No movement in the bulrushes. No hum of insects or twitter of night birds. I walk along singing, loudly and stridently, but then as I walk deeper into the thicket, my voice becomes soft. "I worship you, my King. I worship You, my King! Ohhhh, yesss…I doo…I dooo."

I come to a standstill and listen. It is so quiet I can hear my hair growing (just kidding). It is so quiet it is as though the lagoon is holding its breath. I stand there listening and waiting because I know how the Lord loves to spring surprises on a person. I stand there alone out in the middle of the dried lagoon with darkness and silence around me, when all at once I lift my eyes and see the sky magically light up with millions of twinkling lights. It is so spectacular I immediately flip on the "flesh alarm" for an explanation of the spectacle before my eyes. My first thought is that clouds have moved and stars have simply poked out of the overcast night. Or perhaps it could be explained that I was seeing reflections of the city in the sky. (I was in the country.)

But no, above me is an explosion of sparkling lights with no earthly explanation for their appearance.

I am seeing the sparkling presence of angels, of heavenly beings. I had entered inside the heart of their presence and had become one with their song.

At that instant the Lord Jesus appears and sweeps me up in His arms. He twirls me around and, as He does so, I feel the chaos of the universe. I feel cold and heat. I feel space and time. I feel matter and energy in the swirl of His embrace. I hold on to the folds of His sleeves. He whispers that we must appropriate the power of His name. He tells me we have far more authority over far more than we realize. He tells me that angels don't stop speeding trains by holding up their hands. They take *authority* over molecules, energy, atoms, and matter—all in His name. Angels perform miracles on our behalf in *His name.* We also have this authority in His name. We are to counteract the powers and principalities described in Ephesians 6 in His name. We are not to be victims. The anointing is ours as His sons and daughters. We have authority in His name. We are to exercise authority in His name.

A COMMON EXPERIENCE

The explosion of lights I saw that night greets me now each night before I go to sleep. (At first I wondered if the mysterious phenomenon was due to a weird eye malady, but now I know better.) This nightly explosion of sparkling lights is like a display of brilliant fireworks or like my galaxy screen saver, and no matter where I am, no matter what city, country, hotel, dorm, or guest room I'm in, before I close my eyes the angels are there. I always thank Jesus and stare as long as I can before my eyes grow tired and I close them. At times I don't know if my eyes are open or closed because the explosion of lights remains. You can see them, too. When you begin to praise the Lord, ask the angels to join you. Become at home with your angels and with worshiping along with them. They'll light up the air and your life.

ANGELS WHO SING ALONG ON RECORDINGS

Have you heard the angels singing on your Christian music CD's and DVD's? Musicians are reporting that when it comes time to do the final edit on their recordings, lo and behold, there are other unidentifiable voices and sounds praising the Lord on the tracks. Experts say these sounds can't be duplicated by any high-tech, state-of-the-art recording equipment. On a particular recording I heard some singing in the spirit and there suddenly emerged unfamiliar sounds like a lovely sort of twittering and chirping. According to the sound engineers, there was no practical explanation for the sounds. I'll talk more about the sounds of angels in later chapters.

ANGELS IN WORSHIP SERVICES

We know that God's angels like to join a rousing worship service and sing along with the worshipers. Many people who knew Robert Sadler, a great man of God who traveled the Midwest preaching and singing and leading worship in the '70s, remember how, in glorious worship with him at the piano, he would jump up to dance and the piano kept right on playing! I wrote the biography of this incredible man of God in a book called, *The Emancipation of Robert Sadler*, later entitled, *Help Me Remember, Help Me Forget*, published by Bethany House.

I like the following testimony from a choir director in an Assemblies of God church in California. He told me that one Sunday morning half the people in his choir were out sick. He panicked. He said that he couldn't imagine how the music would sound without all their voices. He prayed a desperate prayer as the few singers stood to their feet to sing. He swears he then saw angels take the place of the missing singers. The choir never sounded better! *"Oh come, let us worship and bow down"* (Ps. 95:6), we sing, and when we do so, we can expect the angels to join us. *"Oh, worship the Lord in the beauty of holiness!"* (Ps. 96:9). This is what draws us into the Presence of the Lord, and worship is the holy key that draws Heaven to earth and earth to Heaven.

I've been in worship services when the angels entered and stood alongside us singing away like there was no tomorrow. When the angels are present, I've noticed we keep on singing much longer. Sometimes we can't stop for hours on end. It's because we are one with the angels and we have brought Heaven to earth.

When I was ministering in Nigeria, the praise and worship in the Nigerian church would go on for hours on end. They just didn't stop praising the Lord. Church services began early in the morning and we worshiped for two or three hours, followed by a two-hour sermon and more praise and worship; I'm telling you, we had church all day.

You know the angels are present when you don't want to stop singing and praising God. Here's something for you to do: next time you're in church worshiping the Lord, open the eyes of your spirit and see how many angels you can see in your midst.

Sometimes when I'm speaking in a church, I'll look out into the audience and who do I see walk in and sit down right in front? The Lord Jesus Himself, along with a few angels on each side. It blows my mind every time. The first time I saw Him walk in and sit down with a few angels on each side I was so overcome that I began hyperventilating. I didn't know what to do! How could I preach about Him when He was right there in front of everybody? All anyone had to do was reach out and touch Him! He had such a loving smile on His face, and I kept on preaching, gasping, and wheezing, but not missing a beat, and let me tell you, that night the miracles flew forth.

"He's here," I told the people. "Just reach out and touch Him." (It was a cliche to say, "He's here, reach out and touch Him," when He actually *was* there and anyone could have touched Him. And the people did so! It was wonderful! We received healings, deliverances, restoration, prophetic revelation, and angelic visitations all in one service!

I prayed and laid hands on everybody that night because I knew the Lord had something big for each one of them. I didn't think He would have allowed me to see Him walk in and sit down with His angels if He didn't have a dynamic plan and purpose for His people that night, and at one point the pastor and I were the only ones on our feet. The people were laid out all over the church, in the aisles, on the pews, and around the altar.

By "laid out" I mean what we call, "slain in the spirit," or "going down under the power." This is when the Holy Spirit touches us through the laying on of hands and we physically collapse under the power of His Presence. We literally can't stand up! Once we are in this collapsed, vulnerable state, He can minister to our spirits in a uniquely personal way. It's a brief time of being alone with God with no interference from anything or anyone. There hasn't been a revival in history without this supernatural phenomenon being present.

At some dynamic meetings in Kansas City in 2004, the angels visited in our midst and the prophet Bob Jones laid hands on every one of us. Fifteen hundred people were lifted up into glory at those meetings. Heaven came down. Don't you love those services when the angels show up? And when you and I worship with the angels, we become *one* in glory.

Just as the explosion of lights has now become a common marvel for me, He has many marvels to show *you* which will become common to you in time. They will become common so you can pass them on to others who are stuck in earthbound, soul-stuck lives. You never know who is sitting next to you in church or what invisible glory is visiting you today. That's why He tells us to *walk in the Spirit*—so you will recognize Him when He shows up because He absolutely, positively *does* show up.

He tells you He is with you always, and He truly is. When you praise and worship the Lord, you are never, ever, not for a millisecond, alone.

ENDNOTES

1. H.A. Baker, *Visions Beyond the Veil*. (Tonbridge, Kent, England. Sovereign World Ltd., 2000).

2. Ibid.

chapter 8

HEAVENLY JOURNEY

I ask the Lord about my relationship with my personal angel and about angels in general. As I say the word, "angel," my angel appears. He wears white and stands before me in his unutterable beauty. I am always stunned by his appearance. It is as though I am seeing the perfect light of kindness. It's not easy to stare at this angel, though I always want to just stare and stare. I look and then I avert my eyes and then I look again. The angel shines with the beauty of the Lord! It's as though he's been dipped in the glow of Heaven, the same glow that fills and surrounds Jesus.

After a time of staring, averting, staring, averting, I try to speak. The Lord, who is standing on the other side of me, says, "*Yes,*" before I utter a word. I was going to ask Him for permission to ask the angel a question. The Lord knew my thought and so He answers before I speak. Much of the time when the Lord and I talk together, we speak with thoughts. I think a thought to Him and He thinks one back to me.

Finally I ask the angel, "Do you always travel alone?" He doesn't say a word, and without moving his head, his eyes turn to the side. I follow his gaze. What I see startles me. There, before me, filling the sky are scores and scores of angels! They are singing glorious praises to Jesus. I instantly join them. (There is nothing at all to talk about when we can praise the Lord, even though my voice comes out tinny and small as compared to theirs.)

Our praising the Lord Jesus filled every inch and millimeter of the universe. I don't know how long we praised the Lord. Minutes, hours, I don't know. Time has no influence in the spirit realm. Time is a substance within the eternal dimension, so when we are "in the spirit" we can see into time as the Holy Spirit directs. Earth's time becomes subject to eternity's time.

My angel smiles at me. I think I might just dissolve into a pool of blubber at such a smile. He is so incredibly beautiful. He looks like Jesus! I look over at Jesus and I can see how sweet their fellowship is. I'm in a flood of tears, utterly undone. From somewhere in my throat I find my voice and I ask my private angel, "Do you–do you have a–name?"

"Sam," he says.

Sam.

Then with a sudden flourish, the Lord takes me up into the heavenlies. I can hear the praises of the angelic host, but all I see is the Lord Jesus. We are in the heavenly realm and He is perched kingly on a great white horse. How spectacular He looks seated so majestically on His great white horse! He reaches down and lifts me up in His arms, which are at once above me and around me. He places me very gently behind Him on His horse. As the horse begins to move, I cling to the Lord's back. I put my face close to His beautiful hair to smell it. His hair smells like a thousand spring mornings.

I think of the line of a poem I once read, "I want to do to you what cherry blossoms do to spring." Oh, Jesus, let me adore you. Let me cover you with blossoms of my adoration."

We ride at a quick gallop in this heavenly realm and I notice throngs of people along the way cheering and singing and praising Jesus, the King of kings, as we ride past. I call out to Him in thought and ask if the people who are cheering and praising Him as we ride past could see me. He answers in thought back to me, *No, because I am from another realm. It is not given for them to see me at this time. Also, I am not able to communicate with them. I know they are human beings who have crossed over into Heaven, but I can't see them clearly or make out their features.* I remember the verse, *"Let the dead bury the dead"* (see Luke 9:60), and I realize I won't be chatting with any of the people I know who now live in Heaven. *"It is not given to you at this time,"* He said.

We ride on His great white horse through space and time until we are back on earth and at the top ridge of a high canyon. I am shocked to be back on earth and the Lord, seeing my shock, holds me tightly with one arm. With His other arm, He reaches out, and with one gesture of His little finger He creates a field of flowers; with another touch of His finger He creates a glistening city. I see it happen before my eyes, recognizing that these are spiritual creations on earth! I begin to cry as I realize how little of the spirit realm we see in our midst. Right above our heads is a brilliant, glittering city, and just over there, a field of radiant, divine flowers that thrive in every season. If only we would all look and see with our spirit-eyes!

I bask in these sights and in the goodness of His touch. I ask Him if with one touch of His finger He is able to create such wonders as these, would He also, with one touch, heal hurting, sick people? I begin to name some hurting people. One touch of His finger and they'd be healed.

Immediately He takes me to another place in the spirit with the words, *"Come with Me."* I ride on the back of His horse and hold Him around the waist. I feel His warmth; it's bigger than life. His warmth and His scent become the source of everything.

I become dizzy riding on His horse with Him. I don't know if I'm dizzy with love or from the ride. We arrive at a place in the heavenlies where He has taken me before. It's the place of body parts. He says to me, ***"You touch the sick and hurting in My name. Bring these healed parts back to earth with you."***

At this I burst into more tears. I slide off the horse and pick up a pair of eyes, some feet, a kidney, and a healthy, pink heart. I can feel the warmth of the heart beating in my hand.

I have been thrilled to discover that many other people have traveled in the spirit to this very same place in the heavenlies! People like Todd Bentley, Patricia King, and others who are called to healing ministries.

The Lord now brings me to another room, His armor room. He says, *"When you are sad, tired, or frightened, put these on."* He instructs me to lift up the breastplate. I hoist it onto myself by heavy straps, both front and back. Then He tells me to put on the helmet. I do as He says, and I put a very heavy beautifully ornate brass helmet on my head. It presses against my temples. Then He says to put on the shoes. They are little shoes with flames shooting out of them. He says they are on fire because everywhere I step I will bring the fire of the Holy Spirit. He tells me that He fashioned every one of these pieces of armor *Himself!*

Suddenly His appearance expands like an exploding balloon and His Presence utterly fills everything. His arms stretch across the entire horizon and fill all that my eye can see. He says that we must decrease so He can increase. He says the meek and humble are most like Him. His voice comes from everywhere. He says we often love what is ours more than what is His.

These words sting and I cry, "What is yours, Lord?"

He answers, *"Look and I will show you."*

Before me appears miles of streets and buildings, structures so gorgeous my eyes hurt to look at them. Mountains, prairies, deserts, fields of grain, orchards, lakes, rivers—then wind, wind coming from all directions. And rain, snow, and hail. A blinding sun and pale moon, stars too many to take in at once, galaxies, worlds. I feel the earth beneath my feet shake. I see the winds moving across the deep. He shows me teeth and mouths and eyes and wrists and feet, muscles, cells, babies being born, adults at work. I see bakers and farmers, doctors, and scientists. Dancers, chefs, plumbers, and violinists. I see every human race, all that grows and all that walks. I see an explosion in the heavens and constellations hurl like sparks into space. I see animals and fish and human beings, and then I see ideas and thoughts. I see the acumen of humans. All of it—His.

chapter 9

SERVANTS AND MINISTERS OF FIRE

PSALM 104:4 says that God *"...makes His angels spirits, His ministers a flame of fire."* Angels ministering to us and with us are ministers of fire. And we, as ministers of the Lord Jesus, are "flames of fire." As servants of God, you and I and the angels are as terrible and commanding as fire. We are a burning force, dynamic, victorious, and impelled with holy power. We are more than conquerors, as He is, because His Spirit lives and burns in us. Hebrews 1:6-7 repeats Psalm 104:4: *"Let all the angels of God worship Him. And of the angels He says: 'Who makes His angels spirits and His ministers a flame of fire.'"*

The angel of the Lord appeared to Moses in the midst of a flame of fire from the midst of a bush (see Exodus 3:2), and when leading the Israelites across the desert, the Lord became a pillar of cloud by day and a pillar of fire at night (see Exodus 13:21).

THE FIRE OF JUDGMENT

The fire of God is also one of judgment. Psalm 97:3 tells us, *"A fire goes before Him, and burns up His enemies round about,"* which we also see when He rained fire and brimstone out of the heavens on Sodom and Gomorrah. (See Genesis 19:24.) Our God is a consuming fire (see Deut. 4:24,36) and He will not tolerate worship of false gods.

THE FIRE OF MERCY

The Lord ordered the perpetual burning of the flame on the altar of the Tabernacle in Leviticus 6:13, thereby informing His people of His continuous readiness to cleanse, forgive, and bring restitution.

ELIJAH AND THE FIRE

Elijah prayed for fire to come down from Heaven to consume the Samarian king's 50 men, and that's exactly what happened. Fire came down from Heaven and consumed them. Just before this horrific deed took place, an *angel* of the Lord partnered with Elijah by appearing to him and giving Him instructions to meet the king's men who were on their way to inquire of Baal-Zebub, the false god of Ekron, about the king's state of health. Elijah was to hand them the king's death warrant. The king sent another 50 men to capture Elijah and again Elijah called down fire from Heaven and they were consumed—cooked on the spot! You'd think the king would have wised up by now, but no. He sent yet another 50 men to capture Elijah, but this time the captain of the 50 men prostrated himself before Elijah, begging for mercy. The *angel* of the Lord again partnered with Elijah and told him not to be afraid of the captain and to go down to the king with him, which Elijah did. (See 2 Kings 1:2-17.)

Elijah was a prophet of fire. Earlier, when he was contending with the wicked King Ahab and his equally wicked wife, Jezebel, he single-handedly called down fire in a competition with Ahab's 450 prophets of Baal. The prophets and Elijah each prepared a bull for sacrifice on the altar and, in effect, Elijah said, *"You boys call down fire in the name of your gods and I'll call down fire in the name of the* [true] *LORD God who answers by fire; He is God."* Of course, the prophets of Baal failed miserably. So Elijah, to really prove the power of the living God, threw water on his sacrifice three times and made a trench of water around it until all was drenched. Everybody knows fire doesn't burn something that is drenched with water. *"Water can't quench the fire of love"* (see Song of Sol. 8:7). So that day Elijah called down the fire that even licked up the water in the trench, and afterward Elijah killed the 450 false prophets of Baal (see 1 Kings 18:20-40). Wow! Elijah's ministry is breathtaking and worth reading and re-reading.

HOLY SPIRIT FIRE AND *YOU*

John the Baptist prophesied concerning you, did you know that? He said, *"He who is coming after me is mightier than I,...He will baptize you with the Holy Spirit and fire"* (Matt. 3:11). That's you! Fire in this instance is like lightning. It jolts you out of complacency, out of the cozy rut you tend to fashion for yourself. It includes the lightning wisdom your mind craves; it includes a holy resolve, Holy Spirit energy, and supernatural vitality. We have to take a good look at ourselves and ask whether we are baptized with the Holy Spirit and with *fire*. This fire is the power in the Holy Spirit that enables us to live a supernatural, ignited life of intimacy with the Lord Jesus—knowing Him, His will, His heart, His mind, and His power, and serving Him with ministry miracle fire. Does that describe our lives?

Angels work in and through fire. We, as children of God, filled with His Holy Spirit, are to be, as John the Baptist prophesied, "...baptized with the Holy Spirit and fire." The angels are ministering spirits who are sent forth to minister to us and *with* us. They assist by igniting our hearts and minds with the power of God.

IGNITING OUR HEARTS IN TIME OF NEED

Elijah was a prophet who was a powerful influence on shaping Israel during the reign of Ahab and Jezebel, a reign which spanned approximately 21 years. He moved in supernatural gifts that outshone any prophet before him, save Moses. He was a prophet whose ministry is distinguished by angelic visitations, but at the lowest point in his career, he took off in fear, running from Queen Jezebel for his life. He ran into the wilderness, sat down under a broom tree, and longed to die. Miserably depressed, he despaired of life.

What's so touching about this story is that God saw Elijah in his misery and was *with* him in his distress.

He is with us, too, when we feel the fire has gone out inside us. When we're dejected and depressed, He is there. The Lord was right there with Elijah. Omniscient God was there. The God who knows all was there with Elijah.

✢ ⊕ ✢ ⊕ ✢ ⊕ ✢ ⊕ ✢ ⊕ ✢

No sorrow is so bleak that the Spirit of God cannot penetrate it.

✢ ⊕ ✢ ⊕ ✢ ⊕ ✢ ⊕ ✢ ⊕ ✢

Anguished in heart, Elijah fell asleep—and what did God do? He sent an *angel* to him. God sent an angel to gently wake him up by tapping him on the shoulder.

How long had he been sleeping? Nearby, on the ground at Elijah's head, a cake baked on some burning coals and a jar of water had materialized. The angel nudged him again and told him to wake up and eat his breakfast.

God sent His angel to cook him a little breakfast and ignite his spirit at the precise moment when Elijah thought the fire had gone out in his life and all was doomed.

Psalm 34:19 tells us, *"Many are the afflictions of the righteous, but the LORD delivers him out of them all."* But, we may ask, "Why the afflictions?" It's a fair question. Remember, we said earlier, affliction can often come as a subtle gift from God. "Ouch!" you say. But affliction can wean our hearts from attachments to things below and cause us to set our affection on things above. This is what happened with Elijah. He ate the angel's breakfast, obeyed, and was supernaturally energized. The Bible says that on the strength of the angel-cooked meal, Elijah was fortified for 40 days and 40 nights and walked all the way to Horeb, 200 miles south of Beersheba. The Lord delivers us out of all afflictions. How? By His Spirit, and He will use angels to lend a hand, even to cook us breakfast and inspire us to go on.

Notice something else here, something that reveals a fascinating compound in the DNA of angels. Compare the angel cooking a meal of cakes and water for Elijah with the broiled fish meal the resurrected Lord Jesus prepared for His disciples in John 21. We see in this picture how God's angels are an expression of Jesus Himself and the love of the Father. Their function is to reflect His heart and His will in everything they are and do. They do not create. God creates, and all miracles they perform are performed through the will and power of God. He sent an angel to cook a meal over the coals in the wilderness for Elijah. And centuries later the resurrected Jesus cooks a meal over coals for His disciples on the beach.

PAUL'S DEMON ANGEL

The apostle Paul relates to us the story of being caught up into the third heaven in Second Corinthians 12. He tells us that it had happened 14 years before, and he preceded the story with, *"I knew a man who...."* (We know, of course, that he's talking about himself. He is simply being very humble.) He goes on to explain, *"...whether in the body or out of the body I do not know, God knows"* (2 Cor. 12:3), and then continues with his account of being caught up into paradise and hearing inexpressible words, which he doesn't think are lawful for a human to utter (see 2 Cor. 12:1-4). The experience blows his mind. Perhaps he worried that such supernatural experiences in the heavenly realm would puff him up or make him boastful. "I'm nothing," he insisted. "Don't think of me as anything special." And, in fact, to keep him humble he tells of a demon—yes, a demon, who nailed him with a thorn in the flesh (see 2 Cor. 12:7).

I know a little something about a "thorn in the flesh." I had the unpleasant experience of falling headlong into a cactus garden not long ago. (The Catholic St. Sabastian who was shot with arrows comes to mind.) A month later I was still pulling thorns from my body. The clothes I wore that day were permanently bloodied and ruined by that blizzard of thorns. Cactus thorns have little hooks on the end, so when you pull them out of your flesh, a part remains which often festers and

ANGELS IN OUR LIVES

gets infected. Some of the thorns that were driven into my arms, hands, and legs were two inches long and, though I yanked them out as best as I could, many of them broke off and remained stuck under my skin, causing aching, swelling, and pain until they surfaced enough to allow me to pull them out with tweezers some weeks later. Some of the thorns were tiny, sharp, hair-like needles that were impossible to pull out even with tweezers. I figured I'd be pulling out thorns till Jesus returned. I have remained swollen, black-and-blue, and scarred from this less-than-pleasant tumble. Let it be said that cactus plants are not the friendliest work of God's creation. Paul used a most appropriate metaphor.

Paul says, *"A thorn in the flesh was given to me, a messenger of Satan to buffet me, lest I be exalted above measure"* (2 Cor. 12:7). The word "messenger" here is the Greek word, angellos. It is used 180 times in the New Testament, and many Bible scholars take this to mean Paul's thorn in the flesh was a demon-inspired person who was sent by satan to torment him. I tend to agree, though I've heard other speculations about physical illnesses such as a runny eye disorder, etc. Nobody knows for sure, but the verb that is translated as "buffet" always refers to ill treatment from other people. (See Matt. 26:67; Mark 14:65; 1 Cor. 4:11; 1 Pet. 2:20.)

Paul pleaded with the Lord to take this demon thorn in the flesh from him and what did the Lord do? He answered with a message. The message was, *"My grace is sufficient for you"* (2 Cor. 12:9). This is an example of God using a demon angel for His glory, much like He did with Job when Job's life came crashing down around him, only to be doubly blessed later.

This is a message God repeats to us again and again. *"My strength is made perfect in weakness"* (2 Cor. 12:9). And He will use angels, both His holy angels and demon angels, to prove it.

I have learned so much from God's missionaries who are out on the front lines in hostile, desperate places of the world. Take the missionary Rolland Baker and his wife, Heidi, who are serving in Mozambique.

They tell stories of ghastly persecution and suffering on the mission field—while laughing.

Laughing.

Living in God's sufficient grace removes the terror the devil wants to lay on us. His strength made perfect in weakness is something to be happy about. I'm happy to tell you that when I fell into the cactus garden I laughed. I was not exactly amused, but laugh I did. We can laugh at trouble because God has overcome it. Paul surely had read Proverbs 1:33: *"Whoever listens to me will dwell safely, and will be secure, without fear of evil."*

✤ ✤ ✤ ✤ ✤ ✤ ✤ ✤ ✤ ✤

God always gives us the resources that are equal to our journey, equal to our calling.

✤ ✤ ✤ ✤ ✤ ✤ ✤ ✤ ✤ ✤

BE DISCERNING

It is important for us to exercise our gift of discernment to know what is from God and what satan is trying to defeat us with. John, who did his share of suffering, realized this and warned us in 1 John 4:1-3:

Beloved, do not believe every spirit, but test the spirits, whether they are of God; because many false prophets have gone out into the world. By this you know the Spirit of God: Every spirit that confesses that Jesus Christ has come in the flesh is of God, and every spirit that does not confess that Jesus Christ has come in the flesh is not of God. And this is the spirit of the Antichrist, which you have heard was coming, and is now already in the world.

Let's examine a Scripture verse that will help to keep us on a straight course. (Uh-oh. Here comes the "flesh alert!") Our life in Christ stands on Scripture for our base and foundation. In Paul's time the church at Colossae had been invaded by false teachers who were teaching the worship of angels as a means of gaining spiritual heights. Paul reacted with rage to these false teachers and their heretic teachings in Colossians 2:18. Here's what he said:

> Do not let anyone who delights in false humility and the **worship of angels** disqualify you for the prize. Such a person goes into great detail about what he has seen, and his unspiritual mind puffs him up with idle notions. He has lost connection with the Head, from whom the whole body, supported and held together by its ligaments and sinews, grows as God causes it to grow" (NIV).

Paul is adamant about the absolute supremacy of Christ. In Colossians 1:15-20 he writes, "He [Christ] is the image of the invisible God, the firstborn over all creation. For by Him all things were created that are in heaven and on earth, visible and invisible...."

It is an indisputable fact: Jesus Christ is Head over all. We do not pray to angels. "...whether thrones or dominions or principalities or powers. All things were created through Him and for Him."

The book in your hand honors angels and the supernatural, and it documents angelic manifestations, visitations, and wonders in the heavenly realm. Its purpose is to encourage and help you enter and understand some of today's amazing outpourings of Heaven to earth, and to learn of God's desire for the future. But let me emphasize we must never, not for an instant, worship angels, pray to them, or give them more attention than they're due.

We must never seek heavenly visitations above a relationship with the Lord Jesus Christ. We must not seek signs and wonders and miracles above a relationship with the Lord. The heavenly manifestations and miracles I share with you in this book are directly related to and a response and result of intimacy with Jesus. I encourage you to know Jesus intimately. Nothing is more important than that.

Throughout history, God's visionaries, mystics, and holy men and women sought one thing—the Lord Himself. The visions and supernatural phenomena were secondary. Walking with angels and miracles were secondary. And all through history those who touched the hem of God's robe, who beheld visions and heaven's glory—couldn't keep quiet about it.

Church leaders today cry out for miracles, signs, wonders, and supernatural manifestations in their midst. This is not God's way. His way is to love Him first and then to be surprised by the miracles.

Paul preached against false teachings regarding angel worship, ceremonialism, asceticism, and the Gnostic idea of "secret knowledge." He especially opposed reliance on human wisdom and tradition. But most of all, he puts to rest any notion of things human, material, or spiritual, being on a par with the majesty of the Lord Jesus Christ, who is the King of Heaven.

He wrote, "*He is before all things, and in him all things hold consist. And He is the head of the body, the church, who is the beginning, the first-born from the dead, that in **all things He mat have the preeminence**. For it pleased the Father that **in Him all the fullness shoud dwell**, and by Him to reconcile all things to Himself, by Him, whther things on earth or things in heaven, having made peace through the blood of His cross*" (Col. 1:17-20).

We must take care to always ask permission of the Lord before talking to angels. And if we thank our personal angels who are assigned to us, be sure to thank Jesus first. Angels accept no compliments for themselves.

Is It Scriptural to Call For Angels?

Is it scriptural to ask to see angels, to recognize them, to ask God to send angels to help in time of need? The answer is yes. Joel prayed for the Lord to send angels. (See Joel 3:11 AMP.) He prayed, "*Bring down Your mighty ones—Your warriors, O LORD!*"

Angels are holy warriors. God wants you to be a holy *human* warrior to partner with his holy *angel* warriors.

The angels are encamped around you because you belong to God and love Him. They are not encamped around you to simply hang out and twiddle their holy thumbs. They are encamped around you to be your partners in bringing the glory of the Lord to earth.

The Bible says that He has made His angels spirits, or winds. God is Spirit and His angels are pure spirits who tend to God in His royal courts, and they are the ones God sends to us as glory envoys.

ANGELS AND SUFFICIENT GRACE

The Greek word *charis* is used for graciousness, or the divine influence upon the heart and its reflection in the life. A Hebrew word that is used for "grace" is *chên*, and the definitions for both of these words give the idea of favor, kindness, benefits, and something precious. The word appears 69 times, mainly in the Pentateuch and in the historical books through Samuel. The New Testament definition is "unmerited favor," which is portrayed in this verse: *"For by grace you have been saved through faith, and that not of yourselves; it is the gift of God, not of works, lest anyone should boast"* (Eph. 2:8).

Here is a sufficient-grace angel story: In the Book of Exodus 23:20, God sends His Angel (spelled with a capital A) before the Israelites to keep them in the way and to bring them into the place which He had prepared for them. He tells them that it is not their military skill that will be the key to their victory over the upcoming attacks of enemy armies, but the Presence and help of God through His Angel (who happens to be the pre-incarnate Christ).

The Angel goes on to say something incredible! He says that the name of the Lord is in them, not upon them, around them, or near them, but in them. And because of this, the Angel tells them, "If you indeed obey His voice and do all that I speak, *then I will be an enemy to your enemies and an adversary to your adversaries. For My Angel will go before you…"* (Exod. 23:22-23).

These words tell us so much about His grace! Look at what His Angel does:

1. He keeps us in the "way." This is the job of God's angels.
    They keep us on track. They are right there to help us

because they want us to be in a position for God to claim our enemies as His enemies!

2. He brings us to "the place God has prepared" for us. Don't you want to fulfill your destiny in God? I do! Lord, bring us to that place! Bring us to the place you've prepared for us, where our lives are a glory to you!

I know you're seeking to fulfill your destiny in the Lord. Ask Him for a vision. I don't mean a vision for a certain ministry; I mean a vision of *Him*. Once you connect intimately with Him, ask Him for the spirit of revelation to visit your spirit. Ask Him to let you be able to see more clearly with your spirit-eyes. Ask Him to send His angels to keep you in the way and bring you to the place He has lovingly prepared for you. Surrender to God your dreams, your hopes, your mind, your eyes, your heart, and watch how your enemies become His enemies. He said it another way in the Book of Isaiah:

> *'No weapon formed against you shall prosper, and every tongue which rises against you in judgment you shall condemn. This is the heritage of the servants of the LORD, and their righteousness is from Me,' says the LORD* (Isaiah 54:17).

God's grace is so much more than we realize. In modern Hebrew the word *chanan* is translated as meaning "to pardon or to show mercy," and it occurs around 80 times in the Old Testament. The Lord God is merciful, gracious, longsuffering, and abundant in goodness and truth. His mercy is without end. Be in agreement with your angels, and let yourself be swept up in the glory of His incomparable grace.

REFERENCES

Graham, Billy. *Angels: God's Secret Agents*. New York: Doubleday & Co., 1975.

Noll, Stephen F. *Angels of Light, Powers of Darkness*. Downers Grove, IL: InterVarsity Press, 1998.

Sumrall, Lester. *Angels to Help You*. New Kensington, PA: Whitaker House, 1982.

Willmington, H.L. *Willmington's Guide to the Bible*. Fort Washington, PA: Christian Literature Crusade, 1995.

chapter 10

POSSESSING THE MYSTERIES OF THE KINGDOM

JESUS said it has been given to us to know the mysteries of the Kingdom of Heaven. (See Matthew 13:11 and Luke 8:10.) You must be able to enter the mind of the Spirit if you are going to connect with God's Spirit-mind. The entrance to that Mind is through Jesus. First Corinthians 4:1 says, *"Let a man so consider us, as servants of Christ and stewards of the mysteries of God."*

Consider yourself a steward of the mysteries of God. A steward is a person who manages another's property or affairs, a person who is in charge of overseeing things for someone else.

✤ ⊕ ✤ ⊕ ✤ ⊕ ✤ ⊕ ✤ ⊕ ✤

You are a person called by God to manage His mysteries.

✤ ⊕ ✤ ⊕ ✤ ⊕ ✤ ⊕ ✤ ⊕ ✤

How do you become a steward of the mysteries of God? How do you become a person God trusts with visions and dreams and signs and wonders? How do you become a person God can ask to perform outrageous deeds like demanding a pharaoh to set all his slaves free or laying your only son on an altar as a burnt sacrifice?

Only one way. You become His friend. The Love Chapter, First Corinthians 13, says it well:

... though I have the gift of prophesy, and understand all mysteries and all knowledge, and though I have all faith, so that I could remove mountains, but have not love, I am nothing.

You cannot love people the way they deserve to be loved if you don't love God first. Everything in your life hangs on one determinant: *the intensity of your love for God.*

When I conduct seminars on the prophetic and releasing angelic activity, I always remind the people that God keeps His secrets hidden for us to find. Before Adam and Eve ate the forbidden fruit, they had a perfect relationship with God. They could share thoughts with Him. They were intimate. This is what God had in mind when He created the human race. In Revelation 4:1 John looks and he beheld *"...a door standing open in heaven. And the first voice which I heard was like a trumpet speaking with me, saying, 'Come up here and I will show you things....'"*

The door to the throne room stands open, waiting for its activity to be released. Jim Goll's definition of an "open heaven" is a vision where "a hole seems to appear in the immediate sky, the celestial realm is disclosed and heavenly sights of God become seeable." He goes on to say we are now moving from an era of prophetic renewal into a new epoch of the Holy Spirit. He explains, "We are crossing a threshold into a period of apostolic open heavens for whole cities and regions to be visited by the presence of the Almighty."[1]

I've been to Bible college and seminary, and I know the programs we put ourselves through to learn how to minister. I've served in enough churches to know how many programs there are to build memberships, get more volunteer workers, and urge people to tithe—all in order to get more programs running. God enjoys our programs, sure, but what He wants first and foremost is a living relationship with us. Relationship first. He wants our love. You don't have to love God to sing in the choir, serve on a committee, lead a Bible study, or teach three year olds to sing "I'll Be a Sunbeam for Jesus." You don't have to love God to bring soup to the sick or toss a fifty in the offering bucket, or even pray.

I'm reminded of something we were taught in Bible college: "You can pin the Gospel message on the back of a dog and set the dog loose and people will get saved."

What about your *relationship* with that Gospel message?

You have to love God to be His friend.

Abraham was called His friend. (See James 2:23.) Can we be called His friend?

What does it mean to love God? Let me quote Madame Jeanne Guyon, a woman of the 17th century who wrote in her commentary on the Song of Songs,

> *What manner of love does God ordain? O Love!*
> *O God of charity! You alone can reveal it!*
> *He causes this soul, who, by a movement of love,*
> *desired for herself every possible good in reference to God,*
> *to forget herself wholly so that she may only think upon her*
> *Well Beloved. She becomes divested of every selfish interest*
> *in her own salvation, perfection, joy or consolation, so that she*
> *may only think of the interests of God.... She no longer asks*
> *anything for herself, but only that He may be glorified. She enters*
> *fully into the purposes of the Divine Righteousness,*
> *consenting with all her heart to everything*
> *He decrees in her and with respect*
> *to her, whether for time or eternity. She can love nothing in*
> *herself or in any other person, except in and for God ...*
> *Such is the order of love that God ordains in this soul.*[2]

Angels accompany such a soul. The early church understood that its first ministry was to the Lord. In Acts 13 we see that the leaders of the church at Antioch had discovered a powerful secret. They knew that it was as they ministered to God that God ministered to them. And from that point of closeness, the Holy Spirit ministered *through* them.

MINISTERING TO THE LORD

Many of our prayers are demands and orders. "Lord, do this for us. Lord, please bless our work. Lord, send us angels. Lord, do this, do that." We have it all mixed up. First we are to minister to the Lord. We are to minister to Him, be filled with His mind, His love, His heart, His power. Then, as we wait on Him and listen, the Holy Spirit can imprint God's sovereign will into our spirits. And we know how to pray.

Angels love to minister to the Lord. Look at Revelation 8:2: *"And I saw the seven angels who **stand before God**, and to them were given seven trumpets."* And Revelation 7:11: *"All the angels stood around the throne and the elders and the four living creatures, and fell on their faces before the throne and worshipped God...."*

The early church knew the beauty of ministering to the Lord. They gathered together and ministered to the Lord *first*. From that point of intimacy, the Holy Spirit directed their work and empowered them to go out in ministry. How can we dare call forth His holy angels when they only respond to *His* direction and we don't know what His direction is! Intimacy leads us into the knowledge of the mysteries of God. *"He [or she] who dwells in the secret place of the Most High shall abide under the shadow of the Almighty"* (Ps. 91:1).

In the Old Testament the priests' duty was to minister to the Lord first and then to the people. The Lord came *first*. In Ezekiel 44 we have a clear example of two types of ministry: to the Lord and to people. Some of the Levites had led Israel astray by worshiping idols because they had put material things before God. God became furious and, in effect, He told them that they were still His Levite priests, and this meant they could minister in the Temple and do the work of the Temple, but they would never again minister to Him. God said they'd never again be able to *"...come near Me to minister to Me as priest, nor come near any of My holy things, nor into the Most Holy place"* (Ezek. 44:13).

This has to be the worst punishment on earth! The other priests in this passage of Scripture, the sons of Zadok, were pleasing to God because they put ministering to God *first* in their lives. (*Zadok* means "righteous." Jesus Christ is our Righteous One.) Here's what the Lord has to say about the sons of Zadok: *"They shall enter My sanctuary, and they shall come near My table to minister to Me, and they shall keep My charge"* (Ezek. 44:16).

As a type, the rejected Levite priests represent those Christian workers who evangelize the lost and do good works in the church, but "they shall not come near to Me." Does this give you chills or what? These Levites still worked in God's house, but they never were to enjoy a real sense of nearness to the Lord as His priests. They could do the work of the Lord, but they could never again minister to the Lord of the work.

Don't let anything come between you and your sacred time with the Lord. Years ago I incorporated a minimum of two hours each day during which I take off for the woods or the hills or the beach (or anywhere private—sometimes it's in an empty school playground or a city park) to be alone with the Lord. Rain or shine, summer or winter, I head out for my Jesus walk. I've walked in snow up to my knees, rain up to my ankles, in winter storms and in blinding heat, no matter what the weather conditions are. This two-hour time slot is not my Bible study time or my intercessory prayer time. This is my time, the time when I go out with Him to minister to Him and to hear from Him.

You might be the kind of person who likes to sit on a chair when you have your prayer time, or you might love to lie on the carpet and soak in His Presence. Or you may dance your love to Him. No matter how you like your sacred time to be set apart with Him, if you want to hear from God, minister to Him first. Go into a room for several days, shut the door behind you, and spend time alone with the Bible and the Lord. Don't come out of that room until you've blessed the Lord, until you've gotten hold of Him and He's gotten hold of you.

Did you know that if you've been washed in the blood of Jesus and your sins are forgiven, you're a priest? Did you know that? *"To Him who loved us and washed us from our sins in His own blood, and has made us kings and priests to His God and Father, to Him be glory and dominion forever and ever...*" (Rev. 1:5-6). As a priest, you have the right to enter His Presence.

Let's be Zadok priests.

CAN ANGELS READ OUR MINDS?

In answer to that question, we must remember that spiritual beings don't possess human tongues or eardrums, and they don't share our human limitations. Our human constraints are not their constraints. They can walk through walls, open prison gates, roll back two-ton stones, appear, and disappear. They speak, hear, and move as *spiritual* beings. They see and listen *in the spirit*. Do they read your mind?

Now let me ask you: Why would an angel *want* to read your mind? They are not interested in eavesdropping on your temporal daydreams, your complaints, your self-centered mutterings, or your mind wanderings. No, the angelic host is not sneaking around and peeking into your head to check you out.

However, when you think a thought to God, He hears. He will send angels to nudge your thoughts much like your conscience, but angels don't eavesdrop. You can pray in your head and God hears. God hears and dispatches His angels to your aid.

The devil sends little sharp-fanged demons to harass your thoughts, but they can't hear you think. They figure out what you're thinking by your actions and your words. Then they figure out a way to nail you. You mutter woefully, "I'm such a loser," or some dumb thing like that and the devil's consort will oblige you by helping you feel worse.

We are told by God to fix our minds on things above, and we're told to pull every thought into captivity to the obedience of Christ. (See 2 Corinthians 10:5.) God's angels love Kingdom Thinking. They love God's thoughts toward us, and they love it when we exercise the mind of Christ (see 1 Cor. 2:16), as they do.

When angels appear to humans in physical form, it is because God has sent them on a mission. The angels are fully prepared by God to complete the task they're sent to fulfill. They already have been informed of what we're thinking about if it's important information. I have received reports about suicidal persons who were on the brink of taking their lives when God sent divine intervention and stopped them. The angel didn't have to hear their thoughts. God already told them what the person was thinking.

Elisha had the supernatural gift of knowledge when he could hear the plundering plans of the king of Syria several miles away at night in his royal chambers. Did Elisha actually, with his human ears, hear the king's thoughts and plans? Did he hear the king's voice all those miles away? No. He heard in his *spirit* what was taking place. He simply *knew*.

Elisha could not only *hear* in the spirit, he could *see* in the spirit. The next day God sent a mountain full of angels with horses and flaming chariots to surround and protect him. (His servant couldn't see them until Elisha prayed, then he could see in the spirit.) When the Syrian army showed up, Elisha prayed again, and the Lord blasted the entire army blind. The dazzling light of the angels and fiery chariots blinded them! God knew the secret plans and thoughts of the Syrian king and his army. He let Elisha in on the king's secret plans in order to save Israel. (Read this story in 2 Kings 6:8-18.)

Every supernatural gift of God, first of all, is mandated by Him. When you walk in the spirit like He tells you to do in Galatians 5, and when you practice seeing and hearing in the spirit, God can trust you with information that only He knows.

RECOGNIZING THE ANGELS: GOD'S OR THE DEVIL'S?

Here's a good test: If any thought comes to you that is contrary to biblical principles, it isn't from God. If your thoughts are being attacked by demonic influence or your own evil desires, rebuke them immediately. Use the 3 R's: *Rebuke, Renounce,* and *Repent,* which I explain later in this chapter.

Sometimes I'll be in the middle of prayer and some nasty thought will fly across the landscape of my beautiful mind. I immediately rebuke the thought. I yank it out of me like I'm pulling thorns out of my wrists. "Get behind me, satan," I will say out loud, like I once did on the train when I scared a couple of people out of their seats. I'll tell you the story.

I was silently praying while I was boarding the train from San Diego to Los Angeles when all of a sudden I got a disturbing picture in my head. It was a fear-thought about train accidents. (Do you ever do that? Does your mind ever take off to a never-land of futility like when you're boarding a plane and your mind strays to the last plane crash you saw on the news? Squelch and cover those thoughts in the blood of Jesus immediately!) I *always* come against these unprofitable thoughts. I absolutely refuse fear-thoughts. I always come against them. They're right from the pit of hell. So there I was, boarding the train in the midst of a morning rush-hour crowd, and I blurted out in a loud voice, *"Get behind me, satan!"* Two people near me got up and changed seats! I thought that was pretty funny and started to laugh and, of course, I must have appeared like a total nut case. Here I was, first thing in the morning on the crowded Amtrak, chuckling and hollering at the devil.

CHIEF OF THE CROW PATROL

Recently I had an experience with crows. One thing I do not like in this life is crows. Where I live the crows are loud enough to rattle the shingles on houses. Their raucous voices could break glass. Aggravating!

On this particular sunny afternoon I sat outside in my back yard praying and studying my Bible when about 20 enormous crows lighted on various neighbors' trees and were cawing back and forth and screeching like troops of tuneless brass instruments. It was giving me a serious headache. I flipped to Genesis 1 and reminded the crows in a loud voice that I had dominion over the birds of the air, and I commanded them to shut up. Well, I commanded for about half an hour for those crows to shut up. I just wouldn't quit and neither would they. I kept on taking dominion over the birds of the air, as it said I could in Genesis 1 and commanding the crows to shut up, but they kept on screeching and giving me a headache. Finally, I went inside and closed the door. Even the cat had his paws over his ears under the table. I'm telling you, those crows were loud!

That night I awoke around 3 A.M. and I heard a tinny, creaking voice in the far distance: "I don't like it when you tell us to shut up," it said. Do you know, those crows haven't returned? I hear them cawing their heads off down the block in other people's trees, but they stay away from my place.

Just as God's angels will take on a variety of forms, so do the evil spirits. I never converse with evil spirits. I don't care what they have to say. Those crows were not just loud birds of prey, they were carriers of bad spirits. The bad spirits didn't like it when I told them to shut up because they had to obey. We must take dominion over our thoughts in the same way I got rid of those squawking crows.

CAN ANIMALS BE DEMON-POSSESSED?

Picture this: My neighbor above me on a hill has two big German shepherd dogs. Every time I would so much as step a foot outside my back door, those dogs went wild. I'm telling you, their barking could scare gorillas. They have bass-baritone voices and they would hurl themselves at the fence, snapping and snarling and barking. (My poor cat—if it's not crows, it's dogs!) Even the gardeners wouldn't go near that hill. Friends looked at me aghast when they came over. "*What's that?*" they'd ask, their faces suddenly turned ashen. I would tell them, "Oh that? You mean the wild howling and heaving of 125-pound animal bodies against the fence? Ferocious beasts barking their heads off? Oh, nothing. Just killer dogs, not to worry."

Finally, I took dominion. Sometimes we have to suffer awhile before we realize the authority we have in the Spirit. That word "dominion" may be overused, but that's what it says in Genesis 1, that I have dominion over the animals and everything that "creepeth" (KJV). With this in mind, I got very brave, ran up that hill and started commanding those dogs to shut up in Jesus' name. I prayed in tongues, I commanded, I decreed, I took authority, I cast out generational curses, I did everything I could think of. And the dogs went goofy with rage. I mean to tell you, they would have swallowed me whole if they could have gotten over that fence. I was full of faith, though, because of my recent experience with the crows, so I just kept on praying and telling them they had to shut up because I, the woman of God, was on the scene and they had to obey what I said in the name of Jesus.

(Friends drove by and when they saw me up on the hill waving my arms around and jumping up and down, the wife asked her husband what on earth I could be doing. He told me that he just sighed and told her, "Oh, you know Marie—she's just communing with the angels.")

He was right, of course. But it wasn't God's angels I was communing with. I was addressing the spirits that tormented those dogs. If the Angel of the Lord could shut the lions' mouths for Daniel, surely a couple of dogs would be no problem. What do you suppose happened after I took authority over those spirits? I'll tell you what happened. Those dogs became the sweetest, most docile creatures. They bark because they're dogs, after all, but the mad, ferocious howling and frantic leaping at the fence is a thing of the past. What peace we're all enjoying! It seems like even the trees on the hill are smiling with relief.

THE BLESSINGS YOU GIVE

This reminds me of something else. I also command the trees to be healthy, be blessed, and be beautiful in the name of Jesus. I do believe angels like trees. God's angels appeared twice in the Bible by terebinth trees, not to mention their appearance near the myrtle trees in Zechariah 1, and the broom tree that Elijah slept beneath. Genesis 2 says that God made every tree grow that is pleasant to the sight and good for food. First Chronicles 16:33 says that the trees will sing out and rejoice at the presence of the LORD, and Isaiah 55:12 says that one day the trees of the field will clap their hands. There are 357 mentions of trees in the Bible. We ought to bless the Lord's creation in His name. And, if you have a garden, pray over your garden. Bless your plants, your trees, your flowers, and your soil.

THE TALENT OF THE GERANIUM

Several years ago I became a divorced person and a single mom. It was a very difficult time for me. I had no money and two beautiful children to raise. During that difficult time I took the Parable of the Talents very much to heart. I knew if I proved faithful with little, the Lord would bless me. After all, He said, *"You have been faithful over a few things, I will make you ruler over many things"* (Matt. 25:23).

I wanted a home for my children; I wanted land and beautiful growing things so we could have a place we called our own and property to skip around on. So I bought a geranium plant and stuck it in the window of our rented apartment. I took care of that plant like it was another baby. I fed it, talked to it, prayed over it, ran from window to window with it so it could get enough sun. And then I bought another geranium plant, so I had two geranium plants in the window. I explained to the children that these geranium plants were our future farm.

In time we moved to a nicer apartment with a balcony and I bought tomato and pepper plants to grow on the balcony. I took care of those plants like they were fields of corn, as if our lives depended on the harvest. I became Farmer Marie with those tomato and pepper plants. "Jesus, I am being faithful in a little," I reminded Him. (The tomatoes were the size of marbles and the peppers not really worth mentioning, but we celebrated anyhow.)

Then came the day when we moved from apartment living to a rented house. I ran out every day and picked up the leaves falling from the trees *by hand!* Call me nutso, but I was really going to prove to the Lord I was serious about being faithful over a few things.

And guess what. The day arrived when I was finally able to buy my first house. I was able to landscape the property and plant about 20 trees, including rare guava and cherimoya trees, and a zillion flowers. I even bought a couple of fountains that were on sale and put in a trellis of cascading bougainvillea, and a velvety lawn for the children and me to skip around on.

I took care of that property like it was another baby. Do you know why? Because I had (and still have) a dream, and I am *still* being faithful over "a few things."

This brings me to another point. We never stop being faithful with a little, or with a few things. I do a regular spiritual clean-up of the place where I live. I call forth God's angels to hug the trees. I cast out all negative spirits from the grass, flowers, trees, etc. The Lord wants to bless what is ours. He wants us to be cognitive of what He has given us and He wants us to maintain what He gives us for His glory. There's no glory in screeching crows, mad dogs, and hassles like root rot and aphids. Ask the Lord to send His angels to hover over the gifts He has given you. Bless your land! Bless your geraniums in the window. Bless your multi-acres! Bless your ministry office! Bless the sidewalk outside your home. Bless all that is yours in Jesus' name.

Discern the Spirits in the Things You Own

No book about angels is complete without talking about the bad angels. I had been experiencing nightmares and I couldn't figure out the cause. I knew the nightmares were spiritual attacks, and I thought I was doing everything right to protect my sleep hours, but the nightmares continued. When you begin to bless what is yours (and I suggest you begin by blessing the things you have in your cupboards, on your shelves, in your closets, the glove compartment of your car, your garage, basement, and attic), ask the Lord to show you what you might need to get rid of. I say this because of what happened that really took me by surprise. I've done a lot of spiritual cleaning up, mind you. I'm very experienced in this department. I've studied with the best teachers, including the great Paul Cox, from whom I have learned much about the activities of the angelic realm as well as generational curses.

One day my cousin, Naomi, was visiting me and she said she saw a powerful black force come flying at her one night as she was going to sleep in my home. I was shocked. Something ugly in my house? So I asked her what direction it was coming from. She pointed ahead, which led me to a high shelf of a bookcase. I had a basket full of some antique folk dolls up there. You couldn't see the dolls because they were inside the basket. (I used to collect very old folk art and folk dolls and I had given most of them away, but I kept these three very old dolls because I really liked them.) I showed the dolls to Naomi and she reacted with shivers. She said she thought there could be some curses connected to them; maybe they were used as voodoo dolls at one time, so I tossed them outside in the garbage, and when I did that the atmosphere in the room changed! We both felt the atmospheric change. It actually became brighter in the room. Not only that, I noticed in the weeks that followed that the nightmares I had been having stopped.

Now you might ask, why didn't I just cast off whatever negative ungodly curse or spirit might have been attached to those dolls? In so doing I could have kept the dolls and had a good night's sleep because they would have been cleansed. That's a good point. I did pray over the dolls before tossing them, but I just didn't like them any more. They didn't interest me any more.

Sometimes we keep stuff just because we think we should or because we think it might have some monetary value, but I say chuck it if it's not a blessing to you or your house.

Never forget that we live in a spiritual world. Bless what is yours in the name of Jesus. Get rid of that which attracts the wrong spirits. *Things* can have spirits attached to them. False religions worship statues after all. Are statues of various gods and goddesses mere statues? No. They are nesting places for evil spirits. Ministers, like Paul and Donna Cox, who work in the area of deliverance, have heard audible screams of protest when they have burned false idols and fetishes in order to destroy them.

God's angels *love your house* and love your things because they love *you*. They want to bless and watch over you and all that is yours. *"As for me **and my house**, we will serve the Lord ..."* (Josh. 24:15). My children, my grandchildren, my great grandchildren, my great great grandchildren, and *all I have* and am—as for everything associated with me, we belong to God.

I speak over my car and I tell it to serve the Lord. I speak to my stove, my computer (especially my computer), my hair dryer, toaster, teapot, and everything in my house by saying, "You will serve the Lord."

I have a cat, and this cat was a feral thing, off the streets and abused by rock-throwing boys. This cat has been delivered of nasty cat spirits and prayed over and hugged and loved, and it is the sweetest thing ever to clutch a chew toy. Bless what is yours. Leave nothing unblessed.

When I dog-sit for my daughter's huge standard poodle, Moses, I anoint his curly head with oil and bless him. I swear, the dog practically becomes like a bird fluttering around, for he becomes happy, light, and full of slurpy kisses.

SPIRITUAL RADAR

The more spiritually discerning you become, the more radical your prayer life becomes. You no longer pray little wimpy prayers as if you don't know who you're talking to. No, you begin to resemble a fire alarm for Jesus. You can walk into a place, whether it's a store or a church, and you discern the spirits in the place, whether they're of God or not. You'll see angels and you'll sense when agents of darkness are at work, too.

I've been at prayer meetings where I wanted to get up and go someplace else because the spirit of contention was so heavy. I can tell when two people don't like each other. I can tell when there's disharmony at hand. I can tell when there's someone with an adverse spirit and especially a spirit of unbelief.

And so can you! Send out your spiritual radar. When we dare to open our spiritual eyes, the Lord will show us the truth so we might be able to be useful in His Kingdom!

What's really fun is to watch the angels during good preaching. Angels love to accompany good, Spirit-filled preaching. Angels come to purge hearts and to burn the Word of God into hearts. Sometimes I'll see unusual angelic beings in meetings. For example, at the Prophetic

Conference at Harvest Rock Church in Pasadena in 2006, I sat in Rick Wright's meeting and, as he preached, two very unusual-looking angels showed up to the right and the left of the platform. They were box-shaped and covered with eyes, like cherubim, and they twirled around on the platform and were having a great time as Rick opened the Word of God to us. Angels *love* good preaching. Those angels were just ecstatic with the Word going forth. When I listen to the CD I can still see them, their eyes ablaze and whirling around. I can't describe Rick to you, what he was wearing, etc., but I can remember every detail of those two delighted angels.

Frankly, I would never want to be at a meeting or fellowship and not see angels.

DO CHRISTIANS EVER NEED DELIVERANCE?

Are you kidding? Of course! Oh, but Marie, you say, how can a *Christian* need deliverance? Most of us who call ourselves Christian are in need of deliverance of some kind. Our minds are renewed by the power of the Holy Spirit, yes, but this renewing of the mind takes work on our part. For instance, you and I both know Christians who are bound by *religious spirits.* These people are in need of deliverance from their religious spirits. You know the type of person I'm talking about: that super-religious, legalistic person who puts down other Christians, other denominations, and everything else that they don't understand about God's Presence in the world today. They're on the radio and in pulpits; they're always in an awful snit about God doing something without their approval. These poor folk probably don't even believe angels are at work in the world today. Isn't that sad? They know the Word of God, but they don't know the loving power of God.

We also all know those Christians who are what I call, "asleep in the light."

(I've been there. I've done time in that prison.) It's the spiritual state of being where a person is simply "out to lunch." Lots of hard work, but no power, no oomph, no joy—no *relationship.* If you're "asleep in the light," or if you are feeling any of the symptoms of the presence of bad spirits, you need deliverance. Jim Goll, in his excellent book, *The Seer*,[3] gives us a list of some of the common symptoms of the presence of bad spirits:

- An oppressive atmosphere
- A sense of confusion
- A pervading sense of loneliness or sadness
- A feeling of pressure and depression.

I would add to that list a sense of restlessness and feeling of futility which lead to addictive behaviors, including drinking and overeating.

Jesus came to set the captives free, and He took every weakness of the human personality on the cross with Him. When you find yourself being pulled down into those low valleys of the soul, you can get out. You can get free to be alive in the Light.

MARIE'S THREE R'S

Think the 3 R's: Rebuke. Renounce. Repent.

1. **Rebuke**: In Jesus' name, I rebuke every false thought and influence in my life that exalts itself above the authority of the King of the universe, Jesus Christ, the Son of the living God.

2. **Renounce**: In Jesus' name, I renounce every false thought and influence (name them as you think of them—this could take days and weeks—a lifetime even) in my life that exalts itself above the authority of the King of the universe, Jesus Christ, the Son of the living God.

3. **Repent**: Lord Jesus, I repent of every false thought, influence, and action that I have accepted into my life and exalts itself above your authority. I repent of every sin (name them) in the name of Jesus Christ, the King of the universe, the Son of the living God. I willingly turn from this (these) sin(s) and commit myself to a holy, pure, wise, beautiful, and Holy Spirit-led life in the everlasting, all-powerful name of Jesus Christ, the King of the universe.

If you will incorporate these 3 R's into your life, you can expect your life to be lifted to a higher level of power and authority in the Holy Spirit. I think you will find that calluses which have formed on your soul will fall away and you will be able to enter into an intimacy with your Savior and Lord that will surge you forward into a Spirit-dominated life that will be like Heaven on earth.

A 4-Year-Old Boy and an Angel

John Paul Jackson tells this story about a Christian man who came to him and told him that his 4-year-old son was talking to angels. The boy not only talked to the angels, he could see them quite plainly. John Paul told the father to ask his little boy if he was talking to God's angels (and not demons) and so the boy asked the angel whose angel he was. Was he God's angel or the devil's angel? The angel answered that he was God's angel. The little 4 year old asked the angel if his father could please also see the angel. The angel told him to tell his father that he couldn't see angels because he had seen too much evil. This puzzled the boy. He asked his father what was meant by "evil."

The father then asked the boy to ask the angel if his daddy would *ever* be able to see an angel. So the boy did so and the angel told him to tell his father, "Yes, but he's got a very thick callus around his soul." The little boy didn't know what a callus was, and the father knew without a glimmer of a doubt that he needed to do some serious praying. What he needed to do was some serious renouncing, rebuking, and repenting in order to live on the same spiritual level as his 4-year-old boy!

God loves to reveal Himself to children. Children have an easier time of moving in the supernatural than most adults do. They barely need our tutoring in the supernatural, either. Little orphan children of Kunming, a remote village in the province of Yunan, China, lived in a Christian orphanage called Adullam Home. Uneducated, undisciplined, half-starved, and unwanted, the Holy Spirit fell on these little children and they not only spoke in tongues, they prophesied, preached, and were taken up in heavenly trances and visions. They saw angels. They saw Jesus. They saw Heaven and hell. They saw wonders nobody had ever told them about. They preached with wisdom and authority and many, many Chinese people were astonished and ushered into the household of God as a result.[4]

I pray for faith like that of a child.

Lord Jesus, being an adult is not easy. We adults don't make the best believers. We're so full of the world, and past hurts and disappointments. We're so educated and so ignorant.

Lord Jesus, I want the faith of a child, for you said of such is the Kingdom of God. You said we can't receive the Kingdom of God unless we enter as little children. O God, help me become as a little child.

Endnotes

1. Jim Goll, *The Seer*. (Shippensburg, PA. Destiny Image, Inc., 2004).
2. Jeanne Guyon, *Song of the Bride*. (Shippensburg, PA: Destiny Image, Inc., 2004).
3. Goll, *The Seer*.
4. Baker, *Visions Beyond the Veil*.

chapter 11

THE ORDER OF ANGELS

THIS chapter deals with the categories of angels that Christ rules over. The Scriptures refer to the order of angels, both good and bad, and the Lord rules over them both. All angels, whatever their rank, holy or fallen, are subject to their Creator, the preeminent Lord Jesus Christ, for *"All things were created through Him and for Him. And He is before all things, and in Him all things consist"* (Col. 1:16-17).

God ranks the angels, and Jesus even used a military term when referring to them. In the Garden of Gethsemane, when Jesus was about to be arrested, Peter took out a sword to protect Him. The Lord rebuked him by exclaiming, *"Do you think that I cannot now pray to My Father, and He will provide Me with more than twelve legions of angels?"* (Matt. 25:52-53). The word "legion" was a Roman military classification for 6,000 soldiers.

RANKS OF ANGELS

Seraphim and Cherubim

The Seraphim and Cherubim are God's highest order of angels. They are the guardians who stand before God's throne. Night and day, the Seraphim praise the Lord, crying, "Holy, Holy, Holy is the Lord of Hosts." The Cherubim show forth God's power and mobility as His holy attendants. The Seraphim and Cherubim have intimate knowledge of God and give Him continual praise and adoration. We'll share more about them in the next chapter.

Thrones (thronoli) refer to those who sit upon them, both good and evil angels.

ARCHANGEL

The word "arch" means "chief." *Michael*, whose name means, "Who is like God?" is like a general. He is a powerful fighter with a particular responsibility for Israel. In Daniel 10:21 and 12:1 he is called "the prince of Israel." In the famous account in Daniel 10:13 Michael arrived to answer Daniel's prayers after being withstood by the Prince of Persia for 21 days. In the New Testament Jude 9 recounts Michael winning the battle with Lucifer over the body of Moses. And in Revelation 12:7-9 we see Michael as the commanding officer of legions of angels casting satan and his cohorts out of heaven:

> *And war broke out in heaven: Michael and his angels fought with the dragon; and the dragon and his angels fought, but they did not prevail, nor was a place found for them in heaven any longer. So the great dragon was cast out, that serpent of old, called the Devil and Satan, who deceives the whole world; he was cast to the earth, and his angels were cast out with him.*

GABRIEL

Gabriel, whose name in Hebrew means "mighty one of God," or "God's hero," or "God is great," serves God as His messenger. Gabriel actually isn't called an archangel in the Bible, contrary to John Milton and popular opinion. There is only one archangel and he's Michael.

Gabriel appears in the Book of Daniel imparting revelation concerning future events in God's Kingdom. God sent Gabriel to Daniel to interpret Daniel's vision in Daniel 8:15-16:

> *...suddenly there stood before me one having the appearance of a man. And I heard a man's voice between the banks of the Ulai, who called, and said, 'Gabriel, make this man understand the vision.' So he came near where I stood, and when I came I was afraid and fell on my face....*

Gabriel also appeared in Daniel 9:21 with loving words for Daniel from God and an interpretation of another vision. In the New Testament Gabriel came to Zacharias to tell him he would have a son named John the Baptist (see Luke 1:11, 19), and it was Gabriel who appeared to Mary announcing the birth of Jesus (see Luke 1:26-27). Gabriel is primarily a messenger of mercy and promise, whereas Michael is the general of the army, a chief warrior. All angels are warriors, but some angels serve solely in battle against the enemies of God.

THE HEAVENLY HOST

These are the legions and legions of angels who populate the heavens. Most references to angels in the Bible don't give us their names, but they are powerful agents of God. One example is the solitary angel in Second Kings 19:35 who killed 185,000 Assyrian enemy soldiers in a single night. That's what I call a warrior. These are your personal angels and mine.

Let it be said that these angels, for the most part, do not have wings. Angels do not need wings to fly. These are the angels we personally partner with under the leadership of our Commander-in-Chief, the preeminent Lord Jesus Christ. They are our personal angels.

"Are they [the angels] *not all ministering spirits sent forth to minister for those who will inherit salvation?"* (Heb. 1:14).

Jesus said, *"Take heed that you do not despise one of these little ones, for I say unto you that in heaven their angels always see the face of my Father who is in heaven"* (Matt. 18:10).

THRONES, DOMINIONS, PRINCIPALITIES, POWERS

These are the *ruling angels* we read of in Ephesians 1:21; 3:10; Colossians 1:16; 2:10; and 1 Peter 3:22, which speak of principalities, powers, might, authorities, and dominions that Jesus Christ is Lord over.

Paul lists four kinds of angels among those who rebelled with satan against God:

1. Principalities: Chief rulers, those of highest rank in the satanic kingdom. (See Col. 2:10; Eph. 1:21; 6:12.)

2. Authorities: Fallen angels whose power is derived from satan, and they do his bidding. (See Eph. 1:21; 6:12; Col. 2:10.)

3. Rulers of darkness: Spirit-world rulers who assist the plans of satan in the world. (See Dan. 10:13-21; Eph. 1:21; 6:12; Col. 1:16-18.)

4. Spiritual wicked spirits: Operating from the heavenlies where satan has his seat of operations. (See Eph. 1:21; 6:21; Col. 1:16-18.)

Two passages of Paul's speak in particular of *thrones, dominions, principalities, and powers:*

*He [Jesus] is the image of the invisible God, the firstborn over all creation. For by Him all things were created that are in heaven and that are on earth, visible and invisible, whether **thrones or dominions or principalities or powers**. All things were created through Him and for Him* (Colossians 1:15-16).

*Put on the whole armor of God, that you may be able to stand against the wiles of the devil. For we do not wrestle against flesh and blood, but against **principalities, against powers, against the rulers of the darkness of this age, against spiritual hosts of wickedness in the heavenly places*** (Ephesians 6:11-12).

GOD IS IN CONTROL

God is in control of the evil angelic forces we are to stand against. Jesus said, *"Now is the judgment of this world; **now the ruler of this world*** *be cast out. And I, if I am lifted up from the earth, will draw all peoples to Myself"* (John 12:31-32).

> *"I will no longer talk much with you, for the ruler of this world is coming, and* **He has no power over me**, *but I do as the Father has commanded me, so that the world may know that I love the Father"* (John 14:30-31 NKJV).

At this very moment Jesus is preparing for mortal combat with satan, a combat that will cause satan to lose all his authority. The world, which belongs to God and will always belong to God, is under the influence and power of the evil one (see 1 John 5:19), but the Lord is counting on us to overcome the evil one in our lives, because He has already conquered him and the demon ranks. We, who live with big spirits, who live with our spirits so highly developed and educated by the Holy Spirit of God, can and will overcome this world (the invisible, spiritual system of evil dominated by satan) and its ruler's wiles, because Jesus has already done it for us. *"In the world you will have tribulation;, but be of good cheer, I have overcome the world"* (John 16:33).

LUCIFER

Lucifer has many names which emphasize his evil constitution. He is known as satan or the devil. Jesus called him "the evil one" (John 17:15). The Book of Revelation calls him the old serpent, the great dragon, the destroyer, the accuser, and the deceiver. He is also the tempter (see Matt. 4:1,3).

We know from Scripture that lucifer was a high-ranking angel; in fact, Ezekiel 28:12-19 tells us, among other things, that he was appointed to be the anointed guardian cherub with access to the holy mountain of God. When he sinned, God cast him out of the mountain of God like a common sinner:

> *"I destroyed you, O overshadowing cherub, from the midst of the stones of fire"* (TLB).

Why was he cast out of heaven? Because of his pride and ambition.

How you are fallen from heaven, O Lucifer, son of the morning! How you are cut down to the ground, you who weakened the nations! For you have said in your heart: 'I will ascend into heaven, I will exalt my throne above the stars of God; I will also sit on the mount of the congregation on the farthest sides of the north; I will ascend above the heights of the clouds, I will be like the Most High (Isaiah 14:12-14).

The passage concludes with God pronouncing satan's doom, *"You shall be brought down to Sheol, to the lowest depths of the Pit"* (v. 15).

PARTNERING WITH GOD'S HEAVENLY HOST

We can see that there are many ranks of fallen angels. The demon that harasses our neighbor's tormented German shepherd dogs is in a different class from the principality that rules our city. We are to be wise and alert, but never, ever fearful. We are to be prepared at all times, wearing the full armor of God, as Paul tells us to do in Ephesians 6. We are to be strong in Him because we can't and don't achieve anything without Him. The angel of the Lord appeared to Zechariah to encourage the building of the Temple by Zerubbabel by saying, *"Not by might nor by power, but by My Spirit says the LORD of hosts…"* (Zech. 4:6 NKJV).

Those words ring true for us today. They tell us that no might or power, whether of this world or of the spirit realm, can overcome the Holy Spirit of God and His purposes. Those blessed words tell us that the Spirit of God cannot be counterfeited. No power, no matter how terrible and fierce, can defeat us when we have the Holy Spirit. We conquer evil not with our human cleverness, our human resolve, or any human effort, for it is only *"…by My Spirit says the LORD of hosts."*

As we partner with the Lord's heavenly host, joining forces with them to bring to pass God's will on earth, we step onto a plateau of overcoming joy that is truly heavenly. We enter into the joy of the Lord—a place of such extreme power and beauty that the whole world will know we're here!

chapter 12

IN GOD'S GLORY ARENA

INTRODUCING THE CHERUBIM AND SERAPHIM

CONSIDER for a moment how you came into the world. You were born into the world because God knew you before He created the world. You were formed in your mother's womb as the image of God. He loved you and embraced your birth from the holy beginning of time. Angels celebrated God's genius when He created you. Angels celebrated, and they continue to celebrate every time you choose Him and bless Him with your beautiful life. Angels understand that you were created for His pleasure.

Your birth was God's planned and perfect strategy. Your heavenly Father chose you from the foundation of the world. He knows every hair on your head and every cell within your body. He knows every particle within the air you breathe. He knows your thoughts, your hopes, and He wants you to be aware that you are never alone with your thoughts, hopes, and your time in this world. He is with you always. And you are surrounded by a great a cloud of witnesses. You are encircled with thousands of heavenly beings, the angels. They are your partners who have come to help you and to perform the Lord's bidding on your behalf.

Look up and see the angels. In God's order of the Glory Arena the first and highest order of angels is the cherubim and seraphim. They remain in a fixed position before God's throne.

THE CHERUBIM

Cherubim is plural for the word, *cherub*. The letters of the Hebrew root word for cherub mean "holding something in safekeeping," and the name "cherubim" means to "be near." These angelic beings render the most intimate service to the Almighty. The plural form of cherub, "cherubim," occurs 64 times in the Scriptures. A real cherub is nothing like those cute, chubby, baby-like creatures we see in paintings and on the shelves of gift stores. A cherub is actually very curious-looking.

You probably have never sent a picture of a *real* cherub on a birthday card or Valentine's Day card. Magnificently full of light and so close to God, they appear as "whirling balls of fire." Ezekiel describes the cherubim as living creatures with four faces and four wings. He describes these four living beings as having bodies like men, but with four faces each—a human face in front, an eagle's face behind, a lion's face to the left, and an ox's face to the right. When these creatures move, their knees do not bend, but they remain straight and stiff. Their feet are like the soles of calves sparkling like burnished bronze. Each figure has four arms, two attached to each shoulder, and attached to their arms are wings. Of these four winged arms, two are outstretched above them, and two cover their bodies.

Ezekiel describes what he saw, "*As for the likeness of the living creatures, their appearance was like burning coals of fire, like the appearance of torches going back and forth... [they] ran back and forth, in appearance like a flash of lightning*" (Ezek. 1:13-14).

Does this description sound like the cuddly figures you're accustomed to seeing decorating calendars, birth announcements, and valentines? (Not to mention garden ornaments, bathroom walls of restaurants, and bird baths.) Ezekiel goes on to tell us that the four living beings stood together facing in four opposite directions, and between them were four huge wheels, each wheel being double so that it could roll forward or sideways forming a wondrous sort of angelic chariot. In each of the four directions it moved it always presented the same viewpoint (see Ezek. 1:15-21).

The cherubim not only have four faces, four sides, and four wings, they are covered with *eyes*! (The eyes are important features. The seraphim, another angel classification, are also covered in eyes.) The tops of the outstretched wings of the cherubim touch a great expanse of crystal, and on this crystal is a sapphire throne. It's wonderful to compare the ecstatic vision of Ezekiel (593-571 B.C.) with those of John on the Isle of Patmos (A.D. 94-96).

How are we to interpret these incredible heavenly reports? Read the account for yourself and notice the colors, the sounds, the fire, and the terrifying and sublime majesty Ezekiel describes. But what do the faces, the wings, and the eyes of the cherubim mean?

Theologians have interpreted the faces of the cherubim to signify the intelligent wisdom of humans, showing man's authority to rule for God over His creation, as in Genesis 1:28. The strength of the lion, the servility of the ox, and the soaring swiftness of the eagle are each in harmony with the other. In this way the four faces correspond to the New Testament Gospels— Matthew, Mark, Luke, and John—God's completed message to humankind. The number four, symbolic of the world in Scripture, can refer to the four corners of the earth, implying that God's angels execute His commands everywhere. The eyes tell us that the eye of the Lord is everywhere. He is all-seeing.

Many people report visions where they see an eye or many eyes during their prayer times. I often see eyes in the spirit, and one early evening, as I was walking on the beach in prayer, I looked up at the gray sky just as it broke apart, sending fog and clouds scattering until there formed across the clear expanse *one gargantuan eye*. This eye extended as far as I could see. I mean, it was huge. I fell to my knees on the sand, utterly stunned. Just before the eye appeared, I had been asking the Lord to help me know more of His love, and now, stretched on the sand beneath a gigantic eye in the sky, I knew how little I understood of His love.

I didn't know what to do with myself. I couldn't look at the eye directly, because it was so piercing, so monumental, and so alarming. I began to weep and praise God. I quoted Scripture, I asked for forgiveness, and I repented. The strange thing was that I was alone on the beach; there was not another soul in sight, which was unusual, so I don't know if anyone else saw the giant eye in the sky. It remained for several minutes, and then the white and gray sky blended together, and the eye dissolved. Darkness moved across the sky. I sat on the sand weeping as the night fell around me.

I believe what I saw was an image of the eye of God. I want so much to live inside the "apple of His eye" that David prayed for in Psalm 17:8: *"Keep me as the apple of Your eye;"* he prayed. *"Hide me under the shadow of Your wings."* David knew the only safe place in this life was in the very center, the pupil of the eye of God. And I had just experienced the very presence of God's eye! There are some 630 "eye" references in the Bible, not counting eyesalve, eyeservice, eyesight, or eye witness. I thought of Second Chronicles 16:9: *"For the **eyes** of the Lord run to and fro throughout the whole earth to show Himself strong in behalf of those whose heart is blameless toward Him."* This could be one of the jobs of His cherubim! These angels continually run to and fro seeking to encourage and empower us in the Lord. If only we could see the love and power we are surrounded with. If only we knew and trusted all that God has done for us through Christ.

THE WINGED CHERUBIM

The popular impression most people have of angels is that they are winged creatures. You never see an angel ornament without wings. But this is man's idea of an angel. Most angel art—paintings, sculptures, bas-relief, statuary, etc.—portray angels as being encompassed about by swirling wings, and perhaps this idea originated with the descriptions of the cherubim and seraphim. Rarely do artists attempt to render angels' true forms. God's angels don't have wings for the most part. They don't need wings to fly.

The other ranks of angels, which we will discuss next, may not be quite as extraordinary in appearance, with four heads and a lot of eyes and all those wings, but they soar, zoom, and translate themselves from one place to another in a flash, and they perform incredible deeds that no human can comprehend or execute.

The cherubim are the first angelic beings the Bible speaks of. They appear as guardian keepers in Genesis 3:24 after God drove Adam and Eve from the Garden of Eden. He stationed the cherubim with whirling, flaming swords to keep them from eating of the Tree of Life in their fallen condition. The tree of life, the cross of Christ, would become humankind's entrance into fellowship with God.

The cherubim appear again in Exodus 25:18-22 when God commands the construction of the Ark of the Covenant. *"And you shall make two cherubim of gold; of hammered work you shall make them at the two ends of the mercy seat"* (Exod. 25:18). He instructed the cherubim to face each other with their wings stretching out as a canopy to cover the mercy seat.

Cherubim are always associated with the glory and Presence of God. They are the bearers of the throne of God, and they guard the mercy seat. (See 1 Samuel 4:4 and Isaiah 37:16.) The two cherubim on either side of God's throne are His chariot, or honor guard, upholding His glory. A repeated phrase that is used to describe the Lord is as One who: *"...dwells between the cherubim"* or *"Who sits upon the cherubim"* or *"Who dwells above the cherubim."* (See 1 Samuel 4:4; 2 Samuel 6:2; 2 Kings 19:15; 1 Chronicles 13:6; Psalm 80:1; 99:1.)

Cherubim were even woven into the Tabernacle curtains and the veil for the Holy of Holies, *"...with...fine woven linen, and blue, purple, and scarlet thread"* (Exod. 26:1). (See also Exodus 26:31.) Solomon had huge, 15-foot-tall cherubim figures carved in olive wood and covered in gold in the inner sanctuary of the Temple and carved on all the walls of the Temple, both the inner and outer sanctuaries. (See 1 Kings 6:23-29.) He also made carts and panels for the Temple with cherubim designs. (See 1 Kings 7:28-29.)

Cherubim are the angelic guardians of God's Presence, and they become His chariot as He requires. (See 1 Chronicles 28:18.) God *"rode upon a cherub, and flew..."* (Ps. 18:10), and *"He bowed the heavens also, and came down with darkness under His feet. He rode upon a cherub, and flew; and He was seen upon the wings of the wind"* (2 Sam. 22:10-11). When the Lord Jesus comes in future judgment, He will come *"with fire and with His chariots, like a whirlwind…"* (Isa. 66:15).

THE SERAPHIM

Close relatives of the cherubim are the seraphim. The plural for seraph is seraphim. Isaiah describes them as having *six* wings, unlike the cherubim who have four wings. They have two wings to cover their faces (so they wouldn't gaze directly into God's glory), two to cover their feet (acknowledging their subservience to God), and two with which to fly (serving the Lord who sits on the throne). They worship God day and night, crying out in antiphonal praise, *Holy, holy, holy is the LORD of hosts; The whole earth is full of His glory!"* (Isa. 6:3).

Eight hundred and thirty-three years later, the apostle John on the Isle of Patmos, writes of the very seraphim Isaiah saw. He, like Isaiah, describes them as four living creatures (full of eyes in front and in back)—one like a lion, one like a calf, one like a man, and the fourth like an eagle. They each have six wings and are "full of eyes around and within." Their eyes are not omniscient like God's, but nothing escapes their scrutiny, and they worship the Lord continually.

The seraphim do not rest day or night, for they are constantly crying out, *Holy, holy, holy, Lord God Almighty, Who was and is and is to come!* (Revelations 4:8)

One of the seraphim touched Isaiah's lips with a live coal from the altar and gave him a message from the Lord who sat on the throne, *"Your iniquity is taken away, and your sin is purged"* (Isa. 6:7). Then the Lord asked, *"Whom shall I send, and who will go for Us?"* (Isa. 6: 8). Notice the pronoun *Us*. Was He referring to the Holy Trinity? (See Gen. 1:26.)

Isaiah responded full of enthusiasm, "Here am I! Send me." So we see the seraphim helping to launch Isaiah's ministry, and we can pray for hot, purifying coals to visit our own lips as God sends out more workers in this day. We'll talk more about this later.

Referred to as fiery serpents, the singular noun, seraph, designates the brazen serpent in Numbers 21:8 and the flying seraph of Isaiah 14:29 and 30:6. The holy seraphim Isaiah and John saw are celestial beings who praise God night and day and are right at this very moment shouting their praises to God in Heaven.

You have to admit, the cherubim and the seraphim are fascinating.

When we praise the Lord, and when we shout and sing, "Holy, holy, holy," we are joining the seraphim and a heavenly host who love to praise Him. The substance and essence of Heaven is praise, and that means when we worship God with our praise, we enter the atmosphere of Heaven. It's incredibly encouraging, during dark hours of the soul, to know that when we love God we are never alone, not for a minute. We need only begin to praise the Lord and we're lifted spiritually into the same attitude of the seraphim and cherubim. Theologian C.H. Spurgeon wrote, "When we think of the extraordinary powers entrusted to angelic beings, and the mysterious glory of the seraphim and the four living creatures, we are led to reflect upon the glory of the Master whom they serve, and again we cry out with the Psalmist, 'O Lord, my God, thou art very great!'"

CELESTIAL CHARIOTS

Cherubim and seraphim are but two classifications of angels. Cherubim, as we see, actually become chariots for the majesty of God to ride upon. God also created the angels who commandeered the chariots of fire that whisked Elijah up to heaven in a whirlwind. (See 2 Kings 2:11.) I love to think about Elijah being whisked up to Heaven with flames roaring around him and angels cheering and pressing upward to the arms of God in their flaming chariot.

MY MOTHER'S WHIRLWIND RIDE

Let me tell you my mother's whirlwind story. She died in September 2005, and my grief over losing her was overwhelming, really awful. I was just a wreck, to be honest. Even though I knew she was in Heaven, I missed her terribly and couldn't shake my sorrow. Then one day as I was moping around, the Lord said He wanted to show me something. I said, "What do you want to show me, Lord?"

He said, *"Open your eyes and look."*

So I looked and there before me I saw a vision of my mother dancing with the Lord. Big as life, there was my mother dancing with the Lord. The wonderful thing was, the Lord was beside me talking to me, and also several feet away He was dancing with my mother. Jesus, the omnipresent One. My mother wore a long, white gown on her perfect spirit-body, and she was healed and beautiful. She was radiant with happiness and peace. I saw her hands and her feet, which were now perfect. I saw her move with ease and grace.

Jesus was still standing nearby at this point, and all at once in my vision a great whirlwind rose up around my mother, and with a sound of a great roar, that of a tremendous fiery explosion, she was lifted up in the whirlwind. I stood in amazement, watching my mother lifted up in the whirlwind and I watched until she was out of sight. I felt very much like Elisha must have felt in Second Kings 2:12, only I cried out, "My mother! My mother!"

After the experience of watching my mother rise up into Heaven in a whirlwind, I felt a sense of release come over me. I believed I'd be able to enter the process of recovery and rebuilding my life in a world without my mom and without the daggers of grief cutting so deeply into my heart. My recovery had begun. The Lord had given me a vision to encourage and comfort me. How loving He is!

OUR SPIRIT-SELF

Inside us we have a spirit-self being that is formed in the image of God. We don't always listen or pay attention to our spirit-self being that was formed in us by the Holy Spirit, but that doesn't change God's order of things. You and I are spiritual beings. We are body, soul, and *spirit*. Our spirits are made alive by the Spirit of God who has taken up residence inside us. The Source of everything created lives in us. This is God's plan, and it has been His plan since He created Adam and Eve. He created us humans as eternal beings with spiritual DNA to live forever. You and I (our eternal selves), because we are born again *of the spirit*, will go on with God forever.

We know that when we die we don't take our bodies with us. Our bodies stay here. Before my mom went to Heaven, as she was lying in her hospital bed, I watched her soul slowly leave this realm, and when I held her dead body in my arms, she clearly was not with me in the room. Her perfect spirit-self had been lifted up and she was gone from this world. Even though her body was still warm in my arms, her dear body that had struggled for breath only minutes earlier, she was not in her body. In the flash of an eye she had entered and taken permanent hold of her real, perfect, eternal spirit-self.

When you and I talk to God or hear from God, we hear and speak with our spirit-self's mouth and ears. We hear from God *in the spirit*. We hear with our eternal ears that one day we'll take home to Heaven with us. When we came to God through His Son, Jesus Christ, we opened our hearts and lives to Jesus, receiving Him as Lord of our lives. At that moment, *zing*! The Holy Spirit fused Himself into our human spirit and we became eternally connected with God. At the moment we inherited salvation, angels were dispatched to us. (See Hebrews 1:14.)

But the Third Person of the Trinity, the Holy Spirit, is not only fused with our human spirit, He has taken residence *inside* our human frames. So now, as Christians, we have God living inside us. That's something to sit back and meditate on no matter how many years (or seconds) you've been a believer. Inside us! That means *God* is in our minds, our hearts, and our bodies.

Without the Holy Spirit dwelling in us, we are consigned to living as body, soul, and *human* spirit. We are, as the poet May Sarton wrote, "Men carved out of sleep who wish to pray but have no prayers...." Without the Holy Spirit, we can't see God.

FREE TO CHOOSE

The celestial host and humans share one thing in common. This one thing we share in common shapes our relationship with eternity and affects the history of the world. We, along with the angelic host, are created by God with a *will*. Angels and humans alike have the power to *choose* God, to love Him, and live in the glories of His Kingdom—or not.

God's angels know God intimately; they live and move in His divine perpetual Presence. The cherubim and seraphim exist to praise, honor, and glorify God. The angels we are about to study in the following chapters also live to obey Him, and when God speaks to them, they listen, understand, and act immediately—without question. They *always* obey the Father. They jump to obey each fine detail of the Lord's Word, not missing a hair or breath of His will. They know God. They love God. And they obey God. They are ready to act on our behalf at all times. What's so marvelous is that they love to act on our behalf. They love to come to help us and to partner with us to fulfill God's best plans.

✤ ⊕ ✤ ⊕ ✤ ⊕ ✤ ⊕ ✤ ⊕ ✤

A free spirit is a trained spirit.

✤ ⊕ ✤ ⊕ ✤ ⊕ ✤ ⊕ ✤ ⊕ ✤

The five-fold ministry of apostle, prophet, evangelist, pastor, and teacher is secondary to our knowing and having an intimate relationship with the Lord Himself. The gifts and callings of God are without repentance the Bible tells us (see 2 Cor. 7:9); in other words, the gifts will always thrive. God wants our *hearts*. He wants our obedience. He wants our worship. He wants our surrendered discipline.

When I wrote the *Free to be Thin* books, (*Free to be Thin, There's More to Being Thin*) with Neva Coyle, and then later when I developed the Blessercize program and wrote *Fun to be Fit* (the last two are now out of print), I shared a lifetime of continual hard work, study, prayer, and the dynamics of discipline. Training our spirits is not easy, and training our souls is hard work, too. Training our will, our tongue, our appetites, our thoughts—this all takes work.

I'm free to choose, but I also tell myself I'm set free to be trained. Mark Twain called this kind of freedom "riding loose in the saddle." A free spirit is a trained spirit.

References

Elwell, Walter A., Editor. *Evangelical Dictionary of Theology.* Grand Rapids, MI: Baker Book House, 1984.

Illustrated Dictionary & Concordance of the Bible. Ed. Geoffrey Wigoder, et al. Jerusalem: The Jerusalem Publishing House Ltd., 1986.

Jansen, Jan. *Global Fire Ministries.* 2005.

Lockyear, Herbert. *All The Doctrines of the Bible.* Grand Rapids, MI: Zondervan Publishing House, 1964.

MacArthur, John, Editor. *The MacArthur Study Bible.* Nashville: Word Bibles, 1997.

Roundtree, Anna. *The Heavens Opened.* Lake Mary, FL: Charisma House, 1999.

Spurgeon, C.H.. *The Treasury of David, Volume 2.* Grand Rapids, MI: Zondervan Publishing House, 1968.

chapter 13

WITH AN ANGEL

THE tall being in white does not speak as we walk along the trail in the woods. He has not spoken since joining me on my prayer trail, my outdoor sanctuary. As I walk along, I worship the Lord in prayer, and the tall being in white prays and worships the Lord along with me. He begins to sing. I am quiet for some time but then I begin to sing too, my voice almost imperceptible at first. Before long I am singing with more resonance, and little by little, I become more comfortable until together our voices sing out the praises of the living God throughout the trees of the woods. Eventually, we're dancing, this tall being in white and me, dancing and singing along the trail in the woods, celebrating the majesty of the King of kings. I soon begin to hear other voices joining ours and presently the woods become alive with joyous voices praising the Lord. I look up at the sky between the trees; it is now filled with figures in white, and they are singing and dancing with us. Heaven and earth have broken forth in praise, exalting the Lord Jesus, King of kings, right here in my little woods.

Much later, after the sun has set and the cicada are chirping at the moon, I sit in my study praying for words to describe what I experienced in the woods. I had celebrated the living God with His heavenly host! Oh, such sounds the angels made: high trills and whirring, humming, and cheering. I sit in my study praying as the night crowds in upon me when, in the shadow of a single lamp, I see Him. My Lord! He has entered my study! And beside Him is the tall being in white.

The air of my study is at once filled with praise.

The night has become praise!

Nothing exists but the voice of Heaven joining earth in praise.

The tall being in white has become one large, smiling face on the wall.

I look at the face and begin to weep.

How much time passes I do not know.

I want to talk to the angel, ask questions.

I ask permission of the Lord to talk to the angel.

"May I speak to the angel?"

"*Yes.*"

I am able to ask at last, "Do you all have names?"

"Oh, yes," responds the beautiful one. "And each hair on our heads is numbered."

At this I burst into such a storm of tears that the night itself is shaken, a woven quilt

of tears.

Exhilarated, and yet weeping, I sink into my chair.

The room becomes still.

It's all so beautiful. Language has left me.

REFERENCE

Lockyear, Herbert. *All The Doctrines of the Bible.* Grand Rapids, MI: Zondervan Publishing House, 1964.

chapter 14

SPIRITUAL LIBERTY

"*W*HERE *the Spirit of the Lord is, there is liberty*" (2 Cor. 3:17). This verse speaks of holy, divine liberty. It means He has liberty to move as He will. *He* is liberty. We must not confine Him and impose our will on His. We can take an example from His angels. They never, ever impose their will upon Him. They do exactly as He does, and they are 100 percent at peace. I realize angels are without sin, and we must always be on guard against sin, "*...because He who is in you is greater than he who is in the world*" (1 John 4:4).

"*He must increase, but I must decrease*" (John 3:30) is the kind of liberty where the Spirit of the Lord is in charge, not us or our ideas of how and when He should move. Many times we are impatient for a move of the Holy Spirit and we wonder if He's passed us by. Keep on praying! Plant seeds of faith! Keep on planting! Plant for the harvest. Don't put God on trial. One of God's favorite methods of preparing us for something great is to teach us how to wait. Moses and the apostle Paul had careers that began with fleeing for their very lives, followed by long periods of waiting before God moved them into their miracle callings. Cast aside your notions of how God should do things. I know you long for more. Hang on. Your day will come.

MY DESERT EXPERIENCE

One day the Lord pulled me of my secular university position and ministry and sent me out into the desert with Him. (Not a literal desert; what I mean is, He isolated me with Himself.) The desert expression comes from the years the apostle Paul spent between the Taurus Mountains and the sea, when he dropped from history until resuming his ministry in Antioch in Acts 11:26. God sent him to the Arabian desert.

Similarly, the Lord pulled me out of the busy life I had been leading and tucked me away alone with Him in a desert of my own. This went on for three-and-a-half years! Every day, all day! Daily I poured myself out before Him, and He poured Himself out for me.

Being in ministry doesn't heal us of our past wounds and brokenness. On the contrary, being in full-time ministry or on a ministry team can delay our healing and deliverance; it can put off our spiritual health and growth because we are unprepared internally for what it means to serve the Lord.

All of my training and all the suffering of my life fed into the misbelief that working oneself into a frazzle was somehow spiritually commendable. I repent for allowing such deception to come into my life.

God didn't save us on Sunday to put us to work on Monday. (I'm not talking about telling others about what the Lord did for us when He saved us. This is natural!) It's a given fact, however, that it takes a certain amount of time growing, learning, and experiencing the Lord before we become mature Christians and pliable in the hands of God. To build an arsenal of spiritual weaponry through overcoming hardship, trials, and temptation takes time.

I see with deep regret how ministry and helping people can take the place of true intimacy with God. Even prayer can take precedence over intimacy with God. We can be so busy praying for answers from Jesus that we overlook Jesus! Sometimes the answers to prayer are so urgent and so critical that we concentrate more on needs than on God. Little by little we begin to wear down under the weight and pressure we were not meant to bear. I used to have an expression that I thought was holy. I'd say, "I just want to be burnt out for God!" (And, Lord help me, that's what I became.)

Everything depends on our intimacy with God, not our work. He wants our friendship! He wants us to know Him! Everything in our lives flows from this place of intimacy. Like a body of water with tributaries, He is the body of water, and our ministries, activities, interests, and lives are tributaries springing out from their Source. Burnt-out is what I became because I didn't understand that intimacy with God is more important than the air we breathe, the food we ingest, and the ground we walk on, and it's more important than the ministries we're called to.

I left full-time ministry to go back to college, earn another master's degree and teach and write in the secular world. I became an editor, publisher, book reviewer, lecturer, professor, and I won some writing awards that made me feel good about working so hard. When the Lord pulled me out of the secular life and said, *"No more,"* I followed, but with a bit of hesitation. Why would God want me to leave what I believed was such a blessing?

During my years alone with Him day and night, I learned something valuable. His gifts and callings truly are irrevocable. If He calls us for a certain purpose, He's serious about that call. He is never limited by time or how far away we may meander from what He has purposed for us. If you have a son or a daughter who has not fulfilled their destiny in the Lord, or if you are off the mark of your high calling, brace yourself—God *will* have His way. God had plans for me I was unaware of, and even though I didn't understand at first, I listened and obeyed when He told me to leave secular life.

During the three years that followed alone with Him, I realized I was in the elementary grades of the school of the Holy Spirit. I had been to Bible school and seminary. I had studied His Word most of my life. I had been in full-time ministry. I had preached, prophesied, taught, and ministered. I had seen miracles and signs and wonders. Yet now I found myself in the kindergarten of the Holy Spirit. All my years of loving God now found me like a baby at His knee. I learned obedience and faith on a level I never knew before.

In my isolated years with the Lord He showed me that the broken and surrendered life is the highest calling on earth. Each day as I experienced more of Him, I felt more of me break off. I became broken before Him. There were areas in my life where pain had been my teacher and not the Holy Spirit. The things that can fuel a demanding life like pride and ambition shattered around my feet. (God had a lot of work to do with me!) As I submerged myself in His Word and spent my days walking with Him and His heavenly host, I felt my whole life disintegrate, to then bloom again. I didn't realize it, but these were to become the finest years of my life.

In those years alone with Him, he told me about the unleashing of His presence and power around the globe. He said He was about to pour out His Holy Spirit in unprecendented measure such as humankind has never experienced. At that time, I was not aware that the move of His Holy Spirit had already begun in so many places of the world.

When I was invited to attend a conference in Kansas City with Mike Bickle, I could hardly believe what I was seeing. I heard and saw supernatural wonders just like the ones I had experienced at home when I was alone with the Lord. Then a friend told me about a prophetic teacher named Patricia King in Phoenix; so I got on a plane and attended two of her schools and was thrilled to learn I wasn't "off the wall" at all. I was simply one of countless children of God who were experiencing the supernatural. I was not only completely normal, I was a completely normal *babe*. I realized that, after all those years alone with God, I had just begun.

Moving Forward

I can't imagine you're willing to simply maintain the status quo in your walk with the Lord. I believe you want more, as I do. I believe you want to hear from God, as Moses and Elijah did, and walk in miracles like Joshua, Elisha, and Paul did. I believe you want wisdom like Solomon and Deborah had and courage like Daniel and David had. I know in my heart you are crying out for revelation and illumination from the Word of God. More of Jesus! More Holy Spirit! More! More, heavenly Father! Every day you reach out for miracles in your life, for an impartation of glory, for a divine appointment.

God is answering.

The Lord may not remove you from the world for three years to teach you about Himself and His Kingdom like He did with me, but one thing is for sure—He wants you to know Him. He wants you like putty in His hands. He wants you to hear when He speaks. He wants you to be His friend.

Dear Lord, I refuse to accept less when there is the whole heavenly realm for me to partake of and partner with. Let me never limit You!

THE CHARISMATIC MOVEMENT

I was a student in a conservative Baptist Bible college in the '70s when the Holy Spirit fell on a small group of us students as we met for prayer in a private home off campus. It was amazing. The Holy Spirit didn't exactly fall on us, He *exploded* upon us. Our lives changed. We began ministering with a new anointing on the streets, in our churches, and everywhere we could, and we experienced signs and wonders so wonderful that we believed we were living in the second Book of Acts.

We became part of a move of God that had begun in the 1960s and continued through the '70s and '80s. It was called the Charismatic Renewal. Hundreds of ministries were birthed in the United States at that time. Mainline denominational churches received new life and power in their services and outreaches. Modes of evangelism were sparked with new energy and power to reach those who never heard the Gospel. Storefront churches popped up in shopping centers, garages, and warehouses across the country. Music ministries flourished. (Every other Christian young person had a guitar slung over his or her shoulder and wrote wonderful Scripture songs.)

Catholics and Protestants grabbed arms and danced before the Lord together. We heard new inspired teachings on prayer, on faith, and on how to live as people of faith and walk in the Spirit; we were taught how to operate in the gifts of the Spirit, how to prosper, how to trust God. New Christian communes were formed as well as camp ministries, Bible schools, missionary training centers, and missions organizations. The Jesus Movement was birthed, plus the Messianic Jewish

Movement, Horizon and Calvary Chapel churches, Melodyland, Maranatha, the Vineyard, Third Day, the Catholic Charismatic Renewal, and Christian television.

AND NOW?

A fresh wave of the Holy Spirit is rushing toward us today, and its glory is for every believer, not for just a few radical saints or fire-baptized charismatics. God honors the righteous, and it's His righteous ones who are bringing Heaven to earth as the Lord's Prayer teaches, *"Thy kingdom come. Thy will be done in earth, as it is in heaven"* (Matt. 6:10 KJV). We're living in an open Heaven today if we will only realize it. We've seen great stirrings in Pensacola, Kansas City, and Toronto. Other cities, villages, and towns around the world are experiencing Heaven opening and a powerful move of the Holy Spirit even as you read this. Your town may be next.

The Bible tells us that God's children are positioned with Christ and seated in heavenly places. (See Ephesians 1-3.) We must take this divine inheritance as truth and a certainty. When it really sinks in, our minds can then become centered in our heavenly identity rather than simply accepting the dictates of our natural surroundings.

Jesus repeated Himself three times in the Gospel of John where He explained that He could do nothing of Himself: *"The Son can do nothing of Himself, but what He sees the Father do; for whatever He does, the Son also does in like manner"* (John 5:19). Again He says, *"I can of Myself do nothing. As I hear, I judge; and My judgment is righteous, because I do not seek My own will but the will of the Father who sent Me"* (John 5:30). And again in John 8:28-29: *"I do nothing of Myself; but as My Father taught Me…. I always do those things that please Him."*

He tells us, *"Without Me you can do nothing"* (John 15:5). It's wonderful, isn't it? Isn't it a relief to be led by the Spirit of God and not our own carnal souls? Isn't it wonderful to live a life imitating His?

Our supernatural journey with God will inform and instruct our lives in the natural realm to the point where we can actually reflect the Lord Jesus in our lives as the Bible teaches: *"…be imitators of God, as dear children"* (Eph. 5:1). And, as Jesus said, we can do nothing of any value without Him. Pause for a second. *We see Him* and we can't resist doing what He does, thinking like He thinks, loving like He loves, trusting like He trusts, believing like He believes, and being like He is. Because we *see* Him!

Victory is normal. It's normal for us to live victorious, overcoming lives.

But Is It Real?

Revival and a fresh move of God can come as big surprises, even when they're exactly what we're praying for! We pray and pray for revival and when God pours out His Spirit, we're upset because He didn't do it *our* way. The pastor just wanted more people in the sanctuary, not angels in the balcony bringing healing and deliverance from demons! The prayer group prayed for more people to come to church, not supernatural manifestations, signs, wonders, and miracles! We think revival means increased numbers of people in church, more young people in Sunday school, more volunteer workers, more money, and I don't know what all. Our thinking is skewed.

Zacharias was a praying man and a priest who served God with his life, and yet when the angel Gabriel came to him in person in Luke 1:11, he *argued* with him! By arguing with the angel, Zacharias was protesting the power of God. By arguing with the angel, Zacharias inferred that God's answer to his prayers was the wrong answer, badly timed; in other words, God had no business doing the impossible. God should be nice and do things the proper way.

Look at the spiritual revivals of the past hundred years. For every 10,000 souls praising the Lord and experiencing the miraculous in the revival meetings in tents, churches, and great auditoriums, there were those "doubting Thomases" who cast their religious traditions in concrete, unaware that most of Jesus' preaching was against religious convention and practice.

Today we stand before an open Heaven. Today there are many of us who visit heavenly places on a daily basis, and many of us who walk in the portals of glory all the time, not just occasionally! Soon there will be countless more. The Holy Spirit is given to us without measure. Take!

I prophesy that in the very near future, angelic manifestations and excursions throughout heavenly realms, accompanied by miracles on earth in Jesus' name, will become commonplace. That being said, we can expect some accompanying persecution as well as demonic imitations of the works of God. (But never fear. The truth lasts forever; the lie lasts only for a moment.) (See Proverbs 12:19.)

THE PROBLEM OF ZACHARIAS

Zacharias, the priest, had a problem trusting the supernatural, didn't he? And Zacharias was a man of God! I believe he loved and worshiped God with all his heart. Why, then, did he *argue* with an angelic being? He was actually ministering to the Lord and burning the incense in the Temple when the angel Gabriel appeared to him, and Zacharias just "lost it." He was taken completely by surprise. It's a wonder he didn't have a heart attack and drop dead on the spot.

The angel Gabriel brought the news that Zacharias was going to be a father. Elizabeth, his aged wife, was going to conceive a child. This was just too much for old Zacharias. (He was so "out of it" that he didn't realize *who* he was talking to!) Not only did the angel tell Zacharias he'd have a son, but he gave the child a name and proclaimed his great calling and destiny. His son would go before the Savior in the spirit and power of Elijah! And what did Zacharias do after hearing these glorious prophecies? He *protested*. He tried to explain his situation as though God didn't already know what was what. God was fully aware that he and Elizabeth were old. Zacharias had been praying for decades for a child and now he protested his answer as though God was incapable of answering his prayers. So Zacharias asked the angel for a sign: "How shall I know this?" he demanded.

I scratch my head. Zacharias, I remind you, was a priest! He must have known the Torah, the first five books of Moses; after all, knowing the Torah was his job, which means he had to have known about Sarah and Abraham bringing a son into the world when Sarah was 90 years of age and Abraham was 120. He would also have known about Hannah in First Samuel 1. Hannah was hopelessly barren, yet God miraculously blessed her to bring forth a son named Samson. It wasn't as though Zacharias was the first old man to sire a child.

The God of the universe's chief messenger angel then announced, *"I am Gabriel, who stands in the presence of God, and I've been sent to speak to you and tell you this good news"* (Luke 1:19 TLB). Do you think Zacharias bit his lip at that? Do you think he told himself how blessed he was? No, he didn't; instead, he *protested!* (Zacharias must have been used to talking and not listening. I figure he was probably a big talker in his day.) The result was that Gabriel had to declare Zacharias mute and unable to speak until the day his baby was born. The man was full of arguments and unbelief. He was a chatterbox. He didn't understand the miracle that was taking place. He didn't understand that God never lies, never breaks a promise, and He *always* answers.

I believe Zacharias is a lot like some religious people of today, people who love God with all their hearts, but who are more accustomed to talking about God than talking to Him or *listening* to Him. These people are so stuck in their traditions that if the Lord Himself were to appear to them, they'd either ignore or rebuke the experience. I've been put down for speaking in tongues, for praying for healing, for prophesying, you name it. I'm sure some people think it's downright outrageous to be experiencing an open Heaven. Religious tradition, instead of being a blessing and a solid base from which to learn and grow in the Lord, is a hindrance if the Holy Spirit is quenched in favor of keeping the status quo.

We have two sets of eyes and two sets of ears: our natural physical eyes and ears and our spiritual eyes and ears. We see into the spiritual realm with our spiritual eyes and we hear in the spiritual realm with our spiritual ears. This takes effort. This takes work. It takes a renewing of our minds. It takes thinking on the things of God—on the things that are true, noble, just, pure, lovely, and reputable (see Phil. 4:8). If it's more glory we want, we must train ourselves to receive more glory.

MORE GLORY

Right now worship gatherings are going on for 24 hours, especially in the 24/7 prayer rooms across the nation. People are gathering to worship the Lord and pray around the clock. We have midnight fasting and prayer vigils where we gather together at midnight for intercessory prayer and mighty things happen at these odd times. We expect supernatural visitations. We expect Heaven to open. And it becomes like Second Chronicles 5.

In Second Chronicles 5:13-14 the priests of the Lord praised the Lord in the Temple of Solomon, and His Presence knocked them off their feet. They could not stand on their feet to minister. The power and Presence of the Lord were so great that their knees just gave way and they were brought to the ground. The Lord came as in a magnificent cloud and 120 priests, the singers, the musicians with stringed instruments, harps, trumpets, and cymbals, all wearing beautiful white linen, fell to their faces.

Solomon prayed a magnificent prayer of dedication and suddenly fire roared down from heaven and consumed their burnt offering and their sacrifices, which had been laid out "...*and the glory of the LORD filled the temple*" (2 Chron. 7:1). The priests tried to enter the Temple for their ceremonial duty, but could not get as far as the door. They could not enter the house of the Lord because of the glory of the Lord. The Temple was filled with God's glory, and no human could bear such glory. God's glory singed and burned the particles of air; His glory swallowed all breath, and His glory demolished everything else (see 2 Chron. 7:1-2).

Can we expect God's glory to descend upon our worship services? *Expect* it, I say! *Expect* God to pour out His Spirit as He promised. *Expect* miracles, heavenly manifestations, and visitations. *Expect* the glory!

God's glory will descend upon us as we praise Him. This is *normal*. I've seen sparkling colored lights, gold dust, rain, white lights, and a cloud of glory come over His people while praising the Lord. And there is so much more to come. God inhabits the praises of His people! (See Psalm 22:3.) The angelic host loves praising God with us.

An Angel on a Bicycle

We are seeing and hearing God's angels in our worship services all the time. Angels are showing up with greater frequency in places outside the church, too. Angels are showing up when we least expect them. I heard from a woman this week who described how she was awakened at about 3 o'clock in the morning, looked out the window, and saw an angel riding a bicycle on her front lawn. He signaled a message to her, which was the answer to a particular problem she was facing. I love that. You never know how God will send us help when we need it. Angels show up in many forms. Once, when I was extremely tired, an angel jumped ahead of my car the entire hundred miles from Los Angeles to San Diego in the form of a dancing ball. I was so fascinated by this that I didn't get sleepy once.

An Angel in a Convenience Store

I like a story evangelist Todd Bentley tells about an angel showing up in a convenience store dressed like a street person. Todd and his friend had been talking to some tough guys in the store about the Lord when the angel walked in and told the guys to pay attention to the preacher because what he was telling them was true. The guys jumped back at those words like someone had taken a swing at them. Then the angel turned, walked out the door, and Todd and his friend sweetly led the guys to Jesus. Todd's wife and her girlfriend, who were waiting outside in the car, told them later that nobody had entered or left the store; they said that they knew this because they were sitting there and watching the whole time.

I see angels every night as millions of starry lights surrounding me. I also experience flashes of light like shooting stars or blasts of light exploding. In prayer meetings we experience angelic manifestations such as feathers floating down on us, or our skin becoming covered in gold flecks. But now we're asking for more! *We are expecting more!*

SPIRITUAL PORTALS

We're coming to understand portals better. We're able to sense in the spirit where the angels are or have been. Often when I am on my prayer walks, I feel pockets of heat or waves of a different atmosphere around me. (It's the best way to describe it.) I stop, wait, and listen. I pray and take authority by releasing His blessing on the area. What is Holy Spirit saying and expecting me to do? I then announce to the area that I am there and as long as I am there the area is holy.

Many times when I'm ministering, a person will tell me they feel a cool, refreshing wind as I pass by. (My first reaction is "flesh alert." Maybe I walk too fast and create a breeze, or maybe a window is open or the air conditioning kicked on.) But if it's real, and it is the Presence of the Holy Spirit in our midst, we must reach out and receive what He is imparting.

Once I passed a young woman who was sitting on a rock as I was taking my prayer walk, and I felt a strong wash of heat; it was hot air in the middle of winter. A few feet away, sitting on another rock, was a man who was about her age. I looked at the two of them and discerned that they were having a lovers' quarrel and she was plenty mad. I was right.

Did you know that your attitude can change the air molecules around you? The young woman had built up a real heat wave in the middle of winter. When I'm on my walks in the woods and I sense a patch of air that is suddenly very hot, like the heat you would feel while walking past a puff from an exhaust pipe, I quickly begin to engage in spiritual warfare. This was what happened as I continued my prayer walk. I prayed for the couple and when I circled back to the spot where they had been sitting previously, I saw them walking off hand-in-hand.

The secret is to know whether you're sensing activity in the spiritual or the natural realm.

Jesus once told me, because I walk in many strange and out-of-the-way wilderness places, to *sanctify* the area I walk through.

"Sanctify?" I responded.

"Yes, sanctify. The area."

"OK," I said, and then I went on to the work of sanctifying: "I sanctify this area now in the name of Jesus. I speak forth and bring the Presence of the living God *now* to this area. (I go on to name the place.) In the name of Jesus Christ, the Creator of Heaven and earth! This area is sanctified in Jesus' name!"

I do that all the time now. I also remind the area that as long as I am there it will have to behave itself. There will be no rattlesnakes striking out, no mountain lions lurking around, no scorpions, skunks, animal or human predators—because the woman of God is on the scene. I pray in the name of Jesus. The Bible says in Genesis 1 that we are to have dominion over the fish of the sea, over the birds of the air, and over every living thing that moves on the earth. We are to be fruitful and multiply; we are to fill the earth and subdue it. I know hikers who carry guns, knives, and pepper spray, and I don't even carry water.

You may wonder whether or not I took authority over that cactus garden before I took a nose-dive into it. Actually, no. I did not. But after the fall I sure did. I may be one of the few Christians you know who prays fervently over cactus plants. One often learns the hard way. (Ouch.) I am so thankful for my angel, because I know it was a miracle I wasn't hurt worse. The experience still makes me laugh.

Imagination?

On my hikes with the Lord I am accompanied by scores of angels. I see them physically in the atmosphere. I see them because I am seeing with my spirit eyes and not my natural eyes. I've heard it said that we use our imaginations to enter heavenly realms. Though humans have imaginations, the Holy Spirit does not. The Holy Spirit is real. Heaven is real. Angels are real. Take those little fat cupids they call angels you see everywhere. They were created by someone's imagination, not by knowledge of the Truth. I don't know how anyone could replicate the angelic host. There's not enough marble, granite, clay, gold, wood or *papier-mache* in the world. One day the angels show up as breathtaking, mighty warriors across the horizon; and the next day they're enormous pillars of white standing along the back wall of the church, or they're riding a bicycle on the front lawn. The heavenly host is real and diverse.

Heaven is *real*. Walking in the spirit, seeing and hearing in the spirit, and living in the spirit are all dimensions of being. We empty ourselves of our soulish, natural thoughts and feelings in order to concentrate on God. We concentrate on His goodness, His beauty, His holiness, His glory. Like the priests at the dedication of Solomon's temple, the glory of God causes our knees and our flesh to grow weak and our spirit-self to soar. In that place of meditation, we see Him. In His glory we hear His voice. This is how Moses lived as the deliverer of the Jewish nation. He entered God's glory with his whole being, and the Lord spoke with him "face-to-face" as a man speaks to his friend. (See Exodus 33.)

✣ ⊕ ✣ ⊕ ✣ ⊕ ✣ ⊕ ✣ ⊕ ✣

God wants your freindship.

✣ ⊕ ✣ ⊕ ✣ ⊕ ✣ ⊕ ✣ ⊕ ✣

Let's live in the revelation of the Lord's eternal, inexplicable love that yanks the strength from our knees and collapses us permanently prostrate in the wonder of His glory. It's where we long to live, where we were born to live. It's where Heaven opens its gates and tells us to come on in, come on in where you will find yourself face-to-face with more opportunity and joy than anything you dared dream in your sunniest of dreams.

Come on in.

chapter 15

PREPARING FOR ANGELIC ENCOUNTERS

T HE Jewish historian Josephus wrote, "It was from God, *through angels*, that we have learned the most beautiful of our doctrines and the most holy sections of our laws." One of the finest and most powerful sources of help that God created for us is the ministry of angels. God wants to release the angelic realm, and we must prepare ourselves for angelic encounters and visitations.

When I am asked, "How do I know if it's God speaking to me?" or "Is it just my imagination?" or "How do I recognize God's voice?" Or, "How do I know if God has sent me His angel or if the devil has sent a counterfeit?" My answer is always to test the message alongside the Word of God. As D.L. Moody said, "You know whether or not a stick is crooked by laying it down next to a straight one."

But how about when the angel Gabriel appears and tells you that your prayers are answered for a son when you're old enough to be a great-granddaddy, which is what happened to Zacharias?

How about when you're facing a life-or-death situation and an angel of the Lord comes and wrestles all night with you and knocks your hip permanently out of joint, but then blesses you and changes your name and character forever, as happened with Jacob?

How do we prepare for the unexpected and what God has in store for us? We make the unexpected *expected*. What's more, *we expect God to be outrageous*. We expect God to do the amazing, the unusual, the marvelous. Wasn't it outrageous when an angel appeared to Mary and told her she'd conceive a child by the Holy Ghost? Wasn't it outrageous when God sent an angel to shut the lions' mouths so Daniel could get a decent night's sleep? Wasn't it outrageous when the angel came and rolled back the stone from the door of Jesus' tomb and sat on it?

One day you're like Gideon, nervous, scared, and hiding from danger. The next thing you know, an angel of the Lord appears to you and calls you a mighty person of valor. (See Judges 6:11-12.) Are you talking to *me*, Mr. Angel? Are you *kidding*? Am I dreaming? Huh?

Again I say: expect God to do the amazing, the unusual, and the marvelous. Also, expect God to see you through *His eyes*, not yours. You always think less of yourself than He does.

Number one in preparing for the unexpected is to know your worth. Really. Work hard at this. Re-read Marie's 3 R's. You're in trouble if you don't know who you are in the Lord. People with inflated, disturbed egos come up with off-the-wall encounters with false spirits. Remember that Joseph Smith, who founded the cult of the Mormons, claimed it was an angel who guided him. What deception! Know who you are in *Christ*.

Start here.

YOU ARE:

Beloved. *"My **beloved** brethren..."* (See James 2:5; 1 Cor. 15:58).

*"My **beloved** is mine and I am his"* (Song of Sol. 2:16).

The Apple of His eye. *"For thus says the Lord of hosts: 'He sent Me after glory, to the nations which plunder you; for he who touches you touches **the apple of His eye**"* (Zech. 2:8).

Loved. *"I have **loved** you with an **everlasting love**; therefore, with lovingkindness I have drawn you"* (Jer. 31:3).

Clean. *"You are already **clean** because of the word which I have spoken to you"* (John 15:3).

Anointed. *"Now He who establishes us with you in Christ and has **anointed** us is God..."* (2 Cor. 1:21).

Strong. *"A wise man is **strong**, yes, a man of knowledge increases strength"* (Prov. 24:5).

A Partaker of Divine Nature. *"By which have been given to us exceedingly great and precious promises, that through these you may be **partakers of the divine** nature, having escaped the corruption that is in the world through lust..."* (2 Pet. 1:4-5).

A Success. *"This Book of the Law shall not depart from your mouth, but you shall meditate in it day and night, that you may observe to do according to all that is written in it. For then you will make your way prosperous, and then you will have good **success**"* (Josh. 1:8).

Prosperous. *"Beloved, I pray that you may **prosper** in all things and be in health, just as your soul prospers"* (3 John 1:2).

Faithful. *"For He is Lord of lords and King of kings; and those who are with Him are called, chosen, and **faithful**"* (Rev. 17:14).

Blessed. *"Blessed be the God and Father of our Lord Jesus Christ, who has blessed us with every spiritual **blessing** in the heavenly places in Christ..."* (Eph. 1:3).

Called. *"You also are the **called** of Christ"* (Rom. 1:6).

A Treasure. *"Now therefore, if you will indeed obey My voice and keep My covenant, then you shall be a special **treasure** to Me above all people; for all the earth is Mine"* (Exod. 19:5).

The Light of the World. *"You are the **light of the world**. A city set on a hill cannot be hidden"* (Matt. 5:14).

A Vessel of Honor. *"Therefore if anyone cleanses himself...he will be a **vessel for honor**, sanctified and useful for the Master, prepared for every good work"* (2 Tim. 2:21).

Number Two in preparing for the unexpected is to be armed. The best way to arm yourself for God to work in your life is by gaining *experience in His Presence.*

Nothing can take the place of solid experience with the Word of God and the Holy Spirit. It's the armor you wear when you face the world. And by experience I mean those hours you spend in prayer and the Word of God each day. Those hours you spend on your face before the Lord soaking in His presence, studying His Word, and listening for His voice of instruction and guidance. The more experience you have *alone* with God, the more you position yourself for an open Heaven and an overcoming life.

The time I have spent alone secluded with Him hour upon hour, day upon day, month upon month, and year upon year has reshaped my life. Nothing is the same for me now. The more time you spend with Him, the more familiar you will be with His ways, His personality, His character, His voice, and His ways. When the apostle Paul started his ministry, he really didn't know the Lord. He got blasted with the Shekinah glory of God on the Damascus road and then he started preaching right off. But he really didn't know the Lord personally yet. The Lord had to pull him aside for a few years to teach him—and it was *then* that Paul got to really *know* Him. In Galatians 1 Paul speaks of his years in solitude. Let's look at what he said.

WHO DO I WANT TO PLEASE?

For am I now seeking the favor of men, or of God? Or am I striving to please men? If I were still trying to please men, I would not be a bondservant of Christ.

For I would have you know, brethren, that the gospel which was preached by me is not according to man. For I neither received it from man, nor was I taught it, but I received it through a revelation of Jesus Christ. For you have heard of my former manner of life in Judaism, how I used to persecute the church of God beyond measure, and tried to destroy it; and I was advancing in Judaism beyond many contemporaries among my countrymen, being more zealous for ancestral traditions. But when He who had set me apart, even from my mother's womb, and called me through His grace, was pleased to reveal His Son in me, that I might preach Him among the Gentiles, I did not immediately consult with flesh and blood, nor did I go up to Jerusalem to those who were apostles before me; but I went away **to Arabia**...(Gal. 1:10-17 NAS).

Exactly where Paul went in the Arabian desert we don't know. The desert stretched as far south as Sinai near Egypt and north to the lower boundaries of Syria. Paul doesn't give any details, except to tell us that he was in the desert for three years. But it was there he had Jesus all to himself for three years. In Galatians 1:18 he says, *"Then **after three years** I went up to Jerusalem to see Peter, and remained with him fifteen days."*

THE FAVOR OF MEN OR OF GOD?

Paul had been a passionate Pharisee who was zealous to earn the approval of the Sanhedrin. He had been an ambitious and ruthless man. Now he could say that he no longer cared about the favor of men, good or bad. He was no longer interested in pleasing anyone except God. What happened to him to make this drastic change in his character? He met the Lord deeply and intimately, and from a place of intimacy he could now exclaim in triumph, *"I count all things to be loss in view of the surpassing value of knowing Christ Jesus my Lord, for whom I have suffered the loss of all things, and count them but rubbish in order that I may gain Christ"* (Phil. 3:8, author's paraphrase).

We become strong through the lessons we learn in solitude. We become broken and undone when we're tucked away alone with the Lord. It's a place that is at once sublime and terrible. Life cannot offer us anything so beautiful.

Number Three: Intimacy with the Lord teaches you how to receive from Him. You can't give without being able to receive. You can't give mercy if you can't receive mercy. You can't be a light in the world unless you receive the Light of the world.

You don't glow with blessings from God unless you *receive* His blessings.

Moses didn't just wake up one morning with his face shining in Shekinah glory. Moses spent time in the Presence of God, talking with

God, communing with God, receiving from God, and his face took on the reflection of that communion.

HOW TO RELEASE ANGELIC ACTIVITY

God's angels love to partner with us. How do we release angelic activity in our lives? We begin by getting ready, by preparing ourselves. Just as we are constantly in a state of readiness for the imminent return of the Lord, we prepare for Him to move here on the earth now. Whenever there is a great move of God, there must be a time of expectation, a time of consecration, a time of making the necessary preparations in our midst and in our hearts for Him to come.

Let's pretend for a minute that you and I are going to host a dinner party. What's the first thing we do? We prepare the invitation list. And then, because we know who our guests (or Guest) will be, we know how to prepare.

Knowing what your guests will enjoy is the key to the success of every party.

Let me illustrate: I once cooked a rather fancy continental dinner for a group of my relatives in Minnesota (who consider pasta a gourmet food, ha ha), but what I thought would be a great time of eating interesting food turned into a big fizzle. My guests hardly nibbled a thing on the table. My lovely stuffed grape leaves, my bubbling moussaka, and my snappy tabouli sat there getting suspicious looks. (I thought my family would enjoy something they weren't used to eating since we weren't Greek. Was I ever wrong!)

Did I say knowing what your guests enjoy is the key to success? We cook for our guests and their enjoyment, not for ourselves, right? We prepare for *them*. And to do that, we figure out what would best bless them, right? Oh, how I failed. My family would have been completely at home and happy if I had served fried chicken on that occasion. They didn't need the Greek music and the decorations either. There was a game on TV they had to miss. And what was with that sticky looking tray of honey and walnut-soaked baklava? They still laugh about it.

A MEETING WITH ANGELS

What did Abraham do when the Lord and His two angels came to visit him in Genesis 18? Let's set the scene. Here is Abraham, minding his own business, sitting in the doorway of his tent. He's hot. He's tired. Sarah is busy inside and Abraham is just sitting there trying to keep cool in the blistering heat of the day. Maybe he's thinking about taking a nap, washing his socks, who knows? He looks up and what does he see but three men standing at the edge of his grove of terebinth trees. Abraham leaps to his feet as if he had been shot through with a bolt of lightning. He races from the tent door and throws himself down on the ground at the feet of the men.

"My Lord, if I have found favor in Your sight, do not pass on by Your servant..." (Gen. 18:3).

Notice he only addresses one of them: *"My Lord...."* God Himself had come as a human being, a theophany.

And first thing, Abraham makes them comfortable.

When you are praying for an open Heaven, prepare a place where the Lord will be comfortable. *You* are that place. Is He comfortable with and in you? Is He comfortable in your skin? In your life? Have you made a place for Him?

✛ ⊕ ✛ ⊕ ✛ ⊕ ✛ ⊕ ✛ ⊕ ✛

Is the Holy Spirit comfortable in your skin?

✛ ⊕ ✛ ⊕ ✛ ⊕ ✛ ⊕ ✛ ⊕ ✛

The next thing Abraham does is to prepare food for his holy guests. He prepares what he believes they will enjoy because he knew who his guests were. He cooks a tender calf from his herd and prepares it with butter, milk, and unleavened cakes. He knew just how to honor them.

COOKING FOR GOD

In three miraculous biblical instances we see the Lord Himself coming to earth in person and consuming a meal that was prepared by humans. In these three instances we see the Guest as the supreme key, and we see Him appear:

1. With Abraham under the terebinth trees where He ate meat, milk, butter, and unleavened bread. Abraham *prepared for the Lord.*

2. With Lot in Genesis 19. The angels came to Sodom and stayed at Lot's house to escape the ignoble intentions of the street crowd. The Bible says that Lot "*... made a feast, and baked unleavened bread, and they ate*" (Gen. 19:3). Lot prepared. He made them welcome, and he fed them a nice feast.

3. Later, in the Book of Judges, Gideon has a divine visitation from God. Here again the "Angel of the LORD" is the LORD Himself. (See Judges 6:11.) After a discussion about God's mandate for Gideon to defeat the Midianites and Gideon thinking there's been some mistake, he prepares an offering for the Lord. He prepares a young goat and unleavened bread and a pot of broth. The Lord then consumes it with fire.

Then the Angel of the LORD put out the end of the staff that was in His hand, and touched the meat and the unleavened bread; and fire rose out of the rock and consumed the meat and the unleavened bread (Judges 6:21).

BLESS THE LORD

In each of these three visits from heaven God accepted the human preparations. The preparations blessed Him. This is why we command our souls to get into position to bless the Lord. "*Bless the Lord, O my soul; and all that is within me, bless His holy name!*" (Ps. 103:1). Know what pleases and blesses Him!

Because Your lovingkindness is better than life, My lips shall praise You Thus I will bless You while I live (Psalm 63:3-4).

I will bless the Lord at all times; His praise shall continually be in my mouth (Psalm 34:1).

Bless the LORD, O my soul! O LORD my God, You are very great: You are clothed with honor and majesty... (Psalm 104:1).

Notice how Abraham, Lot, and Gideon each responded in like manner, which gives us a determinant to help us get into position for angelic encounters. The secret? Know how to entertain an angel!

Purging Ourselves of Sin

Did you notice the three men prepared *unleavened* bread for their heavenly guests? Why? Because they knew how to entertain an angel. They knew how to bless the Lord. Leaven represents sin. The chemical definition of ferment or yeast is a substance in a state of putrefaction. The Law forbade the use of leaven in all offerings made to the Lord by fire.

First Corinthians 5:6 tells us that a little leaven spoils the whole lump.

Therefore purge out the old leaven, that you may be a new lump, since you truly are unleavened. For indeed Christ, our Passover, was sacrificed for us. Therefore let us keep the feast, not with the old leaven, nor with the leaven of malice and wickedness, but with the unleavened bread of sincerity and truth (1 Corinthians 5:7-8).

We see the sacrifice of Christ foreshadowed as our perfect Passover in the offering of unleavened bread. We prepare for God's visit by removing the leaven, or by purging ourselves of sin. *"Search me, O God, and know my heart...see if there is any wicked way in me"* (Ps. 139:23-24) should be our regular prayer, followed by a grateful heart:

Thank you, Lord, for taking my sins on your own body so that I can be free to live a dynamic life pressed in close to you in the spirit. Thank you for forgiving me, for cleaning up my mind, my body, my heart, and my soul. Thank you for the blood you spilled on my behalf to bring me clean and whole before the Father. Oh, I thank you.

God is looking for those who will allow the Holy Spirit to reveal their sin, and then rid themselves of it.

What Is Sin?

Sin is enmity toward God. It's a violation of His nature and His Word. It's separation from God, a delusion. Sin renders us guilty. Sin is darkness, emptiness. Sin makes us slaves. Words like *otseb* in Psalm 139:24 and *amel* in Job 20:22 (*"In his self-sufficiency he will be in distress; every hand of misery will come against him"*) show us the bitter, hard servitude and miserable dissatisfaction the devil offers his dupes.

Sin results in distortion, ruins our hopes, and corrupts our soul.

The tiny Hebrew word *ra*, which is often used for "wicked" or "evil," means the ruin of a soul by breaking it into pieces. Because of sin, the soul is dashed, as in the word, "wickedness" that we see in Proverbs 15:26:

"The thoughts of the wicked are an abomination to the LORD, but the words of the pure are pleasant [pleasing words to Him]."

The Amplified version says, *"The thoughts of the wicked are shamefully vile and exceedingly offensive to the Lord, but the words of the pure are **pleasing words to Him.**"*

In the words "pure" and "holy," we see wholeness and completeness. In the word "wickedness" we have ruin, brokenness, and destruction. Sin begins not only with an impulse, but with a thought. How important it is to clear ourselves of all unclean thoughts, bitterness, anger, self-indulgence, carnality, fear, and unbelief. These are what break us, crush us, and make slaves of us.

WHEN GOD SHOWS UP

When you plan a dinner party, you're not only going to cook a terrific meal that you know your guests will enjoy, but you're going to be sure the place is clean and neat, you're going to set a nice table, you're going to prepare a comfortable, welcoming ambience, and what else? Oh, yes. You're going to get yourself ready. You're going to dress and present yourself in a manner that tells your guests you're glad they've come.

Your supernatural dinner with Jesus is a banquet of love and closeness. When He comes to you, you'll sit down with Him, you'll be quiet with Him, and you'll eat and drink in all that He has to tell you, give you, and teach you.

This is because you're prepared.

It's God's desire to fulfill His promises in our lives. Many of us have been praying for God to answer certain prayers for 10, 20, and 30 years, but the breakthrough we're seeking still hasn't come. The dinner isn't served. Think back now on a promise that the Lord made to you. Think of the prophetic word you received that hasn't come to pass. Think of that vision, that dream, that promise of God you are still waiting to be fulfilled in your life. I tell you, God is about to move on your behalf now! Prepare to receive!

He's about to move because you're preparing for Him. He's going to come to you because He said, *"Behold, I stand at the door and knock. If anyone hears My voice and opens the door, I will come in to him and dine with him, and he with Me"* (Rev. 3:20).

IN WHAT FORM DO ANGELS COME TO US?

So here we are, getting ourselves prepared. We're waiting and expecting. We're training ourselves to see in the spirit and look with our spiritual eyes and listen with our spiritual ears. How do we recognize an angel when he shows up?

The apostle Paul told us, *"Do not forget to entertain strangers, for by so doing some [of you] have unwittingly entertained angels"* (Heb. 13:2).

You may not recognize an angel if he (or she) comes in human form for some purpose of God. I am continually receiving stories from people who tell me things like this:

A lady named Jane was out in her driveway washing her car a week before she was to have major surgery. A lady jogged by whom she had never seen and called out a friendly, "Hi, Jane. Nice to see you!"

Jane turned, gave her a polite smile, and wondered how this stranger knew her name. She called back with a hesitant, "Hi."

The woman, who Jane described later as happy and bubbly, was about 35 years old, and she was jogging in place by the fender of the car. She was quiet for a while and then said, "Listen, Jane, I'm here to tell you not to worry about your surgery. God will be there with you. He's got it all under control."

At that, Jane dropped the sponge and stared at the woman.

The woman gave her a warm smile. "He wants you to know everything is going to come out fine."

Jane bent down to pick up her sponge. "Well, thanks, but how did you know?" She stood up, looked around, and guess what?

Right. The woman was gone. She was nowhere to be seen up or down the empty street and sidewalk.

How will you recognize an angel? Maybe you won't. God often sends what I call the "stranger test." Jesus gives us this example in Matthew 25:

> Then the King will say to those on His right hand, "Come, you blessed of My Father, inherit the kingdom prepared for you from the foundation of the world: for I was hungry and you gave Me food; I was thirsty and you gave Me drink; I was a stranger and you took Me in; I was naked and you clothed Me; I was sick and you visited Me; I was in prison and you came to Me" (Matthew 25:34-36).

How would you respond if the Lord came to you and spoke those words directly in your ear? What would you do? What would you say? Would you respond with these words:

Lord, when did we see You hungry and feed You, or thirsty and give You drink? When did we see You a stranger and take You in, or naked and clothe You? Or when did we see You sick, or in prison, and come to You? (Matthew 25:38-39).

And the Lord takes your beautiful face in His hands, strokes your chin, and whispers, *Dearest one, listen: "Assuredly, I say to you, inasmuch as you did it to one to the least of these My brethren, you did it to Me* (Matthew 25:40).

We can interpret Jesus' illustration to mean that caring for children of the household of faith, the nation of Israel, and needy people around the world in general is ministering to Him, but we must also always be ready for the "stranger test."

Jesus said, *"Whoever receives one little child like this in My name receives Me"* (Matt. 18:5).

Will an angel appear as a little child? Will an angel appear as a beggar on the street? Will an angel show up as a jogger, a rider on a bicycle, three men for dinner, a voice in the desert, or a stranger sitting next to you in church? Will God show up in a burning bush, on a mountaintop, in the stillness after a storm, in handwriting on the wall?

Yes, yes, yes, yes, yes, and yes.

And what are we to do? Goodness gracious, what are we to do? One thing only.

Be prepared.

chapter 16

ANGELS IN THE LIFE OF JESUS

ANGELS, both seen and unseen, were active every minute of Christ's life on earth. Jesus was never out of their sight because He was never out of the sight of the Father. Angels were a vital presence in the earthly life of Jesus, and they attended Him through each stage of His sojourn here. Let's look at the Lord's relationship with angels from His conception to His resurrection.

1. The angel Gabriel appeared to Mary and announced the miracle she would carry in her body. He explained to her that, though she was a virgin, she was about to bear the Redeemer of the world. (See Luke 1:26-37.)

   The angel Gabriel not only appeared to Mary to announce to her that she would give birth to our Savior, but he appeared to Zacharias, the priest-husband of Mary's cousin, Elizabeth, with the news that they would conceive a child, too. Elizabeth and her husband were old and long past the child-bearing age and had given up all hope of having a child. Childlessness was like a reproach from God in biblical days. From the time of Sarah, not to bear children, when family and lineage were so vitally important, seemed like punishment.

   However, there are no time restrictions in God's economy. We despair, waiting for God to answer prayer, if He makes us wait year after year after year after year, as He did with this old couple, and then one day, *zap!*

2. It was an angel who enlightened Joseph in a dream, explaining that Mary was pregnant by the Holy Spirit. This angelic visitation convinced Joseph not to divorce Mary, for he realized it was ordained of God, and, though he was not the Savior's physical father, he would be his legal father. (See Matthew 1:20.)

3. The birth of Jesus was not without hardship and peril, and when He was born in Bethlehem, it was an angel who appeared to a group of shepherds in the field outside of town. The glory of the Lord shone all around them. The angel told them not to be afraid, for he had great news—a baby had been born, a Savior, Christ the Lord, and He was waiting in a manger in Bethlehem. (See Luke 2:9-12.)

4. An enormous host of cheering angels replaced the stars, proclaiming His arrival and filling the skies with their praises. (See Luke 2:13-14.)

5. An angel of the Lord appeared in a dream to Joseph and told him to hurry and get out of town with the baby Jesus and His mother because Herod was after him to kill him. Joseph did exactly as the angel told him to do. (See Matthew 2:13-15.)

6. An angel appeared to Joseph again after Herod died and told him to take Jesus and His mother back to Israel. Joseph obeyed the angel. (See Matthew 2:19.)

Do you see how Joseph partnered with the angels? The angel spoke and Joseph acted. God certainly could have supernaturally accomplished His will without the service of angels and without Joseph's help, but that is not God's way. *God always includes angels in His plans and He always includes us in His plans.* In your life right now, God is partnering with you to fulfill His will and your glorious destiny in Him. He is guiding you with His loving hand, and even if you have a personal wicked Herod snapping at your heels, God has His angels watching over you and helping you come through each trial in triumph.

Notice how the angel didn't say, "Hop aboard, Joseph, and I'll zip you and the family over to Egypt and safety." No, the angel gave directions about how *Joseph* was to take his family to safety. Also, notice how God didn't just zap Herod on the spot to make things a whole lot easier for everybody. God wants overcomers. He wants us to use the power He gives us.

WHAT ARE WE GOING TO DO WITH ALL OUR POWER?

7. Angels ministered to Jesus in the wilderness after His 40 day fast and the temptations the devil presented to Him. When the devil gave up, realizing that Jesus wasn't interested in his foibles or lies, the Bible tells us that angels came and ministered to Him. (See Matthew 4:1-11.) Notice here that the devil didn't lead Jesus into temptation; the Holy Spirit did. Matthew 4:1 says, "Then Jesus was led up by the Spirit into the wilderness to be tempted by the devil." Jesus passed the temptation test with flying colors, and afterward the angels arrived to minister to Him. It's reasonable to imagine that the angels not only embraced Him with encouragement and heaven's love, but they brought Him something to eat and drink to break His fast.

8. Angels rushed to Jesus' side in the Garden of Gesthemene as He struggled in prayer with the certainty of His impending death. He knew He was about to go through a horrible death for the sins of humanity: *"And there appeared to Him an angel from heaven, strengthening Him in spirit"* (Luke 22:43 AMP).

9. When the soldiers arrived to arrest Jesus in the Garden, Peter drew his sword and cut off the ear of Malchus, one of the high priest's servants who was with the soldiers. Angels were waiting for the Lord's beckoning, should He call for them,

and Jesus abruptly stopped Peter and told him to put his sword back in its sheath. *"Do you suppose that I cannot appeal to My Father, and He will immediately provide Me with more than twelve legions* [more than 80,000] *of angels?"* (Matt. 26:53 AMP). (See also John 18:10-11.) In other words, Jesus didn't need human help, and He wasn't going to call for the angel warriors to help Him either. He was going to bear our sins on His body willingly.

The most terrifying and devastating moment for Jesus was not the bloody beatings and the morbid pain of the crucifixion, but that moment when he cried out in agony, *"Eli, Eli, lama sabachthani?... My God, My God, why have You forsaken Me?"* (Matt. 27:46). It was at that instant that the sins of humanity were fixed on Him. At that terrible instant the angels were ordered to turn their faces and lend Him no help. God Himself turned His beautiful, loving Father-face away as the perfect Jesus became the embodiment of the all the sins of the human race. This was God's plan and heaven and its angels were silent. They turned their faces and they were silent.

10. When Jesus was brutally crucified, His dead body was laid in a tomb, but then three days later: *"Behold, there was a great earthquake, for an angel of the Lord descended from heaven and came and rolled the boulder back and sat upon it. His appearance was like lightning, and his garments as white as snow"* (Matt. 28:2-3 AMP). The guards were so terrified that` they became "like dead men." (Yet another example of the magnificence of the angels' appearance.) The angel said to the women, *"Do not be alarmed and frightened, for I know that you are looking for Jesus"* (Matt. 28:5 AMP).

11. After Jesus was crucified, He rose from the dead and walked the earth in His resurrected body for 40 days. Well over 500 people witnessed His appearance during this time as Jesus ate, drank, taught, and fellowshipped with his followers.

Then on the 41st day, as His disciples stood watching in awe, Jesus was lifted bodily up to Heaven. The Bible says, *"And while they were gazing intently into heaven as He went, behold, two men [dressed] in white robes suddenly stood beside them"* (Acts 1:10, AMP). The angels told the disciples that Jesus would return in exactly the same way they were seeing Him ascend.

12. The Lord travels with His angels. *"...when He comes in the glory [splendor and majesty] of His Father with the holy angels"* (Mark 8:38).

When the Lord enters a church service, you'll usually see Him accompanied by angels. I've seen the Lord sitting out front in the pew when I've been speaking, and then after the service someone will tell me, "I saw these enormously tall angels behind you as you were ministering." They saw the angels clearly because they were huge and on the platform with me, but Jesus, who sat in the midst of the crowd, went unnoticed. I'm looking forward to the day when we will all see and recognize Him in our midst.

I believe angels are hovering over you now and they have a message for you this minute. The message is: "Be patient just a little while longer. It won't be long now. Be patient, beloved."

chapter 17

OUR GUARDIAN ANGELS

THE Bible doesn't use the term, "guardian angel," but we refer to our helping angels as "guardian angels." Perhaps this designation originated with the verse in Psalm 91:11: *"For He shall give His angels charge over thee, to keep thee in all thy ways..."* (KJV). They are our "keepers" and we are their "charges." Our angels are wonderful allies. Angels love us because they love God, and they understand our journey. They are assigned to us by God Himself. They are fully aware of the rocky roads we encounter, as well as the temptations and anguish of the soul that we must overcome. They watch as we plow along muddy roads. They are with us when we run up against roadblocks, and they are with us when we fall into life's murky pits, when we're wounded and hurt. *They bear us up in their hands.*

An historian of the ancient Christian church, Origen (A.D. 200), wrote, "All the faithful in Christ...are helped by an angel. We must say that every human soul is under the direction of an angel who is like a father."

We know there is but one Father and one Savior, Jesus. Angels do not take the place of the Holy Spirit, nor of the Lord Jesus or our heavenly Father. They are helpers, ministers, divine messengers. Angels don't make a move without the Father's direction.

Our guardian angels remind us of the Holy One who pulls us out of the miry clay and sets our feet on dry ground, as it says in Psalm 40:2. They watch over us and reach out their long, protecting arms when we stumble and crash headlong on our faces. They hold us in their arms so we don't mess ourselves up beyond recognition. They then carefully help wipe us off and steer us back along the right direction. They show us how to follow God's will, not theirs and not our own.

And they never give up on us. Never. Once an angel is assigned to us, he's ours forever.

BILL'S STORY

The Bible tells us to be spiritually aware, for we may be entertaining angels unaware, without knowing it. (See Hebrews 13:2.) There are many stories of angels who have a big impact on the lives of men and women without the people being aware of it.

Here's a story I like about a very successful businessman and one of the richest men in his city. I'll call him Bill. Bill was also a Christian and well-known for his good deeds. One day a well-dressed, elegant-looking man he didn't recognize showed up at his office. Bill asked who the man might be. The stranger replied, "You may not remember me, but on a cold January night, when you were a young man, poor and unemployed, I was the homeless man you gave a twenty-dollar bill to. Not only that, you gave me your only pair of gloves."

The millionaire scratched his head. "I'm sorry, sir, I don't seem to remember you."

The stranger went on, "God gave that act of kindness to you as a gift, and you received it gladly. For that you are honored in Heaven."

Bill's mouth dropped open. Honored in heaven?

The stranger continued, "I am your angel," he said. "I have been with you all your life, and God sent me here today to bring you a message." With that, the angel gave the man news of a business opportunity that was about to be offered to him, an opportunity that would help many people. He followed this by warning Bill of another business deal he should reject.

Imagine Bill's reaction. Imagine his life from that moment on. Imagine the people who were touched by his simple act of kindness to an angel "unawares." The ripple effect is endless.

Bill's story demonstrates to me some important revelations about the heart of God and His divine and perfect destiny for each of us. Bill was a man who was dedicated to the Lord. He lived a life that was surrendered to God. He often said his business was not his own, but it was a tool for use in building the Kingdom of God. Bill helped younger men and women get started in businesses by showing them how to use the godly principles he had learned. He also tithed much of his income, but most of all, He lived to know the heart of Jesus.

Because of Bill's complete acceptance and openness to God and His Holy Spirit (*"you are in the world but not of the world"*), God could speak to Bill and he could hear Him. God could send angels to test him, and Bill would respond with love and kindness. God could send angels to guide him, and Bill would surely follow their guidance because he was in *tune with the spirit realm* through Jesus Christ, the King of the universe.

An act of kindness to an angel unawares almost thirty years earlier had served to shape his and countless others' destinies.

God is perfect and lovely and true and good. The Bible says, *"At the name of Jesus every knee shall bow and every tongue confess that Jesus Christ is Lord"* (Phil. 2:10-11), and we'll all bow in the sheer glory of His majesty, in the sheer wonder of the King of kings. Some will bow in shame, having rejected Him, but they will see Him and they will bow. It's a given.

HEARING YOUR ANGEL SPEAK

This happened recently. A missionary woman was asleep in her house in the bush country of Africa when her angel woke her and told her some men from another village were coming to kill her. The woman jumped out of bed and fled out the window. She escaped to a church elder's house, and the next morning they found her house burned to the ground and all her possessions destroyed. But because the woman *heard* the voice of her angel, she was able to escape unharmed.

ANGELS IN OUR LIVES

This wasn't the first time this missionary woman had received personal, direct instruction from the Lord through her angel. She was *accustomed* to communicating in the heavenly realm. She knew the voice of the Lord. She is an example of the words we find in Hebrews 5:14: *"... those who by reason of use have their senses exercised to discern both good and evil."* When He spoke, she jumped. This time, and in other times to come, her obedience would save her life as well as the lives of others.

I believe now is the time to be joining with our angels and going forth as partners in this life to bring the Kingdom of God to earth and bring God glory.

Can We Hinder the Work of Angels?

Can we stop or negate angelic guidance in our lives? Frightening as the possibility is, if you answered yes, you're right. The answer is yes; it is possible to miss out.

There are those people who reject the reality of a spiritual realm, and it's difficult for them to recognize or accept God's angelic intervention. Their spirits are dead to the moving of God's Presence and supernatural power in their lives. Then there are those who listen and follow the *wrong* spirits, those who invalidate Jesus Christ as Messiah and open themselves up to demonic forces. These demonic forces masquerade as good spirits, and even show up as angels of light. Their only goal, however, is to lie, destroy, and kill.

I would like to address your spirit again now. Turn your mind to the Person of Jesus. It is through Him that we gain access to the vast heart of God. God created angels and humans alike to fulfill His divine master plan through Jesus Christ. We, like angels, must want what God wants. We must passionately want His will and live solely to fulfill that will. What freedom there is in this discovery. What freedom there is in uniting our human spirit with His Holy Spirit and becoming wholly His.

Sadly, there are some Christians with undeveloped spirits. But here's the good news. An impoverished spiritual state can be remedied. *"He who has ears to hear, let him hear!"* (Matt. 11:15). If you're one of those Christians who has never seen or felt the presence of your personal angel, simply ask the Lord to open the eyes of your spirit. Intimacy with the King of the universe will reveal to you more of His kingdom, more of His wisdom, more of His will.

To Know the Lord

It's the Lord Jesus, not heavenly manifestations, that we want to know more intimately.

We recognize the divine order God has set in place. The first commandment is to love the Lord our God with all our heart, soul, and strength (see Deut. 6:5). We are to love Him with all our energy. Everything spiritual in our lives flows from that place of love, including revelation, wisdom, understanding, and anointing. The nine fruits of the Spirit—love, joy, peace, patience, kindness, gentleness, humility, and self-control—all flow from that place of love.

The nine gifts of the Spirit, the gift of prophesy, the gift of wisdom, knowledge, miracles, healings, tongues, interpretation of tongues, miracles, and discernment of spirits, each flow from that place of love, as well.

In fact everything good in our lives flows from that place of love.

When Do You *Not* Hear From Angels?

Not hear from angels? What do I mean, *not* hear from angels? You may know the Word and be able to quote Scripture from now until forever, but unless you are intimate with the Author, you're way out of line. You're nowhere near His heart. You have a small spirit. There are times when we yammer at the Lord all day but it's just that, yammering. As much as He loves our conversation, there are certain times when our prayers just don't seem to reach God's heart. Have you had that experience? I have. I pray and I wait, I pray some more, and I feel I'm completely alone, as though God isn't anywhere around. How can I hear from angels if I can't hear from God? How am I supposed to get through to heaven if I can't get through to God?

Pause here a minute. If I'm upset about something; let's say some-one has hurt my feelings (real rare, right?), I go to the Lord with the problem. I'll start out by whimpering away, telling Him I don't know how to handle the situation, and it's not my fault, and how so-and-so did such-and-such and won't He please help me, because after all, I try to be a good person and I didn't deserve to be treated so badly, and on and on. I remind Him I'm His humble servant and I live only for Him and then I remind Him of the hurts I've suffered in my life and woe is me, blah, blah, blah, and guess what? *I'm talking to myself!* If I checked the temperature where I was standing it would be mighty chilly.

Awhile back, I got upset over a problem that came jetting at me out of the blue. I muttered my prayers of woe to no response—and then I got smart. I took myself out into the woods and praised the Lord. It was cold and windy and I praised Him in the cold and the wind. The sky was like dark steel, and I praised Him in the dark steeliness of sky. I adored Him. I got down on my face in the dirt. I was thankful! I entered His gates with thanksgiving in my heart. True thanksgiving filled my heart. The more I thanked Him, the more thankful I became. I wasn't thankful for anything particular in this world, I was just thankful for Him! I thanked Him as I looked up at the steely sky and I could see His glory. I saw my own puny, little world in the light of His glory.

And then I entered His courts with praise. I praised Him with all of my heart. I praised Him for Himself, for the honor of knowing Him, for the honor of praising Him. Oh, it was wonderful. I pulled up my collar in the wind and felt myself being ushered into His courts of praise. Inside His courts in His glorious presence, I suddenly heard His voice. My self-pitying muck no longer clogged the air between us. My ears were cold, but no human static drowned out His voice.

Loudly and clearly He said to me, *"Marie, the problem you're con-cerned about is a gift from me. It comes to you directly from my hand. It is for your good."*

What? Excuse me? For my *good?* What a relief! I was back at square one. Lessons I thought I had learned had returned for review.

The entrance of Your words gives light; It gives understanding to the simple (Ps. 119:130).

I hopped homeward, feeling as warm as summer. I was so happy to learn this lesson again. God gave me a problem, which meant He must have trusted me enough to give me the problem, which meant I could act now on my love for Him, which meant I could show Him I was grateful for *all* His gifts, even the ones I didn't ask for, which meant I would no longer be upset, which meant my ears were open to hear from Him, and I was free from myself, my own selfish feelings. What could be better?

I'm not saying I tripped out in a cozy state of denial. No, not at all. What I did was, I returned to the problem with new resolve and within a matter of days it was taken care of.

THE WORD OF GOD

In order to enter the supernatural realm of God I must speak His language, and I learn His language by knowing Him through His Word. *"How sweet are Your words to my taste, sweeter than honey to my mouth!"* the Psalmist writes in Psalm 119:103. And how can I hear His words without ears to hear His words? Matthew 11:15 says, *"He who has ears to hear, let him hear…"*.

When I soak in the Presence of God, asking for nothing, seeking nothing, simply resting, He fills me with such an overwhelming sense of peace and tranquility that I feel myself transported into a heavenly ecstasy that transcends all human knowledge and desire. In this place I ask for nothing; in fact, I don't even speak. I'm in a state of adoration and perfect love. My spirit is united with His and I'm completely content. There is nothing I want, nothing I need. I am complete, and I can decree Colossians 2:10 out loud: *"I am complete in Christ who is the head of all principality and power."*

This high and holy place of divine union with God is the only place where I am not seeking, begging, pleading, imprecating, or interceding. In this place I am overcome with the majesty of His Presence and every breath becomes His breath. It is well with my soul. I am my complete self. I am completely alive.

This experience may last minutes, hours, or days. From this place of worship and adoration I can now face the world. It is from *this* place that I can live out my days in victory and beauty. The years the canker-worm has eaten are past.

THE GOAL OF ANGELS

The supreme goal of angels is to share with us the same profuse flood of love and joy that they enjoy. They are the agents who lead us into intimacy with God. God uses angels to influence us by touching our consciences with certain images, inclinations, aspirations, and desires that direct us to Him. Angels never give up as they gently prod us forward on the good and beautiful path God sets before us. *"This is the way, walk ye in it"* is their silent whisper to our spirits. They have perfect patience and move in our lives with the tender loving-kindness of the Lord Himself.

St. John of the Cross said that angels not only carry our prayers to God, but they also bring God's messages to our souls, feeding them as good fathers with delightful inspirations and communications from God.

When God's people are spiritually mature and full of humility and wisdom, the work of the holy angels can be profound in the world through our lives. As partners with the angels, we herald in the incredible Presence of the One who is the Head of all principality and power.

OUR GUARDIAN ANGELS AS INVISIBLE GUIDES

Listen to what God tells the Israelites in Exodus 23:20-21:

Behold, I am going to send an angel before you to guard you on the way and to bring you to the place which I have prepared. Give heed to him, and listen to his voice, do not rebel against him, for he will not pardon your transgression, for my name is in him (NAS and AMP).

In this historic event, God sends His angel to guard and guide an entire nation of people. He tells them in verse 23 that His angel will go before them and bring them into many enemies' territories, but they aren't to worry because He will utterly annihilate their enemies. God also sends angels to guard and guide us individually. Your angel knows the tough road you have traveled. Your angel is well aware of the pain and suffering you've experienced in your life. He has been there with you, guiding and guarding and watching, for his one goal is to bring your human spirit into oneness and alignment with God's Holy Spirit. Your angel knows that true victory comes through intimacy with the Lord and nothing else. Your angel knows that nothing can separate you from the love of Christ. (See Romans 8:38-39.)

Angels in Israel appeared as divine assistants, identified as "sons of God" and "morning stars." (See Job 1:6; 38:7.) They were called "the host of heaven." (See Nehemiah 9:6; 1 Kings 22:19.) They appeared in human form in Genesis 18:2, Joshua 5:13, and Ezekiel 9:2. They were envoys of God's messages to His people. It was an angel who gave Abraham the promise that he would one day father a nation. (See Genesis 22:15-18.)

The Bible is filled with accounts of angels making personal appearances to guard and guide individuals. When the slave girl Hagar was driven from Abraham's camp and dying of starvation and thirst in the desert with her son, Ishmael, it was an angel who appeared to her and produced a spring of water to drink. (See Genesis 21:17-19.)

It was an angel who appeared to Cornelius, the Roman officer, in the Book of Acts: *"Behold, a man stood before me in bright clothing"* (Acts 10), he explained, and this angel told him to summon Peter who was staying in the house of Simon, a tanner, by the seaside some miles away. The Holy Spirit spoke to Peter at the same time, so he traveled willingly with the Roman soldiers to the house of the Gentile Roman officer where he preached his famous sermon on God showing no partiality between peoples. Peter preached that God loved Jews and Gentiles alike. And, *"The Holy Spirit fell upon all those who heard the word. And those of the circumcision who believed were astonished,...because the gift of the Holy Spirit had been poured out on the Gentiles also"* (Acts 10:44-45). Read Chapter 10 of Acts in its entirety for the full story. It's thrilling.

Jews were the first ones God saw fit to acquaint with the work and presence of angels. As Christianity was preceded by Judaism, not only was the Lord Jesus a Jew, but every one of the authors of our Christian Bible were Jews. Aren't you glad God called the Gentiles, too? Aren't you glad God doesn't discriminate? Aren't you glad for the words, *"For God so loved the **world**..."*? (See John 3:16.)

ANGELS ALONGSIDE US

Angels are our spiritual helpers. They work alongside us to raise our level of spiritual awareness throughout our entire lives. They do not reside *within* us, taking the place of or moving in with the Holy Spirit; no, they travel *alongside* us. To paraphrase one writer, "Angels speak to our hearts constantly as one means by which God leads and helps us, and they continually whisper to us of love and peace and wholeness and how to fulfill our destiny as God's chosen."[1]

You carry the supernatural with you at all times. No matter where you are, you carry the Lord's Presence with you. This means you have signs, wonders, and miracles within you. You walk with the gifts of the Holy Spirit within you. You walk with God Himself in your spirit. You're a walking wonder!

If you and I are not living daily in the supernatural, with signs and wonders inside us, the world will look for the supernatural in other places. They'll go to the occult; they'll go to astrology, necromancers, witches, mediums, psychics, and other realms of the occult. People want to see evidence of God in the world. We're hungry for miracles! We're desperate for miracles. You and I are called to be miracle workers.

I like the following story about Padre Pio, the sainted Catholic Capuchin priest (1887-1968). He apparently held a strong belief in the presence of guardian angels. The account goes that Padre Pio believed that one could send their personal angels to intercede in prayer on someone's behalf, or to help or bring a message to them. It was reported he often sent his angel out when somebody needed help.

If a person wanted Padre Pio to pray for them, but they couldn't come to him personally, Padre Pio told them to send their angels in their place. "Your angel can take your message from you to me and I will help as much as I can," he would say.

One day a small child was worried about a sick uncle who could not come to Padre Pio's for prayer. She decided to send her guardian angel to tell Padre Pio to pray for him. Some time later, the story goes, she met Padre Pio in person and immediately when he saw her, he exclaimed, "Your angel kept me up all night—asking for a cure for your Uncle Fred!"

Granted, the story is fraught with doctrinal glitches, but I share it with you because of the sense of intimacy with the angelic realm it reflects. We need to get a picture in our heads of the divinely appointed partnership we have with God's angels.

YOU'RE A LIVING EPISTLE

You carry within you the activity of Heaven. You are a living epistle, a prophetic message, a manifestation of the supernatural realm breaking into the natural wherever you are. You carry the reality of the supernatural. Though you're on the earth, you operate in the spirit of heaven.

Many ministries today are moving in signs and wonders with angels coming on the scene and bringing powerful anointings that most of us have never thought possible. The Lord is sending angels to help ministries and individuals according to their faith. God's prophets, seers, teachers, evangelists, and pastors who are crying out for supernatural signs and wonders are receiving anointings that the world has perhaps never seen. God's anointed servants are doing the works that Jesus did, living as He lived, and loving as He loved.

The Word of God says signs and wonders will accompany His Word. When we read the Book of Acts we get a good picture of this historical truth. The early church was founded on the Word and the miraculous. We must be very sure we don't accept less than what God has for us in this hour. Read and absorb these verses: 2 Corinthians 12:12;

Romans 15:19; Acts 2:22; 14:3, and Joel 3:28-29. Perhaps instead of being leery of miracles we should be leery when we don't see miracles.

For the Lord God is a sun and shield; the LORD will give grace and glory; no good thing will He withhold from those who walk uprightly (Psalm 84:11).

ENDNOTE

1. Eileen Elias Freeman, *Touched by Angels.* (New York: Warner, 1993).

chapter 18

LEARNING TO THINK
IN THE SUPERNATURAL

PEOPLE always like a little formula to follow. For instance, we fast for a certain number of days a year in order to receive a level of holiness that will touch the heart of God, resulting in earning His and the world's favor. But fasting is not a formula for success. *It's an act of worship.* We fast as an act of worship unto God because we want to break down strongholds; we want to live out Isaiah 58:6-9 to loose the bonds of wickedness, undo the heavy burdens, let the oppressed go free, and break every yoke.

By fasting and intense prayer we receive answers and we find ourselves of greater use in the Kingdom of God. The reality is that fasting breaks us. That's how God can perform the miraculous within us and through us.

IS THERE A FORMULA FOR TALKING WITH ANGELS?

People will sometimes ask me for a formula on how to talk with angels. The other day I was in a meeting with a pastor; we were in his office, and I looked up and who did I see, but an angel standing in the doorway. The angel just stood there watching us. I became completely flustered. I couldn't hear a word the pastor was saying to me. I just kept watching that angel. He was so beautiful, all shining and full of light. The pastor was talking to me about holding some meetings in his church and there I was, dazed in the spirit, completely unable to concentrate. I began speaking in tongues and praising the Lord, and finally I blurted out to the pastor that there was an angel in the doorway, and that I thought the angel wanted to tell him something.

The pastor couldn't see the angel. He expected me to deliver the message the angel had for him prophetically, but I said no. The angel would speak to him directly, if he would listen.

When I left the church that afternoon, my knees were weak. I walked a little crooked. I felt that my voice was somewhere up in my forehead. All I wanted to do was worship and praise the Lord. The presence of that gorgeous angel simply knocked me out! I was confident that the pastor would hear the message the angel had for him regardless of whether or not he could see him at the same moment I did. Just because I saw the angel in the doorway and the pastor didn't, was not an indication that either one of us was in a better or higher spiritual place. Those who have concourse with angels are no more precious or important to God than a pastor who is stuck in tradition, or even a new convert who barely knows that God is a Trinity.

The Lord speaks to us constantly and in hundreds of ways: He speaks to us audibly, through angels, a sermon, a Bible study, our dreams, visions, and spiritual nudges and leadings. He'll speak to us through a word spoken by a stranger or through a child, a word of prophecy, a word of knowledge, a word of wisdom, through His written Word, through music, pain and suffering, and even through silence. The angels don't limit God. God doesn't limit Himself. I never want to limit God.

THE MOUNT OF TRANSFIGURATION

Peter, on the Mount of Transfiguration, in Matthew 17:1-8, was invited up to the mountain by Jesus for a divine appointment. Peter, James, and John were the only ones Jesus invited to see the miraculous event that took place on that day. There, on that mountain, without the crowds or the other disciples around, the three men were witnesses of something shocking, the likes of which have never occurred in all human history. Jesus was transfigured from His earthly self to His divine self, glowing like a torch in glory: "*His face shone like the sun, and His clothes became as white as the light*" (Matt. 17:2), and with Him in a blaze of light, holding conversation with him, up from the dead, were

Moses and *Elijah*. Think about it. Jesus, Moses, and Elijah! The three of them were bathed in blazing light!

A Soulish Reaction to a Miracle

The miraculous appearance of Moses and Elijah proved that the Scriptures looking forward to the Messiah and His Kingdom were fulfilled in Christ. Here, in this moment together, the Bible tells us that they discussed Christ's death (see Luke 9:31), and in such glory Peter became undone, utterly undone. His first response was a passionate, soulish, non-spiritual response. He burst forth with a plan to build three monuments to the miracle on the spot.

A rendezvous with the glory of God will transport us from a soulish Christian life to a bracing new life in the power of the Holy Spirit. God, the Father, interrupted Peter with an audible voice, with the same words He spoke at the Lord's baptism, *"This is My beloved Son, in whom I am well pleased. Hear Him!"* (Matt. 17:5).

The disciples fell on their faces, terrified. That's what we do when the glory of God overtakes us. We fall on our faces. We feel reduced to ash. We can't stand up. Our knees go to putty. Our mouths become full of sand. We see Him in His majesty and we see ourselves for what we are. We become like Isaiah, who in the Presence of God and the presence of the seraphim, cried out in agony, *"Woe is me, for I am undone! I am a man of unclean lips"* (Isa. 6:5). And when the glory of God appeared before Ezekiel, the prophet fell flat on his face in a state of severe shock until God told him to get up. (See Ezekiel 2:1-2.) John, when confronted with the glory of God, fell at His feet as dead. (See Revelation 1:17.) Yes, that's what happens. And somehow we manage to get up.

What Peter had done soulishly that day on the mountain was to place Moses and Elijah on the same level as Christ. God then increased His glory so that Peter could see only the majesty of Jesus, the King of the universe. *"Jesus came to them and touched them and said, 'Arise, and do not be afraid.' When they had lifted up their eyes, they saw no one but Jesus only"* (Matt. 17:7-8).

THE PLACE OF SURRENDER

I need to be in that place of worship and surrender where I see only Jesus and His glory. When I come face-to-face with the glory of God, I lose my worldly, selfish, soulish self. The scales of worldly concerns and bother fall off me like old woollies.

It was in the midst of the Lord's glory that Peter heard the voice of God.

It was in the midst of glory that Moses heard the voice of God.

Moses was so accustomed to being in the Presence of God that every time he went into the Tabernacle to meet with the Lord, a pillar of cloud descended and stood at the door of the Tabernacle and the Lord talked with Moses face-to-face. (See Exodus.33:11.) God spoke to Moses like a friend! Face-to-face!

In the midst of God's glory there is but one visage to behold, the King of Glory Himself. Here is where we hear His voice. Here is where we are taken into His Presence and where we can become not only His servant but His friend.

BREAKING...

Children have a natural instinct to love and praise the Lord. Children will praise the Lord when no one else will. Jesus has a special relationship with children. He is crazy about children, and He loves them passionately. You harm a child, and you are not only in danger of losing your life, you lose your eternity with God.

Children are not theologians; they don't wrestle with church doctrines or denominational conundrums. They have no problem accepting miracles, signs, and wonders as being quite natural occurrences. It's we adults, not children, who get things confused in God's Kingdom. When we break before the Lord, we can begin to become like children.

I write books for children. I write books for children about angels. Children, just like us, make great partners for angels. My book, *Harold and I, an Incredible Journey of Supernatural Events* (Destiny Image), is about a girl of 11 and her angel friend whom she calls Harold. (She thinks all angels are called Harold because of the carol, "Hark! The Herald Angels Sing.")

Angels will talk with and can be seen by children because children have no barriers to separate them from the heavenly realm. At a prayer meeting in her house, my friend's 8-year-old son, who had never sat through an entire prayer meeting without crayons and paper or something to do, sat quietly and peacefully throughout the entire evening. He held no book or art project in his lap and seemed thoroughly engaged in what was going on. My friend was surprised at his interest because it was quite unlike him to sit still for so long with nothing to occupy him.

"Mom, I sure liked the angel," he told her after the meeting.

"What are you talking about?" she said.

"You know. The angel who sat in the middle of the room. I like him. He's really nice."

"You saw *an angel* in the middle of the room?"

"Sure," said the boy. "You know, the one who was helping everyone."

My friend questioned him some more, asking him what the angel was wearing and what color hair he had, those kinds of things. Her son merely shrugged at her silly questions. Didn't she know these things? After all, she was right there the whole time!

It was a revelation and a breaking point for my friend.

GOD'S AUDIBLE VOICE

Sometimes you'll hear God's voice audibly, though this experience is not as frequent because you don't have to be in the spirit to hear an audible voice. Anyone can hear an audible voice. You could be drinking beer in the tavern with bawdy music, whooping it up in your worldly old soul-self and not giving the least thought to God. Then He calls your name. I think you'd hear Him. I think you'd whirl around and gasp, "Who was that?"

But when God speaks to your *spirit*, through *His Spirit*, that's another thing. God wants to connect His Spirit with yours. He wants to call you, and you whirl around, *"Who was that? Lord? Speak, Lord, your servant is listening."*

DEAF MIRACLE

I was holding meetings in Canada, and in one particular town there was a large group of deaf people from different towns and cities who came every night to the meetings. We were experiencing miracles left and right, and the Lord was moving in a very dramatic way in our midst, so I met with the group of deaf people, and I asked how I should pray for them. What was it they were seeking from God? I felt very drawn to this group and loved them on sight. I just loved them! God moved among them and filled each of them with His Spirit in a torrent of glory. I never saw such expressions of ecstasy as what I saw as they worshiped Him. (And they couldn't hear the music!) I assumed they wanted to receive their hearing, so I expected God to work His miracles and restore hearing in the services.

Here is the surprising thing: out of a group of maybe 25 or more deaf people, they hesitated when I asked who wanted to be healed and receive their hearing. Nobody raised their hand. One woman told me, "We see nothing about hearing people that we want." She told me that, as deaf persons, they felt that people with the ability to hear were no more blessed than they were, and in fact, perhaps hearing people were even a bit *less* blessed than the hearing impaired or the deaf. What was there to want that we had?

The miracles they were interested in were miracles of the healed *soul*.

chapter 19

OUR SOUL AND HIS DIVINE NATURE

W E were born to be partakers of God's divine nature. That sounds almost unbelievable, doesn't it? We can be partakers of His divine nature? Really? Would you say your life oozes with the divine nature of Christ? It's an amazing theorem, but it's real and it's in the Bible:

Grace and peace be multiplied to you in the knowledge of God and of Jesus our Lord, as His divine power has given to us all things that pertain to life and godliness, through the knowledge of Him who called us by glory and virtue, by which have been given to us exceedingly great and precious promises, that through these you may be **partakers of the divine nature**, *having escaped the corruption that is in the world through lust"* (2 Peter 1:2-4).

The Greek word used for "partaker" here is *koinonos*, and it means a *partner*. It's what I've been talking about in this book—becoming one with. When our lives are so steeped in Him, so drenched in Him and His love, His Spirit, His life, we begin to resemble Him! The Bible tells us in Ephesians 5:1-2 that we are to be imitators of God and to walk in love as Christ has loved us and has given Himself for us. When we, spirit, soul, and body, are in that place, we are in a place where God can act in powerful ways on our behalf. When we live out the words of Acts 17:28, *"In Him we live and move and have our being,"* we draw Heaven to us, and the angelic host become partners with us. As we live in the full reality of our life in Christ, knowing the power of His resurrection (see Phil. 3:10), we draw closer to the mind of Heaven.

You and God's angels share much more than you realize. The very nature of God surrounds you. You are a citizen of the Kingdom of God, and you possess divine favor. When Joshua was visited by the Angel of the Lord, He introduced Himself as the Commander of the army of the Lord. (That's who Jesus is; He is the Commander of a great, undefeatable army, and this army is on *your* side.) The Angel gave Joshua directions for bringing down the walls of Jericho by having his army circle the city for seven days, and on the seventh day circling seven times. Then the priests were to blow trumpets of rams' horns and everybody was to shout, and the walls would come down.

I ask you. Is that any way to win a war? Does that sound reasonable? Read the full account in Joshua 6. This is a great illustration for generation upon generation to catch on to the fact that God's power and might are beyond all human reason and acumen. We've heard this story since our Sunday school days, we've sung songs about Jericho's walls tumbling down, preached sermons on it, and written books about it. It's time to realize that walls of spiritual strongholds are tumbling down now all over the world as God's people are praying down the miracles and partnering with the angelic host. This we do as we partner with the angels and take our Kingdom authority. This we do as partakers of His divine nature. Is this you?

Your Angels and Your Kingdom Authority

Do you *really* understand your authority and how the angels work with you in the Kingdom of God? Psalm 91:13 states that without reservation you and I will tread upon the lion and adder, *"...the young lion and the serpent you shall trample underfoot."* How does this work? Our angels are with us to help us in every situation, even when we face the wild beasts of life. These invisible beasts chew and gnash at us not only by their bite, but by their roar and their breath.

The lion roars and what happens? How do you meet the terrible roar of the lion who is seeking to devour everything in its way? Perfect love casts out fear, but how do you employ perfect love when you're scared out of your wits? How does perfect love work when you are terrified? The lion is roaring in your face and you don't know which way to turn. You want to run, but you can't. You want to yell for help, but you don't know how. You can't hear anything but the dreaded roar of the beast.

What does this roar sound like? Let's identify this sound because it has many reverberations. Its main attribute is that it is *always* threatening. The roar is meant to tempt you to worry, fret, doubt, shrink back, lose heart, ache, make yourself sick, wonder, go numb in the head, and in general, live in a state of paralyzing fear.

However, if you finally realize it's only a roar, you can take action. Roars can't hurt you, they only startle you. Aha! You see the light. When you see the light, you can turn and face the sound of the roar, pull yourself up, and rebuke the awful noise. You stand up and take your authority. You pray, "In the name of Jesus, I will fear no evil, for the Lord God is with me. Yea though I walk through the valley of the shadow of death and I hear the horrible roar of this temptation, I will fear no evil, for the Lord God Almighty is with me. Greater is He who is in me than he who is in the world!"

The devil is then silenced. He cannot continue to roar when he is confronted with the Word of God. So what happens next? There you are, sailing on in victory when suddenly you come upon another trial, another temptation. A dragon lurks in the grass just waiting for you to trip on him. You naively kick it in the head and it turns its ugly face to you and it *breathes* on you.

Ugh! You're covered in the fiery breath of a foul, stinking, lying dragon.

What is this nasty breath? It's lust. Lust for the things of the world. You're suddenly more concerned with the world around you than with the power and Presence of the living God in your life. Pew! What a stink. You're choking in the putrid odor of self-centeredness. You're trying to figure out your life *without* the power of the Holy Spirit. You're attracted to the things of the world! You're thinking in terms of success, money, possessions, and climbing the social ladder. You're caught in a relationship you have no business being involved with. You're caught in an occult lie that promises false peace and happiness. You don't even realize what has taken you captive.

You're listening to the wrong spirits. You can't hear the voices of the angels and you can't hear God Almighty.

But hang on. Second Peter 2:9 says, *"The LORD knows how to deliver the godly out of temptations."* Throughout Scripture, the Lord sends angels to help His children get back on the right path as he did with Jacob (Hosea 12:4); Balaam (Num. 22:22-25); Elijah (1 Kings 19:5); David (1 Chron. 21:12); and others.

Isaiah 63:9 says, *"In all their affliction He was afflicted, and the Angel of His Presence saved them; in His love and in His pity He redeemed them; and He bore them and carried them all the days of old."*

REPENTANCE AS A WAY OF LIFE

A Spirit-filled Christian minister who is guilty of adultery prays to the Lord to send the angelic realm to come and help in his church services. Now, how can the Lord answer such a request? If He answered him it would be as if He were condoning the man's sin. I think that's what's wrong with a lot of ministries today. They operate in the natural soul realm, doing good works, and some are even Spirit-filled, but without the *power* of the Holy Spirit, because there's a blob of sin at work somewhere. Their sins might not be as flagrant as adultery, but maybe there's envy, strife, anger, fear, greed, dishonesty, you name it. All of these are "little foxes" that are destroying the vine, and God cannot condone them.

What spirit are we operating in if we're not operating in God's Holy Spirit? There's God's Holy Spirit, our human spirit, and the spirit of the devil.

Here's where the beauty of repentance comes in. How I love the gift of repentance! How grateful you and I should be to be able to recognize the sins "that so easily beset us" and then nab those sins by the throat and hand them over to God in deep-felt repentance. "Forgive me, Lord; forgive me, Lord." Oh, blessed release and freedom. Blessed forgiveness!

Let me repeat what I talked about in Chapter 10. Rebuke, repent, and renounce, I say. Say it out loud: "I rebuke the choice of the sin, I repent of giving in to the sin, and I renounce and turn from it in the name of Jesus."

Repentance, like love, takes choice and discipline. I discipline myself to keep a short account with God so that I can have open access to His throne room and His Presence.

Don't laugh, but one day I decided to make a prayer chapel by covering a room in my house with white sheets. I wanted a place to go where I could meet with God each day, a place where I would feel completely set apart. I hung a small wooden cross on the wall and covered everything else in the room with white sheets, including the window, paintings on the wall, bookshelves, the desk, other furniture, lamps, everything, all were carefully shrouded in white sheets. You probably think I was a bit touched in the head, but I wanted nothing to catch my eye, except the cross on the wall.

Well, I spent hour upon hour in that room alone with God with the white sheets hanging from the walls and covering everything. But here's the thing: it took me the longest time just to get into the room, because before I entered, I stood outside the closed door and prayed, "Search me, O Lord, and see if there be any unclean thing in me...." I'd take off my shoes and then pray, "I will enter His gates with thanksgiving in my heart; I will enter His courts with praise...." So then, after repenting and asking for forgiveness for any and all sins, which could take quite awhile, I had to thank Him, because I didn't want to enter His Presence without a thankful heart. And then I praised Him. So really, it could take all day just to get inside the white-covered room to pray!

My prayer chapel was like the inner sanctum of the Holy of Holies to me. It was here that the Lord began to take me up into His throne room. It was here that I learned about the courtrooms of God. It was here that I learned about the angelic realm and about supernatural journeys where I could travel to other places in the spirit and do as the Lord instructed me.

When my prayer chapel was needed for a bedroom again, I took my chapel outside to the woods, and that's where it has remained ever since. Being with the Lord is so exciting it's worth everything to make a place for Him, even if it means being like Susannah Wesley, the mother of John Wesley. She had ten children and she simply pulled her apron over her head when she wanted to be alone with God.

It begins with repentance. A recovered alcoholic told me, "I may not be as much fun as I once was, but I'm a whole lot smarter." I asked her to define what she meant by "as much fun" and she corrected herself. "I guess I mean crazy. I'm not crazy any more. I don't hurt myself and I don't hurt others like I used to." Anger, bitterness, and fear had held her captive, and they were the stimuli that fed her alcoholism. Free and forgiven, she stood on the foundation of a brand-new life. She experienced the power of God because she fell in love with the Presence of God in her life.

Let's look at the difference between the *Presence* of God and the *power* of God. We enter the *Presence* of God in our place of prayer. This is a place of glory and awe. His majesty encompasses the atmosphere. It's incredible. There's nothing like it on earth. In His *Presence* we draw on His *power* to minister, to overcome, to conquer; to prevail in this world. Do you see the distinction? We need His *Presence* to survive. We need His *power* to prevail. If we try operating in the power of God without the *Presence* of God in our lives, we open the door to deception.

We need His *power* to perform miracles, but first, and before all else, we need to live in and know His *Presence* in every breath.

chapter 20

COME BACK

TODAY the Lord took me up into the heavenlies, and He gave me a horse to ride. It was a purple horse. We rode to a field and we stopped to look at it. I gazed out and didn't quite know what it was.

He said, *"What do you see?"*

I said, "Wheat, I think? Fields of wheat."

The Lord said He often used wheat as an illustration, but I should look closer. My horse trotted closer to the rows of what I thought was wheat, but it wasn't wheat at all. What was in the field were miles and miles of rows and rows of *trophies*. Like fields of grain, they were trophies!

I was astonished. I remembered the Scripture verse that tells how the saints throw their trophies at His feet.

I saw the trophies grow and spring forth as human figures praising the Lord. I saw the human trophy figures multiply, and it was a great, unending harvest as far as the eye could see.

The Lord told me to look again, and I looked and saw layers of human forms stretched out on levels like stairs. I didn't know if these were the humble servants who had laid down their trophies. I wanted to cling to the Lord but I was on my own horse. I then saw the figures sprout forth like flowers. They created an immense bouquet and it was quite astounding. They actually *bloomed*.

The Lord began riding again and my horse followed His. We followed the Lord who was galloping on His white horse, as I rode on my purple horse. What I would have preferred would be to ride on His white horse with Him like I had been able to do the day before. He heard my thought and said, *"No, you must ride your own horse,"* and then He told me to look around. I looked and saw millions of other riders on horses riding along with us. *"...Surrounded by so great a cloud of witnesses,"* I thought, and began to enjoy riding on my purple horse and feeling the wind of heaven in my hair. (See Hebrews 12:1.)

Always, we are surrounded by angels. Whenever the Lord takes me up into the heavenlies, I see that we are always surrounded by His angels.

We rode very fast and came to a crystal-clear sea, which seemed to be without water, although we dove into it with our horses as though it were a regular sea. The dive was easy and smooth, and we flew and floated under the sea as though we were swimming. I saw millions of sea creatures shouting their praise to Jesus. The whales, the sharks, the fish, the shrimps, the mussels, every sea creature, even the grasses, the coral, all praising the Lord Jesus as we rode by. It never occurred to me that the little fishes, the shrimp, and the clams could praise the Lord. We rode for some time amid the praise and the hallelujahs of the sea creatures. I thought I even saw and heard the rocks cry out their praises to the Lord!

We came to a great bronze door. The Lord pulled up short in front of it, holding the reins of his horse back. (When His horse stopped, my horse stopped. Every move the Lord made on His horse, my horse followed exactly.)

The Lord told me to open the huge bronze door. I reached forward with my hand and gave the door a push. I was surprised that it opened so easily.

Ugh! What I saw inside was disgusting. It was all brown, murky, ugly, and smelly. The odor from the morass of brown goop everywhere was awful. I knew we weren't in heaven any more, but I was looking down into the earth realm. I saw people (souls) in the muddy stuff, and they were swimming around in confusion.

I said, holding my nose, "Who are these, Lord?"

He told me that they were backslidden Christians and Christians who were making bad choices and didn't ask for help or forgiveness. I felt sick as I looked into the mess and I told the Lord I would rather not look at it any longer. It stunk! Phew!

The Lord said with a very serious face, *"What will you tell these souls?"*

At those words, I immediately jumped off my horse and got down on my knees and shouted to the unhappy lot, "Children! Look up! Turn to God!" I was consumed with love for them.

Some of them looked up when they heard my voice. I saw their faces, so full of defeat. Some wore bitterness like tight-fitting coats. Disillusioned, depressed, looking for happiness in the mud. Such deception they lived under!

Seeing them in this state broke my heart. I called down to them again, "Just ask the Lord Jesus for forgiveness! Come back to the Lord Jesus while there is still time! He is so kind! So good! So forgiving!"

My words were simpler and more direct than the ones I might have used if I had prepared a sermon, but I kept calling down, pleading with them to turn to Jesus, whose loving-kindness was surely better than anything in life. I was crying. If only they knew how incredibly sweet and loving the Lord is. "Come, please! Take my hand! Let me help you! Let me help you!" To my surprise, they began turning around and reaching up for my hand. They began crawling out of the muck! Covered with doubt, fear, and the lies of the devil, they came out. My hand became *His* hand, and Jesus jumped off His horse and welcomed them, holding them, kissing them, frolicking with them, rocking them in His arms. He was so happy!

I broke into more tears as I saw the happiness of the Lord. As I stood there blubbering in awe, more and more souls kept coming up out of the filth and the Lord tenderly washed each one of them, held them, comforted them, frolicked, and even tickled them to make them smile.

And because the Lord was so happy, the angels were happy. They danced around joyfully as though this was a big party. I couldn't stop crying, I was so touched. All those people were saved by the power of the truth. Everyone was so happy. After a while, I saw something even more amazing. I saw the Lord hug His horse! He grabbed His horse around the neck and rolled around on the ground with him and gave his hoof a kiss the way one might kiss the foot of a baby when playing with him.

I was bowled over!

Then my purple horse started talking to me! He said, "I am your gift of provision." I hoped he didn't expect me to roll around on the ground with him or give his hoof a kiss, but by this time I could only stand and marvel.

The Lord laughed. (His laugh is ecstasy. All of heaven laughs when He laughs.) He took me back to the earth realm and set me in a grove of eucalyptus trees. He said, *"Look."* I looked and saw the eucalyptus trees praising and worshiping Him. Suddenly one of the trees spoke to me and said, "We have no voices yet. We can only praise God by what we *are*."

Then the tree said, "You, Marie, can praise Him with everything you have and can be. You are human. You are created in His image."

All of nature knows His splendor and His greatness. Yesterday or the day before, the Father showed me the galaxy of billions of planets.

He said, *"Do you see these?"*

"Yes, Lord."

"So, you see, when I told Abraham he would have children as many as the sand of the sea—that wasn't more than I could handle."

Our God has more planets, solar systems, heavenly bodies, and galaxies than there are sands in the sea.

This is who we are one with.

Father, in Jesus' name, lift up the heart
of the discouraged one right now.
Lift the tired soul, the one holding this book who hurts,

who is lonely and hungers for more of you;
who needs your beautiful kiss.
Pull that one out of the muck. Caress that one.
Love that one. Give them a tickle.
The Lord is speaking to you now and telling you that
He loves you and has called you from the foundation of the
world.
You are to rise up now.
Rise up and receive the good things that are yours
And receive your place in the Kingdom.

chapter 21

DREAMS, VISIONS, AND REVELATIONS

Ezekiel—"Strengthened by God"

EZEKIEL was 25 years of age when he was taken captive and carried into exile to Babylon. (Daniel was also carried into captivity at the time. He was about 15 years of age.) There, God chose to show Ezekiel through explicit, though complicated visions, details of the long-term future of the nation and the world. Ezekiel's name means, "strengthened by God," and he had the most vivid and clear visions of God ever seen by all the major prophets.

Ezekiel was 30 years old when he was called into ministry, the year he was installed as priest. He foresaw the last and greatest temple the Jews would one day build under Messiah's personal direction. God allowed Ezekiel, along with Daniel, the apostle John, and other anointed biblical writers, to look inside the invisible world into the heavenly places. Ezekiel was able to enter the throne room of God and see His plans unfold before his eyes. He saw the shining Presence of the glory of God, the Shekinah glory, the cloud, depart from the Temple in Jerusalem just before its destruction. Both Isaiah and Ezekiel describe the return of the glory to Israel with Messiah's triumphant return when the cloud, the Shekinah glory, will remain over the temple Mount in Jerusalem. (See Ezekiel 43:1-9.) After His resurrection, Jesus ascended from the Mount of Olives in Shekinah glory, and He will return in the same glorious cloud. The Book of the Revelation begins with Jesus returning in a blaze of Shekinah glory and *"...every eye will see him"* (Rev. 1:7).

And the glory of the LORD shall be revealed, and all flesh shall see it together, for the mouth of the LORD has spoken…. O Zion, you who bring good tidings; lift up your voice with strength. O Jerusalem, you who bring good tidings, lift up your voice with strength. Lift it up, be not afraid; say to the cities of Judah, 'Behold your God! Behold the Lord GOD shall come with a strong hand, and his arm shall rule for him; behold, his reward is with him, and his work before him. He will feed his flock like a shepherd, he will gather the lambs with his arm, and carry them in his bosom, and gently lead those that are with young' (Isaiah 40:1-11 NKJV).

In the Book of Ezekiel we see the Spirit of the Lord touch Ezekiel 18 times; he has 5 levitating experiences, and he sees the glory of the Lord 20 times. It is Ezekiel who sees the cherubim. (John on Patmos describes the seraphim.) Thirty times in the Book of Ezekiel, the Lord says, *"That they might know that I am the Lord."*

ZECHARIAH—"THE LORD REMEMBERS"

Zechariah was a priest like Ezekiel, and he ministered about 70 years after Ezekiel. His name means, "The Lord remembers." Zechariah lived during the time of another minor prophet, Haggai, and his calling was specific. The Lord commissioned Zechariah to stir up the people to rebuild the Temple in Jerusalem. Zechariah did as he was told and the Temple was built in four years. The wall was not completed until 75 years later.

What is so exciting about the ministry of Zechariah is that he functioned completely under the direction and instruction of angels and supernatural visions. Although he wasn't lifted up by his hair like Ezekiel had been, nor was he given riddles and dramas, he received eight night visions and spoke and responded entirely with the angel of the Lord and the Word of the Lord of hosts.

The book begins with Zechariah seeing *"…a man* [an angel] *riding on a red horse… among the myrtle trees"* (Zech. 1:8). The angel explains to him each of his subsequent visions, revealing the heart of God for the nation of Israel and the rebuilding of Jerusalem.

Because Zechariah obeyed every word He received from the Lord, he was used to start a revival, calling the people to repentance and reassuring them of their future blessings. He taught them they were building the Temple not just for themselves, but for the Messiah who would one day come to live in it, which would be fulfilled in the millennial kingdom of Messiah. (See Revelation 20.)

Zechariah 9:9 (NAS) is a prophecy fulfilled at Christ's triumphal entry in Matthew 21:1-5:

> *Rejoice greatly, O daughter of Zion!*
> *Shout, O daughter of Jerusalem!*
> *Behold, your King is coming to you;*
> *He is just and having salvation,*
> *lowly and riding on a donkey,*
> *a colt, the foal of a donkey.*

The Book of Zechariah is the most messianic, apocalyptic, and eschatological book in the Old Testament. It is chock-full of signs, angelic visitations, visions, prophecies, and the living voice of God. After Zechariah's death, prophecy would become for the most part silent until John the Baptist, more than 400 years later.

ANGELS IN OUR DREAMS

God will send angels to speak to you in your dreams. Expect the Lord to speak to you through dreams. Dreams are night visions. Numbers 12:6 says, *"If there is a prophet among you, I, the Lord, make Myself known to him in a vision; I speak to him in a dream."*

An angel came to Joseph, the husband of Mary, three times in his dreams to encourage and give instructions from the Lord: *"But after he had considered this, an angel of the Lord appeared to him **in a dream** and said, 'Joseph, son of David, do not be afraid to take Mary home as your wife,* *for that which has been is conceived in her is from the Holy Spirit'"* (Matt. 1:20 NAS).

When they had gone, an angel of the Lord appeared to Joseph in a dream. "Get up," he said. "Take the child and his mother and escape to Egypt. Stay there until I tell you, for Herod is going to search for the child to kill him" (Matt. 2:13, author's paraphrase).

After Herod died, an angel of the Lord appeared in a dream to Joseph in Egypt. (See Matthew 2:19.)

An angel of the Lord appeared to Jacob in a dream centuries earlier: *"The Angel of God spoke to me **in a dream, saying,** 'Jacob.' And I said, 'Here I am'"* (Gen. 31:11).

In the Old Testament we read that the following people were each touched by, led by, or spoken to by dreams: Abraham (Gen. 15:12-17), Jacob (Gen. 28:12-15), Daniel (Dan. 7); Abimelech (Gen. 20:3); Laban (Gen. 31:24); Pharaoh's butler and baker (Gen. 40:1-23); Pharaoh (Gen. 41); Nebuchadnezzar (Dan. 2:1-49); Solomon (1 Kings 3:5); and in the New Testament: Joseph and Herod (Matt. 2:22); Pilate's wife (Matt. 27:19).

Dreams and visions are often delivered by angels. Listen to your dreams. Expect visions.

And it shall come to pass afterward That I will pour out My Spirit on all flesh; Your sons and your daughters shall prophesy, Your old men shall dream dreams, Your young men shall see visions. And also on My menservants and on My maidservants I will pour out My Spirit in those Days (Joel 2:28-29).

chapter 22

ANGELS IN HISTORY

THIS is not the only period in church history in which angels have been well-known on earth. The early church father Eusebius wrote, "Fearing lest sinful mankind should be without...guidance, like herds of cattle, God gave them protectors and superintendents, the holy angels, in the form of captains and shepherds."

Jesus, of course, is our Shepherd, and He sends angels to help us along on our path. Jean Cardinal Danielou in *The Angels and Their Mission*, said, "Beyond a doubt every believer has an angel to guide him as a teacher and shepherd."

The traditional classical approach to the study of angels throughout church history, including Catholic or Orthodox history, is acceptance of the existence and activity of angels based on the joint authority of the Bible, tradition, and church doctrine. Catholic and Orthodox churches invoke angelic presences through prayer, liturgy, and icons, but the Protestant, evangelical approach is a belief in angels based on the Bible alone. There have been differing ideas and beliefs about the existence, mission, and function of angels. All nations and cultures have held some belief in angelic beings. Ancient Egyptians built elaborate tombs for their dead in order that angels would visit and accompany them into the next life. Islamic scholars hold that angels recorded the good and bad, even before the birth of Islam.

In the year A.D. 306 the emperor Constantine had a conversion experience when he claimed to have been visited by the archangel Michael. He said he saw a cross appear in the sky with the words, *Hoc signo vinces* (in this sign conquer) as he and his troops were crossing the Milvian Bridge in Rome. Constantine had a church erected in the archangel's honor south of the city of Constantinople. It's called the Michaelion.

Let's look at some experiences among the Catholic saints such as St. Antonius, a ninth- century hermit who had a vision of the archangel Michael. As a result of his vision, a Saracen attack was miraculously defeated. Monte Angelo Oratory in Castlellamare, Italy, was erected in Michael's honor.

We all know about Joan of Arc and the voices she heard, but what she marveled at most were her visions of angels. She was particularly overwhelmed at the glory and splendor of Michael. She claimed it was Michael who gave her the command to lead the soldiers into battle at Orleans. Many historians now believe Joan's visions were real and have come to recognize Joan's role as being pivotal in the development of Western civilization. Cardinal John Wright wrote, "Certainly, the most important of her voices was the Archangel's. Without his guidance, the future of Europe—and America—could not possibly have been the same."[1]

In the fourth century, St. Rule, custodian of the relics of St. Andrew the Apostle, was shown by an angel the exact route to travel to Scotland. St. Rule traveled to Scotland, following the angel's instructions, and stayed to evangelize the Scots and become their first bishop, thus bringing Christianity to Scotland.

Sister Faustina (1905-1938), a Polish nun who led a quiet, barely noticed life in her convent, kept a diary, and I'll quote from it for you:

"I saw my Guardian Angel who ordered me to follow him. In a moment I was in a misty place full of fire in which there was a great crowd of suffering souls. They were praying fervently, but to no avail…. I asked these souls what their greatest suffering was. They answered me in one voice that their greatest torment was longing for God."

Another time she wrote, "During adoration, I repeated the prayer, 'Holy God' several times and a vivid presence of God suddenly swept over me, and I was caught up in the spirit before the majesty of God. I saw how the Angels and the Saints of the Lord give glory to God. The glory of God is so great that I dare not try to describe it, because I would not be able to do so, and souls might think that what I have written is all there is. Saint Paul, I understand now why you did not want to describe heaven, but only said that eye has not seen, nor ear heard, nor has it entered into the heart of man what God has prepared for those who love him…. Now I have seen the way in which I adore God; oh how miserable it is! And what a tiny drop it is in comparison to that perfect heavenly glory."[2]

Sister Faustina gives the account that, as she was meditating on the rebellious sin of the angels who fell with satan and their immediate punishment, she asked Jesus why the angels had been punished as soon as they had sinned. She says she then heard a voice explaining that it was because of their profound knowledge of God. She was told that no person on earth, even though a great saint, has such knowledge of God as the knowledge of Him that an angel has.

Angels have always played a major role in human history, accompanying humans on our perilous journey through life with one purpose, and that purpose is and always will be to bring us closer to a knowledge of God.

Five thousand years ago, God spoke to Moses after he was presented with the Ten Commandments:

Behold, I am going to send an angel before you to guard you on the way and to bring you to the place which I have prepared. Give heed to him, and listen to his voice; do not rebel against him, for he will not pardon your transgression; for my name is in him (Exodus 23:20-21 NAS).

Ten thousand angels descended upon Mount Sinai accompanying the holy Presence of God when He gave Moses the Law. An earthquake shook the mountain. (See Deuteronomy 33:2.) John, in the Book of

Revelation, saw ten thousand times ten thousand angels ministering to the Lamb of God in the throne room of the universe. (See Revevlation 5:11.)

God uses angels to help to form the history of the world.

But it is most important for us to be able to identify whether or not the angelic activity we speak of and experience is from God Almighty. I repeat this point more than once in this book. Some angelic activity can very well be demonic, as history can prove. (The activities of the devil and his demons will intensify in the days to come, but the supernatural powers of God's holy angels are far greater.) The apostle Paul warned that satan can transform himself into an angel of light to deceive many people—this includes spiritual leaders. Paul writes, *"Therefore it is no great thing if his* [satan's] *ministers also transform themselves into ministers of righteousness, whose end will be according to their works"* (2 Cor.11:15). Satan can masquerade as an angel of light, disguised as a messenger of truth, and so can his demons. The terrifying end for these false teachers and false spirits is God's judgment.

Socrates often spoke of a demon who hung around him, directing and guiding him with instructions and admonitions. Plato taught that the higher kinds of demons were appointed as guardians to men. There are the dreamy fictions of the poets, the skeptic speculations of the philosophers, and the false teachings of the cults with their slipshod ideas and dramas of the supernatural.

God's angels always triumph over the work and purposes of satan and his demons. Daniel and John describe the glories of the angels. Listen to this description John gives us in Revelation 10:1-3:

I saw still another mighty angel coming down from heaven, clothed with a cloud. And a rainbow was on his head, his face was like the sun, and his feet like pillars of fire. He had a little book open in his hand. And he set his right foot on the sea and his left foot on the land, and cried with a loud voice, as when a lion roars. When he cried out, seven thunders uttered their voices.

And how about this description that Daniel gives us in Daniel 10:5-6:

I lifted my eyes and looked, and behold, a certain man clothed in linen, whose waist was girded with gold of Uphaz! His body was like beryl, his face like the appearance of lightning, his eyes like torches of fire, his arms and feet like burnished bronze in color, and the sound of his words like the voice of a multitude.

And this:

And he showed me a pure river of water of life, clear as crystal, proceeding from the throne of God and of the Lamb. In the middle of its street, and on either side of the river, was the tree of life, which bore twelve fruits, each tree yielding its fruit every month. The leaves of the tree were for the healing of the nations. And there shall be no more curse, but the throne of God and the Lamb shall be in it, and His servants shall serve Him. They shall see His face, and His name shall be on their foreheads. There shall be no night there: They need no lamp nor light of the sun, for the Lord God gives them light. And they shall reign forever and ever (Revelation 22:1-5).

HISTORICAL VIEWPOINTS

Let's take a brief look at some of the historical viewpoints and doctrines of angels. It may surprise you to discover that some of today's false interpretations of the angelic world were first presented 600 years ago. Let's start with Augustine (A.D. 354-A.D. 430).

Augustine. Influenced by the Neo-Platonists, he wrote that human beings are fascinated with demons and the demonic realm because both humans and demons are unhappy, whereas the holy angels, happy and immortal, are far above our common experience.[3] To Augustine the angelic realm was distant and unknowable.

Dionysius. The writings of Dionysius were granted virtual apostolic authority until the late Middle Ages. He was a Christian Neo-Platonist who was born in Syria and lived around A.D. 500. He wrote *The Celestial*

Hierarchy. He ranked principalities and powers higher than archangels, which defies Scripture, and he held that his scheme of nine triadic choirs of angels was a vehicle of salvation by which a person could be purified, illuminated, and perfected.[4] Dionysius was wrong.

The Reformation. The Reformers, while accepting the existence of angels on scriptural authority, focused primarily on their function as ministers of salvation.[5]

One of these reformers, John Calvin (1509-1564), emphasized that angels are merely God's helpers. His reserved attitude about the purpose of angels became the norm in evangelical Protestant theology for years to come. Many Puritans defaced the statues and friezes of angels that adorned churches and cathedrals, calling them false idols, which were both sinful and demonic.

The Age of Enlightenment. This era took place during the 17th and 18th centuries. The prevailing philosophies of this age discarded the spiritual doctrine of angels in favor of scientific reason. Descartes' famous dictum, "I think therefore I am," became the voice of the so-called rational thinker. Human reason was to replace God-consciousness. During this epoch, angels became nothing more than mythological.

John Locke (1632-1704). Like Descartes, Locke based his deductions not on the celestial hierarchy or transcendent essences found in the Bible, but on human consciousness.

Modernism. In a nutshell, instead of stating the truths that Scripture is infallible and Christ is infallible, and, therefore, Christ is God—modernism says that Scripture is only reliable as data or a historical record. According to modernism Christ's claims to divinity are not found in Scripture, and therefore most Scripture claims are incorrect.[6]

Post-Modernism. During the 20th century Karl Barth (1886-1968) and the post-modern movement emerged. Barth saw angels as essentially marginal figures who were nameless and faceless messengers of God. Regarding demons and satan, he abandoned biblical theology completely. He claimed that Christians need not wrestle with dark angels and principalities, because they were simply mere shadow existences.[7]

BE AWARE OF THE BIASES

So there you have a sampling of some of the historical biases, but this overview is by no means conclusive or comprehensive. Can you see where some misbeliefs have taken root? How about the class in world religions that you may have taken? Such a class may have taught you that the Bible is just an historical account, and its miracles are mere myths. Or you may have been exposed to a preacher or Bible study leader who didn't recognize the existence of satan or demons and taught that evil exists simply in shadow form. It may even be that the eldership in a church may have told you that your dreams and visions were not acceptable and that miracles, signs, and wonders ended with the Book of Acts. You may have heard a preacher teach that the gift of tongues is not for today. Maybe you've been influenced by the misguided teachings of the New Age. The fact is, many of us are surrounded by misunderstanding, doubt, and unbelief.

Here's what the Lord Jesus had to say when Peter doubted the miracle of walking on water, *"O you of little faith. Why did you doubt?"* (Matt. 14:31 NAS).

Those words must have hurt Peter worse than the lashing waves he experienced on that stormy night. How many miracles do we wipe off Heaven's slate by looking down in fear? We become like fish flopping on sand or frenzied insects in sudden light. What could be more pitiful?

Job was rebuked with these words: *"...do you limit wisdom to **yourself**?"* (Job 15:8). All too often I hear people expounding on their own little ideas of God's supernatural realm. Sometimes they'll mouth the philosophies of misguided teachers, the empty words of people with very small spirits.

WHO TOLD ADAM AND EVE THAT THEY WERE NAKED?

When Adam and Eve were sneaking around the Garden, hiding from God after disobeying Him, God called to them, "Adam, where are you?"

Adam answered, "Well, er, I hid from you because—well, um, I was naked."

God responded with this galaxy-shaking question: *"Who told you that you were naked?"* (See Genesis 3:10.)

God is saying to us today, Who *told* you that having a small spirit won't hurt you and diminish your life? Who *told* you not to dare search out the magnificent depths and riches of Heaven and the spirit realm? Who *told* you angels have not been set in charge over you? Who *told* you miracles, signs, and wonders aren't yours today?

Think of it. There was Adam, the first human, moving in a world of physical and spiritual perfection! Adam romped and played with and communed with God all day long. And then one day, in spite of the immense and unfathomable riches that were his, he committed the one act he was told not to ever do. Adam listened to the wrong voice. *"Who told you that you were naked? Where did you get such an idea? Who told you?"* You can hear the holy furious heartbreak that is contained in those words. God asks us the same question when we limit His power, when we doubt the miracles He wants to rain upon us, when we choose a middle-of-the-road spiritual life.

✛ ⊕ ✛ ⊕ ✛ ⊕ ✛ ⊕ ✛

Who told you God is not a God of miracles?

✛ ⊕ ✛ ⊕ ✛ ⊕ ✛ ⊕ ✛

DANIEL, A MAN OF FAITH

Daniel was an example of a man who refused a middle-of-the-road spiritual life. He was radical! Middle-of-the-road spirituality never worked for him. Even as a captive in Babylon, Daniel was a 100-percent man for God, and, therefore, he was spiritually prepared to receive divine impartations from Heaven. Angels come to those who are prepared!

King Nebuchadnezzar was tormented with dreams his diviners and wise men couldn't interpret. Daniel received the interpretations from God in a night vision and the king was so grateful he promoted Daniel to be the ruler over the whole province of Babylon as chief administrator over all his wise men. Daniel ecstatically praised the Lord for this answer from God:

> *Blessed be the name of God for ever and ever, for wisdom and might are His. And He changes the times and the seasons; He removes kings and raises up kings; He gives wisdom to the wise and knowledge to those who have understanding.* **He reveals deep and secret things;** *He knows what is in the darkness, and light dwells with Him!"* (Dan. 2:20-22).

Daniel was *accustomed* to the supernatural. The false religions of his time were rampant, and magicians, diviners, enchanters, sorcerers, and soothsayers were seemingly everywhere. The supernatural was part of everyday life. The exception was that Daniel was a man of faith in the one true God and to Him he was fiercely faithful. He was prepared for a divine impartation from God. And this was just the beginning.

Daniel faced King Nebuchandnezzar with the utmost of confidence when he informed him that his sorcerers, magicians, and astrologers were of no help. The only One who could truly reveal the meaning of the king's dreams was God. *"…Wisdom and power belong to Him,"* Daniel proclaimed. *"…It is He who reveals the profound and hidden things; He knows what it in the darkness, and the light dwells with Him"* (Dan. 2:22 NAS). Through Daniel, God not only revealed what the king saw, but the meaning of his visions and dreams. To this day we study the interpretation Daniel gave of these dreams and the kingdoms to come, all the way to the final rule by Messiah, the millennium, and the eternal future.

Witchcraft cannot interpret the mind of God. Astrology cannot prophesy or build a healthy society. Philosophy and religion cannot build our spirits, nor can they endow us with spiritual gifts to supernaturally touch and change ourselves and our world. History has taught us a thing or two—wisdom and power belong to God.

A PASTOR'S EXPERIENCE

Former Vineyard pastor Gary Oates sat in a church service one day on a mission trip to Brazil, feeling desperate. He had hit a rock-bottom point in his life and ministry, and he was in a wretched state. He met a man who had been caught up before God's throne on several occasions, a man who experienced angelic visitations on a regular basis. Gary asked how he might activate the same experiences in his life.

The man answered simply, *"Present yourselves and your the members of your body as instruments of righteousness [holiness] to God"* (Rom. 6:13 NAS).

I'd like to point out that this verse is an absolute key to entering the realm of the Holy Spirit and expanding your spirit. The members of our bodies include our five senses—our eyes being open to spiritual visions, our ears being open to hearing from God, our mouth being ready to speak to God and speak forth His words, our nose breathing in the fragrance of Heaven, and our hands doing what we see Him doing.

That night in the tent meeting in Brazil, after surrendering himself, body, soul and spirit to the Lord, Gary had a visitation of the Lord and the angelic host. The gifts of the Spirit were ladled upon him and his wife and their international miracle ministry was launched.[8]

A single divine encounter with the King of kings and His angels can catapult you into a spiritual life that is richer and deeper than you ever thought possible.

ENDNOTES

1. Stephen F. Noll, *Angels of Light, Powers of Darkness*. (Downers Grove, IL: InterVarsity Press, 1998).

2. Sister M. Faustina, *Diary of Sister M. Faustina Kowalska: Divine Mercy in My Soul.* (Cracow, Poland: Misericordia Publications, 2003).

3. Noll.

4. Ibid.

5. Ibid.

6. Ibid.

7. Karl Barth, *Church Dogmatics.* Trans. Geoffrey Bromiley. (Edinburgh: T&T Clark, 1960).

8. Gary Oates with Robert Paul Lamb. *Open My Eyes, Lord.* (Dallas, GA: Open Heaven Publications, 2005).

chapter 23

GOD'S ANGEL
GOES BEFORE YOU

WHEN God appeared to Moses in a flame of fire in the midst of the burning bush, He told him, *"I will certainly be with you"* (Exod. 3:12). Later, as God gave the Israelites His commandments in the desert, He said, *"Behold, I send an Angel before you to keep you in the way and to bring you into the place which I have prepared"* (Exod. 23:20), and *"My Angel will go before you"* (Exod. 23:23).

God never sends you anywhere without going before you and preparing the way. His angels go before you for two purposes: 1) The angels help to keep you on track and to hold on to you lest you trip and lose sight of your goal. The angels gently steer you in the right direction and keep you safe along the path, no matter how rough or difficult the path may be. 2) The angel of the Lord will, without fail, deliver you to the precise place that God has already prepared. See your prayers as having already been answered and your work as having already been accomplished, because if it's in the eternal mind of God, you can't fail. You are fulfilling what He has gone ahead and prepared for you. Your job is to rise up with new resolve and take Him at His Word. It's your call.

MOSES' IMPOSSIBLE TASK

When God told Moses to go to Pharaoh and demand that he let his people go, Moses was stunned. What an idea. He had been living in the wilderness for 40 years after running from Pharaoh for his very life, and now God was telling him to return and make a demand so preposterous even he, Moses, couldn't believe it. The very thought of Pharaoh freeing his slaves who built the pyramids, temples, roads, monuments, and Egyptian houses seemed ludicrous. It was beyond imagination. Could God be serious? Moses was, after all, an Israelite, a *shepherd*. He was a despicable creature in Pharaoh's eyes. In fact, he was no better than a *worm* in Pharaoh's eyes. In Pharaoh's eyes he was less than human. The Hebrews were Pharaoh's slaves, and they were treated no better than animals. Besides, Moses was a traitor who should have been executed 40 years ago. How could he dare make any kind of demand of the great and powerful god-man, Pharaoh? How could he dare even stand before this god-man who was the most powerful ruler in the world?

I've often thought what a transcendent and terrible moment that must have been for Moses when God spoke to him and gave him his orders to go to Pharaoh. Moses, a humble man, felt incapable and intimidated by such an outrageous order. He reminded God he had a speech impediment on top of the other little obstacles, such as being filth in Pharaoh's eyes. Moses' people were lowly, unwashed slaves, and Pharaoh saw himself as the polished god of the universe. How *dare* Moses—?

Moses obeyed, however. Perhaps he thought the same thing Job had expressed, *"Though He slay me, yet will I trust Him"* (Job 13:15), and with his brother Aaron as the spokesman, he forged ahead with his assignment. It's frightening and intimidating to reach out into the unknown and to be bold in the face of extreme danger. But here is something we must realize. When God gives a directive, He never sends us alone. In addition to human partners, we have the Holy Spirit and His holy angels going before us, partnering with us to accomplish what we think is impossible.

When God dispatched Moses with his orders to go to Pharaoh, He also dispatched a legion of angels to accompany him on the mission. Their intention was to see miracles performed to the glory of God. Moses and Aaron did not march into Pharaoh's royal halls alone. God's mighty angels went before them and surrounded them as they spoke the words God gave them to speak.

The angels filled the room as Moses transformed the rod God gave him into a serpent.

Angels sang out God's will upon the snakes of Pharaoh's charmers and watched carefully as Moses' serpent devoured them.

The angels *helped* Moses with his dreaded task by convincing Pharaoh to let his people go.

Not once, but seven times Moses and Aaron made the journey to Pharaoh's court to infuriate the ruler with their demands. God's angels guided and directed their every word and step. The terrible events that were put upon Egypt, including death to the first-born sons, were accompanied by a host of angels.

It was the *angel* of death that visited Egypt at Passover.

FOLLOWING GOD'S WILL

Moses and Aaron never faced Pharaoh alone, and you never have to face your calling alone. Your angels surround you, guide you, prod you, and keep you along in the path of the divinely orchestrated will of God. Angels eagerly partner with you because you speak the same God-language, and you share the same God-passion.

Jesus could completely submit to the Father's will for one reason: He knew His Father. He knew He was perfectly and completely loved by His Father. Your willing submission to the will of God grows out of this same secure understanding of who He is. The love relationship between Jesus and the Father is demonstrated to us at the public revelation that came forth when Jesus was baptized. An audible voice from heaven was heard, *"You are My beloved son in Whom I am well pleased..."* (Mark 1:11 NKJV). And again God's voice is heard from Heaven on the Mount of Transfiguration, *"This is My beloved Son, whom I love; in whom I am well pleased"* (Matthew 17:5 NKJV).

Jesus' selfless willingness to give up His life in a most cruel and inhumane crucifixion for our sakes is expressed in his prayer: *"Father, I want those You have given to me to be with me where I am, and to see my glory, the glory you have given me because you loved me before the creation of the world"* (John 17:24 NIV).

Angels live in the love of Jesus and so do we.

> *Bless the LORD, you angels,*
> *Who excel in strength, who do His word,*
> *Heeding the voice of His word.*
> *Bless the LORD, all you His hosts,*
> *you ministers of His, who do His pleasure*
> (Psalm 103:20-21).

Notice that it says, *"Bless the Lord, all you His **hosts**,"* plural. *Hosts,* not *host*. You think there are a few little angels flipping around here and there helping children go to sleep or giving you a hand in finding your keys? No, no. That's not a true picture of the open Heaven at all. God has more angels than can fill the galaxy. They're tremendous in number. When we open the eyes of our spirit, we can see the angelic hosts, but even then, our spirit-eyes can't take in the whole panorama of their multitude.

ANGELS AND THE SPOKEN WORD

When God gives a word to you, when He gives you an order or a directive, He releases His angels to help you carry out that word. The angels assist with the Holy Spirit's miracles, signs, and wonders, but they wait for you to activate God's will by faith. This is when you become partners in performing His will. Angels perform God's Word; they love His Word, not only His written Word, but his spoken Word as well. Angels love God's prophetic Word. They *live* in His Word.

It's always wonderful to see the angels surrounding prophetic preaching. They sometimes stand right on the platform behind or alongside the person who is preaching. Angels sometimes stand listening along the walls or they will post themselves in the balcony or along the back of the room, hallway, or sanctuary. At times they'll stand sentry at the four corners of the building. Sometimes they dance as the preaching goes on. Always in worship they sing along with

God's children. I've seen them fade away, too, when a false chord has been struck by a given word.

Is It Too Much to Ask?

Angels surround the throne of God, singing His praises continually throughout all eternity. Heaven resounds with praises to the Holy One.

Jesus waits for our embrace and longs for a mutual lavishing of love so He can lavish more upon us. He wants our love. I think often of how He said to me with great consternation, *"Is it too much to ask that My children honor me?"* He wants to be at the center of our celebrations, recreations, parties, work, and play.

Love carries love in its pocket.
Love wears love like a cape.
Love is the skin of love.
Love is the heart of love, the essence of itself.
Love makes us one in a fusion that's eternal.

✦ ⊕ ✦ ⊕ ✦ ⊕ ✦ ⊕ ✦

Miracles are only to be found in
the love of God.

✦ ⊕ ✦ ⊕ ✦ ⊕ ✦ ⊕ ✦

Sometimes we go to church just to give the Lord a little pat on the back. We sing a few songs (or maybe we *listen* to a few songs because they're in a key too high to sing or we don't feel like singing), and once that's over and we've heard the announcements, the vocal solo, and shelled out our money for the offering, we sit down for the message, which we may or may not catch. At the end of the message, if there's an altar call for special needs, we are somewhat stirred, so we get out of our seats to go forward to beseech the Lord for our special needs.

No wonder we scratch at the back door of glory, wondering why we don't have supernatural experiences in the Spirit. The Lord wants our worship and our life. John 4:24 tells us to worship the Lord in spirit and in truth, and when we worship the Lord in spirit and in truth, the angels join us. The sound fills the heavens and the earth. Worship the King of Glory! In worship the Lord inhales the incense of praise. Miracles are only to be found in His love.

chapter 24

PROPHESY

I asked the Lord why He didn't just cut satan off at the chase when satan fell from Heaven, taking a third of the angels with him. Why didn't the Lord fry him on the spot, him and his lousy demons? In that way Adam and Eve would never have been tempted, they would not have sinned, and God would have had a perfect world.

No, it was His will that we be made beautiful through *overcoming*. That's what He tells us. It was His will from the beginning that we be made beautiful to Him through being like Him In order to be *like* Him we have to submit ourselves to Him, fuse our spirits to His, and become, for one thing, *strong*.

He tells us, "I could have called ten thousand angels…," reminding us that He doesn't take easy routes. He never has.

"Be strong in the Lord and in the power of His might" (Eph. 6:10).

God wants an army. He wants an army of lovers who will join Him in His will and His work. The earth was formed just for Him. Every leaf, every stone, every star, every wave of the sea, and every human soul were created just for Him.

I ask and He answers. He tells me to watch the seasons. He tells me to be very discerning, for He is showing Himself in many ways now on the earth. We will recognize Him in the spirit, He tells me. He is being very subtle now in these days, and He tells me to *practice* seeing with the eyes of my spirit, which is what is meant by Ephesians 1:18: "… *the eyes of your understanding being enlightened.*" We are to expect great and terrible things, and we are to be familiar with the moving of angels. We are to look for His hand in all things on the earth. We are to look with our *spirit eyes.*

He tells me to watch closely in this hour because He is going to do a lot of dividing of the wheat from the chaff. Ministries that are functioning without Him are going to experience a dire purging. He said that He is coming for the final altar call. He will appear, and we, at that moment, will have no other gods before Him. There won't be time for the imitators, the false prophets, and the liars to toss their barbs.

First will come signs and wonders in the sky and on earth. There will be dramatic changes in the weather. Fire will rain from the sky, meteors will hurtle toward earth, and the earth will tremble. People will run here and there for protection, but there will be no place to hide. But *"everyone who calls on the name of the Lord will be saved…"* (Joel 2:32 NIV).

We will need each other. Here is where the Body of Christ gets close. Here is where we are no longer Lone Rangers, but a real body of believers who will be caring for and praying for each other with all purity of heart and soul. There will be no division among God's people when that time comes.

Then He will lift us up into His arms and we will become who we were meant to be from the beginning.

The earth will not be destroyed. It will remain. But at that time the earth will remain without God's children. God's Spirit will brood over the face of the waters, ready to empower all those who call upon His name at that time.

God will intervene before humans try to destroy what God created for Himself.

The Lord says, *"You asked why didn't I destroy satan before Adam was tempted?"* He tells me that He *did* destroy satan from the beginning. It was finished then. *"Did My Son not say, 'I have destroyed the works of the devil'?"*

It is finished. Rise and shine for your light has come.

chapter 25

FIFTY THINGS GOD'S ANGELS AREN'T AND DON'T DO

Angels don't earn wings.

Angels aren't good people who died.
(People can't become angels.)

Angels don't cry.

Angels don't answer your prayers.
(God answers prayers.)

Angels don't beg.

Angels don't sleep.

Angels don't worry.

Angels don't desire attention.

Angels don't act on their own accord.

Angels don't marry, nor are they given in marriage.
(See Mark 12:25.)

Angels don't have baby angels.
(They don't procreate.)

Angels aren't dead people.

Angels don't mediate.
(There is one mediator between God and man—
Jesus Christ. (See 1 Timothy 2:5.)

Angels aren't cute, little, fat babies with wings. (Cupid is not an angel.)

Most angels don't have wings,
except the cherubim and seraphim.

Angels don't sin.

Angels don't wear halos. They shine with the glory of God.

Angels don't have temper tantrums.

Angels don't talk dirty.

Angels are never afraid.

Angels never pout.

Angel's don't stress out.

Angels aren't human. (Your Aunt Tess is not an angel. Neither is your husband.)

Angels aren't impatient.

Angels don't gossip or find fault.

God's holy angels don't act as "spirit guides," nor do they "channel," as certain cults would have you believe. Those are false spirits who have nothing to do with God, the Holy Spirit, or Jesus Christ. God's angels live to serve God, not people.

Angels don't act of their own accord.

Angels don't heal. (Jesus dispatches them in His name to do His bidding, which may include healing, but they cannot heal in and of themselves.)

Angels don't deliver us from evil. (They are charged by God in all their actions.)

Angels aren't pretty blonde ladies with large, sweeping wings.

Angels don't appear as females
as often as they appear as males.

Angels don't age.

Angels don't die.

Angels are not subject to the limitations of humans.

Angels are not naive and are incredibly wiser than humans.

Angels are not as smart, wise, or powerful as God is.

Angels aren't God.
(Angels are servant-beings created by God.)

Angels aren't omnipotent.
They aren't all-powerful. Only God is omnipotent.

(Jeremiah 32:27 NIV: *"I am the LORD, the God of all mankind. Is anything too hard for me?"*)

Angels aren't omnipresent. They can only be one place at a
time. Only God is omnipresent.

Angels aren't omniscient. They do not know everything. Only
God knows everything. (See 1 John 3:20.) Regarding preaching
and certain spiritual matters, *"the angels long to look into these
things"* (see 1 Pet. 1:12 and Eph. 3:10). For example, God
knows when Jesus will return to earth, but the angels don't.

Angels don't have the power to create. They are created beings.

(Colossians 1:16: *"For by Him* [Jesus Christ] *all things were created:
things in heaven and on earth, visible and invisible, whether thrones or
dominions or principalities or powers. All things were created through Him
and for Him."*)

Angels don't leave footprints.

Angels don't always show up immediately. (Remember
Daniel 10?)

Angels don't receive any hint of worship. Angels are not to be worshiped.

Angels don't languish around on clouds all day playing harps. They are mighty spiritual warriors. Jesus is the embodiment of their victory and ours as well.

Angels don't eat manna. (Manna is called "angel food" in Psalm 78:25 to denote its superior excellence.)

Angels don't *ever* interfere with God's will.

God's angels will never bring you personal messages from dead persons.

Angels aren't wimps. They possess superhuman physical strength. An angel rolled away a stone weighing almost a ton from in front of Jesus' tomb.

chapter 26

A CLOSE LOOK AT THE CHARACTERISTICS OF ANGELS

Do Angels Have Personalities?

THE answer is yes. You may be surprised to discover that angels definitely have personalities. Let's take a look

First, angels have a will.

We know this from the Word. God's angels lovingly *choose* to worship, praise, and serve the Lord Jesus. It's their *choice*. How do we know this? Because when satan plummeted from God's Presence, one-third of the angels chose to plummet with him. Two-thirds of the heavenly host remained loyal to the living God, the Creator of the universe.

The angel of the Lord *chooses* to encamp around those who fear Him, and *chooses* to deliver them. (See Psalm 34:7.) Why? Because the angels love God and God loves us. Angels are not God's automatons. As we see by the fall of satan, they have a will and a choice. God's angels *choose* to do God's will. And they willingly choose to partner with us to fulfill any and all of God's desires.

Second, angels are intelligent.

Everything angels do is genius—from guiding to protecting to helping to judging. Deuteronomy 33:2 tells us that angels assisted God when the law was mediated to Moses at Mount Sinai: *"The LORD came from Sinai, and dawned on them from Seir; He shone forth from Mount*

Paran, and He came with ten thousands of saints [holy ones, angels]; from His right hand came a fiery law for them...."

And Hebrews 2:2-3 tells us: "*For if the word spoken* through angels *proved steadfast, and every transgression and disobedience received a just reward, how shall we escape if we neglect so great a salvation...*". Galatians 3:19-20 tells us the law was appointed through angels. It was an angel who spoke to Moses on Mount Sinai to give him the oracles of God. Acts 7:53 talks about the law made by the direction of angels.

In Matthew 13:41 the Son of Man sends out His *angels* to gather out of His kingdom all things that offend and those who practice lawlessness. In Matthew 13:49 the *angels*, at the end of the age, come forth and separate the wicked from among the just. Angels are beautiful and good, but they are not naïve, little cupids. You don't trifle with an angel; you don't dare lie to an angel or try to fool an angel. They can tell a hypocrite and a phony a light year away.

Third, angels have emotions.

Angels dance. They sing. They shout. They're talented musicians and thrill Heaven with their passionate music. When Christ was born, a multitude of the heavenly host appeared to the shepherds in the fields around Bethlehem. The angels filled the night air with their exuberant praises. "*Glory to God in the highest, And on earth peace, goodwill toward men*" (Luke 2:14). They were excited! They were happy! (The Greek definition of *goodwill* here refers to God's sovereign good pleasure. The angels were joyfully announcing to all humankind God's peace and the glorious gift of His good pleasure.)

This proclamation of Christ's birth was brought by the angels with great fanfare and holy enthusiasm. The multitudes of angels—too many in number to humanly fathom—didn't all show up for such a spectacular sky show in order to give a ho-hum speech. No, they were loud, effervescent, excited. Not one shepherd cupped his ear with, "Eh? I didn't quite catch that. Say again?"

It was a spectacular sky show of sights and sounds!

The angels were there to rejoice when Jesus was born, and angels were on the scene rejoicing when God created the world. (See Job 38:4-7.) They also rejoice today when one lost soul comes home to God by opening their heart to Jesus. (See Luke 15:7.) Angels love to rejoice! The angel Gabriel introduced himself to Zacharias with, *"I am Gabriel, who stands in the presence of God"* (Luke 1:19). What could be more ecstatic than that?

They love to join in our worship, not only our corporate worship, but our private worship, too. Sometimes while worshiping the Lord, you may hear a high-pitched sort of whistling sound; at other times you will hear a kind of clicking and thumping and a staccato, jubilant, crackling sound. Then there's the whirring like hummingbird wings, or the sound of a thousand-voice, six-part harmony human chorale. You may hear wind instruments at times and bells, too. The sound I love best is the child-like gentle singing, much like giggling and laughing; it is so sweet and pure and happy.

I wish I could express to you how much fun God's angels can be. We tend to think of angels as supremely serious beings wearing supremely serious robes and speaking in supremely serious tones that knock our socks off and make us feel supremely serious. I've seen angels playing merily, laughing, and even tickling each other. I've seen angels dancing, cavorting, hopping around, playing, having fun. You see, they are not burdened with fear or worry! Let me tell you something that happened to me the other day. I was walking in the woods with the Lord as it was getting dark and He said to me, "I'll race you to the trail head."

I thought about it for about two seconds and blurted, "That's not fair. You're God! I'll lose! (ha ha)."

I guess the Lord knew that the sky would be pitch black in a matter of minutes so away we ran. With barely any effort at all I was whizzing through the woods to the trail head and the Lord was running right next to me. He laughed as we ran. Surrounding us in the dark were several angels giggling and cheering us on. I arrived back to my car in the blackest of night with the Lord's arms around me and the angels still giggling.

I pray with all of me that you discover the same sense of fun and delight in knowing the Lord and His angels. These encounters and experiences will fortify you in the bleak hours of life. In trying times I simply remember the sound of His laughter and I'm jerked into His reality, not mine.

Angels are curious.

First Peter 1:12 tells us that the angels desire to look into the very things of God that have been given to us. This tells us that angels are smart and they have a holy curiosity which feeds their holy intelligence. Don't ever forget how incredibly intelligent and *experienced* God's angels are. There's not a language they don't speak, not a thought or dream they're not familiar with; yet, they are as curious as babies. They are always learning. Always alert and 100 percent present. Angels don't daydream, mind-wander, or zone out. An angel will never tell God, "What was that? Sorry, I wasn't paying attention."

Angels are disciplined.

Angels know the Word of God inside and out. They study it more thoroughly than we do. David called them *"mighty ones who do His word"* (Ps. 103:20 NAS).

Angels always do the bidding of God as His messengers. They never react with, "Later, Lord. I'm busy," or like Scarlet O'Hara, "I'll think about that tomorrow." They obey the Lord instantly without question. Why do they obey instantly? Because angels *know* the Lord. They live in the sublime Presence of God, the Father, and Jesus Christ, the Son. The Holy Spirit constantly draws me closer to God. He is always calling me to come closer, closer, closer. The angels constantly nudge me closer to Him. *"Draw near to God and He will draw near to you"* (James 4:8).

I'm sometimes awakened in the middle of the night by a bell ringing. It's a faraway sound, gentle, but distinct. It's my angel, Sam, sounding the bell to rise and pray. Ri-i-i-ng goes the bell. "Get up, Marie. The Lord wants to meet with you." *Closer, closer.*

Can we be as disciplined as angels? Maybe it's not too terribly painful to get out of a cozy bed at 4 A.M. to pray, but how about when we're hit with discouragement or loneliness? How about those fits of depression that seem to overtake us at times? It's at those times that we must fling ourselves into the Lord's arms and cry out for His Presence to overtake us. Bill Johnson says he is always 15 minutes away from depression. I love him for sharing that. A great man of God wrestles with depression? It proves again how desperately we need the Presence and power of God in our lives at all times!

No angel of God is *ever* depressed or wiped out. Why? Because they are living in the Presence of God always. Divine discipline is to remain fixed in the Presence and power of God.

Angels are patient.

One day the angel of the Lord appeared to a weak man who was easily lured by material wealth above obeying the voice of God. The man's name was Baalam. On this particular day Baalam was riding along on his donkey with motives so displeasing to God that He had to send His angel to stop him. The angel of the Lord took His stand right in front of Baalam so he couldn't pass. Baalam was unable to see the angel, but guess what? The donkey saw him! Three times the angel of the Lord repositioned himself to stop Baalam from going further. The donkey was stunned at the sight of the angel and couldn't move. Baalam beat the donkey for coming to a standstill. God gave the donkey a human voice so the donkey spoke to Baalam and asked why he was hitting him. (Think about it. A donkey hollers out at you, "Do you MIND? That HURTS.") That's when Baalam's eyes were opened and he saw the angel standing before him with a drawn sword ready to harpoon him with it.

The angel told Balaam he would have killed him if it weren't for the donkey. A *donkey* saved his life. The angel had shown as much patience as he wished to (see Num. 22:22-35), and Balaam was in big trouble.

I think about this story a lot. I tell the Lord, "If you can put a human voice and human words into the mouth of a *donkey*, please can you use me, too, please?" The *donkey* saw the angel of the Lord. The *donkey* spoke God's words to Balaam. Let us take heart.

Angels are meek.

One who is meek is humble, gentle, patient, easily imposed on, and submissive. Jesus called Himself *"meek and lowly in heart"* (Matt. 11:29), so we find rest from our cares and our burdens in Him. Angels reflect the personality and character of Jesus. Angels, who are greater and wiser than humans, are humble. "Humble" means we think more of others than ourselves. To be humble means to truly love people to the point of being willing to die for them. Paul and the apostles show us this kind of love, this humility embodied in Christ.

Angels don't rise up in "holy indignation" and carry on about their rights and who did them wrong. They do not pound their chests demanding respect. They do not fling insults at the devil or spiritual authorities. The archangel Michael refused to speak evil of satan but called on the Lord to do so. (See 2 Peter 2:10-11 and Jude 8-9.)

Angels have boundless energy.

Angels need no rest. Look at how the seraphim carry on in this passage in Revelation 4:8: *"The four living creatures, each having six wings, were full of eyes around and within. And they do not rest day or night, saying: 'Holy, holy, holy, Lord God Almighty, Who was and is and is to come!'"*

Angels do not wipe out. They don't gasp for breath while climbing hills or running a race. When the angel moved the stone in front of Jesus' tomb, he didn't complain of blisters or a pulled tendon. The angel sat down on the stone with another angel friend and became a welcome committee for Mary and the women.

Angels, just like God, haven't had a wink of sleep since the creation of the world.

Angels have existed since before the creation of humankind, which is, give or take, over 5,000 years. (A debatable figure, I know). Angels do not have to study history. They have lived every minute of it. They understand and are very familiar with human behavior in every possible situation in every possible culture in every possible time and era. We can do nothing to surprise an angel. They've seen it all. Every war, rainfall, snowfall, and tsunami; every birth, every death, every dinner, breakfast, every murder, every marriage—think of it. Angels know about every school of psychology, every cult and religion, every plant, herb, drug, flower, tree, weather pattern, and animal that was ever created. They have been here since Adam breathed the breath of God into his lungs of dust. Angels have seen it all. That's why God used them to deliver His commandments to Moses. Angels intimately know the heart and mind of God, and they know what He thinks of us.

ACCEPTED BY ANGELS

When I'm hard at work in my writing studio I sense the presence of angels. An angel might stand behind me; he is enormous, taller than my ceiling, and his presence fills the room. Always when the angels appear, I feel a sense of confidence and peace. Immediately the tension I may not have been unaware of in my shoulders and neck relaxes and I feel washed over with complete acceptance and a renewed sense of well-being. I breathe in the beauty of the moment and stop working to praise and thank the Lord, and when I resume my place at my desk, it feels as if I had spent hours lying on the beach listening to the surf. I feel loved and beautiful, and best of all, I feel accepted.

Something the Lord is teaching me and I am learning from being in the presence of angels—and not just when I'm in the presence of one angel, but when huge crowds of angels appear before me—I feel *accepted*. Not a single hair of fault-finding or distrust, competition, or intimidation wafts into the air. It's an unfamiliar sensation, this one of *total* acceptance, and one I want to hold onto, become familiar with, live in, and project to others.

The angels' personalities are *accepting*. To feel so much pure, divine acceptance is like taking a bath in a sunrise. Everything feels good, my eyes in their sockets feel good, my toes in their shoes feel good, my fingernails, hair, skin, teeth—every part of me feels good. The world is beautiful. I'm accepted. My mind, brain, thoughts, and hopes—all of me is accepted.

I *know* I'm accepted by the Lord. I know, of course, that *He* loves me. I know what it is to bask in His love, to clothe myself in His love, to wear, eat, chew, walk, talk, run, sleep, breathe, taste, touch, feel, see, hear, and love His love, but romping with the heavenly realm adds a deeper dimension to this reality. So much acceptance boggles one's head.

The arrival of angels in my daily life has me always flopping to my knees to worship the Lord, because in their presence it becomes flagrantly obvious how short of holiness I fall. I like to put all my negative traits in the past tense and say I *once* was nervous, fearful, given to impatience, etc., but I still have to work on those things. It's extravagantly rewarding to know the Lord loves us in our weaknesses (sins), and apparently, so do His angels!

Acceptance is so beautiful. As a Christian counselor, I am always grieved at how alone people can feel in this life. Earning approval is a full-time job for some. (Ask me. I've got the T-shirt.) It's hard work to be accepted, to say the right things, to do the right things, to look the right way, to fit in. Whew! I get tired thinking about it. God wants our spirit-eyes opened and asks us to experience His complete acceptance 24 hours a day. That's worth repeating.

ARE DEMONS SMART?

Demons aren't exactly stupid. James 2:19 tells us, "*You believe that there is one God. You do well. Even the demons believe—and tremble.*"

Second Timothy 2:26 gives us a warning to help people who need correction and proper direction so that they may know the truth and "*...escape the snare of the devil, having been taken captive by him to do his will.*"

God has no mercy for demons, the fallen angels, who chose to leave His glory and follow evil. *"And the angels who did not keep their proper domain, but left their own abode, He has reserved in everlasting chains under darkness for the judgment of the great day"* (Jude 6).

Demons are cunning, vicious, and powerful spirit forces. They are liars and murderers. Their only goal is to steal, kill, and destroy. Jesus said, *"The thief does not come except to steal, and to kill, and to destroy. I have come that they may have life, and that they may have it more abundant-ly"* (John 10:10). Jesus tells us lovingly and longingly again, *"The Son of Man did not come to destroy men's lives but to save them"* (Luke 9:56).

The demons have emotions—mostly rage, hate, and fear. They can never rejoice. To say a demon is happy when they complete an act of deadly damage is ridiculous. They are never happy. Nothing gives them pleasure, nothing. Demons are *never* satisfied. When the demon-possessed man ran into Jesus, the demons possessing him went ballistic, screaming in terror, *"What have we to do with You, Jesus, You Son of God? Have You come here to torment us before the time?"* (Matt. 8:29). Then they begged to be cast out, into a herd of pigs. So Jesus cast them screaming and shrieking to their drowning deaths in a herd of pigs. They are still shrieking in hell.

The devil and his demons hate God and they hate you. Ephesians 4:27 cautions us not to give place to the devil. James 4:7 tells us to submit ourselves to God and *"Resist the devil and he will flee from you."* This literally means to take up arms against him and his cohorts. We're given battle instructions in Ephesians 6:10-18 beginning with: *"Be strong in the Lord and in the power of His might."* We're to put on the whole armor of God so we can stand against every wile of the enemy of God.

The good news is: we win! Almighty God prevails now and forever. *"And fire came down from God out of heaven and devoured them. The devil, who deceived them, was cast into the lake of fire and brimstone where the beast and the false prophet are. And they will be tormented day and night forever and ever"* (Rev. 20:9-10).

References

MacArthur, John, Editor. *The MacArthur Study Bible.* Nashville: Word Bibles, 1997.

Ryrie, Charles C. *Basic Theology.* Wheaton, IL: Victor Books, 1987.

chapter 27

THE FIRE OF GOD

I

T'S a beautiful California autumn afternoon and friends are coming for dinner. We're having whole stuffed bass. I prepared potato leek soup from scratch and it waits in the fridge in a bowl I got from my great aunt Anna. A loaf of sourdough bread twirls and kneads in the electric bread maker, a gift from a student. I've chopped the romaine, trimmed the broccoli, shredded the Parmesan, stuffed the fish, readied the sauce, fussed over the tiramisu, and saved two hours for Jesus (which is not really enough time). I cover the tiramisu with a plate, pop it in the fridge next to the stuffed whole bass and my leek soup prepared from scratch and head out the front door for my hike with God.

I decide to head for the beach. I'm hungry for sky and the sound of the surf pounding on the sand. I'm hungry for God.

ISN'T THAT HOW IT'S SUPPOSED TO BE?

But then I am always hungry for God. I'm hungry for God every minute I breathe. Isn't that how it's supposed to be? Isn't that how we were created? "I just want to be where You are," I'm always telling Him. Nothing in this life in the earth realm compares with being caught up in the Spirit and experiencing the holy Presence of the Lord, *absolutely nothing compares with the divine and glorious experience of being caught up in the Presence of the Lord.*

I quiet my heart and turn my mind off to everything around me. I walk in expectancy. My steps become deliberate and yet extremely light. I feel as though my feet somehow float over the sand; my body is lithe, almost weightless. I concentrate on Him. Still, still, be still my heart. I see my angels. They encircle me. The surf and the sky are gone. Jesus appears.

Caught Up

I am at once caught up in the Spirit, as the Lord lifts me into the heavenlies. He wants to show me more of Heaven and His purposes. We soar through space into a distant place that appears to be *on fire*. We're high up—high, high up. I look down at the fiery place below and I see the flames splattering every which way. I'm holding onto the Lord as down, down we go until we settle on our feet. I look about and realize the Lord has set me down right in the middle of the fire! We are engulfed in flames! I don't like this. I begin to search for a way out. It is quite terrible, this fire. I don't like it at all. I know in the natural that I am walking on the beach in my natural body—but my spirit-body is engulfed in flames!

My natural body is now discomfited. I begin to gag, choke, spew up what tastes like charcoal in my mouth. My knees sway, but I try to keep my natural body upright with one foot moving ahead of the other, weightless on the sand.

In the Spirit I am now in the center of a raging fire! I don't feel any pain in the flames, but it is terrifying, and I think, *"OK, that's enough. I think I get it."* I know lots of Scriptures regarding fire; for instance, I think of Shadrach, Meshach, and Abendnego in the flames. I think of the verse that says, "He made His ministers a flame of fire;" I think of "He will baptize you the Holy Spirit and fire." I think of "He is like a refiner's fire;" I think of "When you walk through the fire you shall not be burned." O Lord. I think of the burning bush, the flaming mountain, and Jesus' words, "I came to send fire on the earth." If Jesus weren't with me, I'd be calling for my mommy. I really want out.

What is the Lord doing to me? This is one raging, horrible fire, not your friendly bonfire like one might see on the beach at night. This fire screams agony!

The Lord Jesus is right beside me. He says without words, *"But I thought you said you wanted to be where I am."* Those words send me spinning because all the times I've prayed to be right where He is at work, all the times I've decreed to only follow where He leads, the jillions of times I've prayed to stand in the center of His will, and to be unmovable, seeking His heart and purposes only—I never imagined *this*.

No, not fire.

The flames howl around me. I look over at Jesus; He is unscathed, at peace, smiling. And I am a wreck of nervous blood and bones. I feel like a child. "Are we there yet?" I think I have to tinkle. I just want out. The Lord speaks again without words, *"Marie, do you feel the flames on your body?"*

I pause. "No, I do not feel the flames burning my body."

"Smell your hand, Marie. Any smoke on you?"

I was certain I stunk. I'd have to shower for a week, and me with guests coming for dinner, the sourdough baking even while I was baking in open flames on the beach.

I sniffed my hands. No smell of smoke.

"Why then do you feel afraid?" He thinks to me. *"I am right here beside you."* Again I feel like a child, less than a child actually. A child would have more faith. I am thankful that the Lord is with me; I am *thrilled* that the Lord is with me and we are standing in the all-encompassing, screeching flames together, but I want to ask Him (*implore* is more the word) to get me out of there, like now! I want to ask that, but I don't. Instead, I begin to praise Him, thank Him, and quote all the verses I can about peace and trust. I squint over at Him and there He is, my Lord and Master, dancing in the flames. *Dancing!*

I begin to dance with Him. What else can I do? I am not overcome with peace, that's for sure, but the Lord is dancing in the fire, so I dance in the fire. Fire is everywhere—everywhere! I cannot see anything but fire. *We are in the belly of a fire storm.* And the Lord of all Heaven and earth doesn't pull me out, doesn't rescue me. We are remaining in the belly of the fire storm for I don't know how long. Too long. It has been a very long time. We are dancing away in the middle of this pit of fire,

ing, dancing, and I am not exactly joyful. He is joyful, though. He is nonplussed, happy as ever, free, and even *laughing*. I love His holy Presence more than life, but here? Here, Lord, in a fire storm?

Finally, eons later, He lifts us out of the flames. *"So, Marie. Any scorching on you? Any sign of burns?"* Of course not. I am totally whole, and in fact, everything about me feels stronger, braver. My skin has the texture of something metallic, gold maybe. I felt as though I had gone through the Zechariah 13:9 refiner's fire.

Here is what He wants us to know. There is no fire that we go through that He is not there with us. He dances through our flames. He says, *"...When you go through the flames they will not scorch you."* He is like a refiner's fire (see Malachi 3:2).

There is no fire storm here on earth that He has not overcome. And He will use the refiner's furnace to purify.

My friends arrive for dinner and in the midst of conversation and fellowship with them I can still hear the thunder of those flames, I can still feel the unthinkable heat of the flames. My friends eat the leek soup I prepared from scratch, the fish, the veggies, the fresh baked sourdough bread, and as we gobble up our tiramisu, I think to myself that the Lord will surely hoist me back into the flames again one day because it is there that I need to learn more of the dance, His dance of overcoming. I need to learn to laugh in the midst of the fire! In the flames I learn to stomp down under my feet the fire of defeat and every peril under the sun—even death.

O Lord, I willingly permit the fire of purification to have its work in me, and may the fire of suffering make me beautiful for You…. I'm willing to dance, Lord. I'm willing to dance.

The night has ended, the friends have gone home, the dishes wait in the sink, the house is quiet. I can't see my angel, but he is here guarding the woman of God and her house. I thank the Lord for His and my angel. I have eaten but now I am hungry. I'm desperately hungry. I am hungry for God. It's how it's supposed to be.

chapter 28

GREATER WORKS
THAN THESE

WHAT would you say if I told you again that you can know God's living Presence 24 hours a day? Am I just one of those far-out folk who live their lives in a trance or in a cave somewhere in Narnia? I'm here to tell you that the surrounding and indwelling Presence of Almighty God for *each of us* should be, and can be, with us all the time. This is the *normal Christian life*. But you have to make it normal.

When you're with your spouse or a best friend, you may not be concentrating on their presence every second you're with them, but you're experiencing their presence, you're *living in it*; they're there with you and you know they're there. The same is true with God. You may not be concentrating on His presence 24 hours a day, but you are with Him 24 hours a day nonetheless. The way to get your 24-hour protection (no, not like a deodorant) is to purpose every hour to embrace His Presence. The way I do it is actually by calling out the days, hours, and minutes. I mean, I practice being aware of where I am and Who I am with. *"Behold I am with you always,"* He says. And I say back to Him, "I'm with you always, too, at one o'clock, two o'clock, at three o'clock…".

I teach my students to "be aware." I tell them to listen to life, to *observe and record*. The best meaning of awareness is to take God's Presence into our daily, hourly consciousness.

When the Bible says that He gives His angels charge over you, it doesn't say angels have charge over you only at night when you're sleeping, or only when you're learning how to wind surf or rock climb, or when you're driving home late at night with the gas gauge on empty. Your angels have charge over you all the time, period.

Ask. Receive. Be aware.

In John 14 Jesus wanted His disciples to understand that they would never be alone again in their entire lives. He told them He would pray that the Father would send them another Helper to abide with them *forever* (speaking of Holy Spirit). He told them that His Holy Spirit would empower them and they would do greater works than He did. What an incredible statement! Read it for yourself: *"Most assuredly, I say to you, he who believes in Me, the works that I do he will do also; and greater works than these he will do, because I go to My Father"* (John 14:12).

Let's look deeper into these words of Jesus. You are never alone and, furthermore, First Corinthians 6:20 says that you are bought with a price. Jesus didn't die for Himself. He doesn't cover Himself with His blood. He covers *you*. He did it all for *you*. That means that God paid a huge price to bring you close to His heart. The price He paid was to send Jesus, His Son, to the earth as a man to be mutilated, tortured, and murdered, taking the sin of the whole world on His innocent body.

> *For you were bought at a price; therefore glorify God in your body and in your spirit, which are God's* (1 Corinthians 6:20).

The Real You, Like Samuel

You have given your heart to the Lord. You've surrendered your life to Him. You believe in and love the Lord Jesus with all your heart. I know you do. You belong to God, body, soul, and spirit. Let me ask you a question. Does this mean His Spirit can move through you as He wills? Does this mean He can nudge you in any direction and you'll obey without flinching a muscle? Does this mean He can wake you in the middle of the night like He did the boy Samuel and you'll answer, "Speak, Lord, your servant is listening"? Does this mean you'll believe the angel when he calls you a mighty man or woman of valor even when you're feeling like a total wimp like Gideon?

If you've given the Lord full permission to have full control over your life, can He do in and through you the same works that Jesus did on earth? Let me reword that. Will you permit the Lord to do in you and through you the same works that Jesus did on earth?

IMAGINE THIS...

Imagine for a minute that it is God's will that the gift of healing be poured out freely on the land. He is not depending on a handful of evangelists to do the work, He's decided to spread the gift of healing out like wildfire all over the land. In order to do this, He speaks through His Spirit and sends out His angels to every church and fellowship, to every prayer meeting, Bible study, Sunday school class, youth group, home fellowship, and wherever two or three are gathered in His name. He sends His angels to every shopping mall, hospital, city, village, and nation.

Imagine this picture. Men, women, and children are laying hands on their sick friends and neighbors, they're praying over their families, church members, and strangers; they're praying and they're believing because Jesus said, *"If anyone loves Me, he will keep My word; and My Father will love him, and We will come to him and make Our home with him"* (John 14:23). These words have given them holy boldness. Christians are praying for hurting people everywhere, just everywhere. They're not waiting to be commissioned or for a financial budget or for programs to be in place, because they are obeying the Holy Spirit. They aren't waiting for a sign from Heaven or permission from a person or department leader before praying for the sick; they are *believing* and they're praying! They are dabbing oil on the foreheads of the sick and dying and they are praying. They are *believing*. Miracles are taking place because God's children are praying. They are answering the call of God and going to the nations in droves. Healings, miracles, signs, wonders, and the salvation of millions are taking place not only in Africa and India and remote villages of the Far East, but in the U.S., Canada, South America, Australia, New Zealand, and even Israel—in rich areas and poor areas, far and near.

The lame are walking, the blind are seeing, the deaf are hearing. Millions of souls are entering God's household and are receiving miracles because people are praying and believing. Cancer victims are rising up whole, leukemia is banished; diabetes, macular degeneration, heart disease, arthritis, aneurysms vanish, paralyzed legs dance again, brain disorders and diseases of the nervous system are healed, feet and hands and skin are healed. Healed, all healed!

"He who believes in Me, the works that I do he will do also... " (John 14:12)

We have taken those words to heart and we *expect* to do the works He did. We expect it of ourselves because we love Him and because He lives, we live. Because the Father lives in us. Because He said, *"He who loves Me will be loved by My Father, and I will love him and manifest Myself to him"* (John 14:21).

"Manifest Myself to him!" Jesus manifests Himself through miracles, healings, and a wondrous outpouring of love through you. *Raising the dead is a normal occurrence.*

EXPECT

✤ ⊕ ✤ ⊕ ✤ ⊕ ✤ ⊕ ✤ ⊕ ✤

Listen and expect.
Live in wonderous expectation of the miraculous.

✤ ⊕ ✤ ⊕ ✤ ⊕ ✤ ⊕ ✤ ⊕ ✤

The angel Gabriel could communicate with Daniel because *God knew Daniel would listen.* God knew Daniel's heart. Daniel lived in expectation of the miraculous. Zacharias, on the other hand, had a problem listening when God brought him a message through the resplendent Gabriel. Another person who had a listening problem was Balaam. Amazingly his donkey not only saw and heard the angel, but was stunned senseless at his presence. Jesus told us that it is the Father's good pleasure to give you the Kingdom. (See Luke 12:32.) We need to see and hear what He reveals. We need to be stunned senseless once in a while.

See your life as a daily adventure. See your day as being loaded with divine appointments that are arranged by Holy Spirit. Let His love be known through you. The world desperately needs God. Let them find Him through you!

You are not only able to do what Jesus did, you are called to produce greater works than He did. Greater in volume, greater in scope, greater in terms of time, and greater in terms of impossibility.

Don't let anyone tell you that you don't have power. Don't let anyone tell you that you're alone in this life. Don't let anyone tell you that angels aren't working on your behalf day and night. Don't let anyone tell you that won't do great and mighty works in this hour. Right now. Today.

You were born for such a time as this.

chapter 29

THAT DAY

I look up into the sky, and I see an explosion of light. The light becomes larger and erupts in a million dazzling shoots and beams cascading across the heavens. The form of a man appears in the midst of the firmament. I cover my eyes, for the sight is like fire and the air itself seems to be afire. I peer out between two fingers. I see the King of kings encircled in a swath of flaming white clouds, accompanied by brilliant, riotous flashes of lightning. His arms are outstretched and He moves across the banks of clouds, as though He is stepping over small beach dunes; behind Him is His throne and beneath Him is the Earth, His footstool. He fills the sky with His luminescence, and, in fact, everywhere the eye can see is at once filled with impossible light and glory.

Glory surrounds the cosmos, the earth, and glory engulfs humanity, overtaking all creation. A thunderous shout rises up from the heavens as angels, in royal apparel, shining as the sun, shout and play their instruments hailing their king, escorting the Lord of lords to earth. Gabriel, the most resplendent of the angelic host, heralds the King, crying out in triumph with the blast of God's trumpet. The universe holds its breath and human time stops for the Chosen. A roar is heard from the earth as it opens its jaws, releasing those it has swallowed in death. A jubilant cry of freedom is heard from the bowels of the earth. I run like crazy toward Him who stands upon the clouds with His arms open. I run to Him and I jump into His outstretched arms. I am lifted up by Him, but I am not the only one running into His arms. Millions upon millions of us leap into Him and are at once wrapped in the luxuriant affinity of His immense esteem and love. The fabric of

His sumptuous robe folds around us and we are at once enraptured, rolling around in the robe, laughing, being lifted up as light as joy, covered in His breath, unaware that the earth is now behind us.

chapter 30

THE FINAL WAR
WITH THE ANGELS

NOW it begins. The shout of the Lord is heard from the ends of eternity. The time has come and the battle has begun. The powerful archangel Michael, the mighty, leads his angels forward. I see an army of angels move forward like many galloping mountains. Each soldier is as tall as a mountain range with peaks stabbing the ribs of heaven. We, God's human army, throw on our armor, and shouting our victory songs, we partner with the warrior angels. Fully trained are we, and we plunge ahead with our swords swirling and fire in our nostrils. We cannot be defeated, for we are *"…strong in the Lord and in the power of His might."* The beast wages war on earth and in the heavens. I hear the words of our brother Paul reminding us that our struggle has never been against flesh and blood.

The enemy of God loses miserably. The shrieking of manacles can be heard as they split and break, and the cloven hooves of demons tear about, crushing one another in a frenzied, defeated last stand. God's radiant beings cast down the gruesome demon forces, breaking their eyes, and sending their teeth clattering. The head of the dragon is chopped off; its putrid smell of hate extinguished. Lightning flashes, thunder blasts, hail smashes the neck of deceit. The seducer of all humanity is destroyed.

Before all creation is a great white throne and seated upon it is the One before whom earth and sky bows. *"I make all things new,"* He announces to creation, and we fall forever at His feet.

The fifth angel has sounded his trumpet and a star falls from sky to earth. The sound is torturous. It is satan himself hurling down. The angel is given the key to the shaft of the abyss, which is the prison of demonic hordes. Scorpion demons leap like hail, greedy to destroy the unsuspecting and naive humanity. But the trumpet call of the seventh angel will be sounded and God's mystery, His secret design, His hidden purpose, as He announced to His servants the prophets, will be fulfilled, accomplished, and completed.

An angel, glorious in light, swings down, carrying the key to the abyss and in his other hand are heavy chains. The angel seizes the dragon, the ancient, stinking serpent who is the devil, and he binds him up for a thousand years. Satan is thrown into the abyss, locked and sealed, forbidden to deceive the nations and nature for a thousand years.

Within His eminence and majesty, a city blooms, the luster of it like jewels, jasper, gold, sapphire, agate, emerald, quartz, beryl, diamond, and amethyst. Can you see it? It is our hallowed consecrated Jerusalem, our home.

The angelic host of Heaven has been prepared for this moment. The children of God have been prepared for this moment. All of creation has been prepared for this moment.

Our angels are utterly ecstatic. We have fulfilled our human destiny to overcome. Our angels fill the halls of heaven, shouting praises to the exalted King who sits in glory on the throne. We are lifted up and seated beside Him in His throne. (See Revelation 12:7-9, 21; 9:1; 10:7; 20:1-3; 3:21.)

Look! It's *you* who is seated there. It's *you* who is sitting with the King of kings. He is kissing your face and whispering love-words in your ear. You are home at last.

Welcome home.

ANGEL REFERENCES
IN THE BIBLE

ANGEL: (The Greek word, *Aggelos*, means messenger, envoy, one who was sent, a messenger from God to bring tidings.)

Genesis 16:7; 16:9; 16:10; 16:11; 21:17; 22:11; 22:15: 24:7; 24:40; 31:11; 48:16

Exodus 3:2; 14:19; 23:20; 23:23; 32:34; 33:2

Numbers 20:16; 22:22; 22:23; 22:24; 22:25; 22:26; 22:27; 22:31; 22:32; 22:34; 22:35;

Judges 2:1; 2:4; 5:23; 6:11; 6:12; 6:20; 6:21; 6:21; 6:22; 6:22; 13:3; 13:6; 13:9; 13:13; 13:15; 13:16; 13:16; 13:17; 13:18; 13:19; 13:20; 13:21; 13:21

1 Samuel 29:9

2 Samuel 14:17; 14:20; 19:27; 24:16; 24:16; 24:16; 24:17

1 Kings 13:18; 19:5; 19:7

2 Kings 1:3; 1:15; 19:35

1 Chronicles 21:12; 21:15; 21:15; 21:15; 21:16; 21:18; 21:20; 21:27; 21:30

2 Chronicles 32:21

Psalms 34:7; 35:5; 35:6

Ecclesiastes 5:6

Isaiah 37:36; 63:9

Daniel 3:28; 6:22

Hosea 12:4

Zechariah 1:9; 1:11; 1:12; 1:13; 1:14; 1:19; 2:3; 2:3; 3:1; 3:3; 3:5; 3:6; 4:1; 4:4; 4:5; 5:5; 5:10; 6:4; 6:5; 12:8

Matthew 1:20; 1:24; 2:13; 2:19; 28:2; 28:5

Luke 1:11; 1:13: 1:18; 1:19; 1:26; 1:28; 1:30; 1:34; 1:35; 1:38; 2:9; 2:10; 2:13; 2:21; 22:43

John 5:4; 12:29

Acts 5:19; 6:15; 7:30; 7:35; 7:38; 8:26; 10:3; 10:7; 10:22; 11:13; 12:7; 12:8; 12:9; 12:10; 12:11; 12:15; 12:23; 23:8; 23:9; 27:23;

2 Corinthians 11:14

Galatians 1:8; 4:14

Revelation 1:1; 2:1; 2:8; 2:12; 2:18; 3:1; 3:7; 3:14; 5:2; 7:2; 8:3; 8:5; 8:7; 8:8; 8:10; 8:12; 8:13; 9:1; 9:11; 9:13; 9:14; 10:1; 10:5; 10:7; 10:8; 10:9; 11:1; 11:15; 14:6; 14:8; 14:9; 14:15; 14:17; 14:18; 14:19; 16:3; 16:4; 16:5; 16:8; 16:10; 16:12; 16:17; 17:7; 18:1; 18:21; 19:17; 20:1; 21:17; 22:6; 22:8; 22:16

ANGELS:

Genesis 19:1; 19:15; 28:12; 32:1

Job 4:18

Psalms 8:5, 68:17; 78:25; 78:49; 91:11; 103:20; 104:4; 148:2

Matthew 4:6; 4:11; 13:39; 13:41; 13:49; 16:27; 18:10; 22:30; 24:31; 24:36; 25:31; 25:41; 26:53

Mark 1:13; 8:38; 12:25; 13:27; 13:32

Luke 2:15; 4:10; 9:26; 12:8; 12:9; 15:10; 16:22; 20:36; 24:23

John 1:51; 20:12

Acts 7:53

Romans 8:38

1 Corinthians 4:9; 6:3; 11:10; 13:1

Galatians 3:19

Colossians 2:18

2 Thessalonians 1:7

1 Timothy 3:16; 5:21

Hebrews 1:4; 1:5; 1:6; 1:7; 1:7; 1:13; 2:2; 2:5; 2:7; 2:9; 2:16; 12:22; 13:2

1 Peter 1:12; 3:22

2 Peter 2:4; 2:11

Jude 1:6

Revelation 1:20; 3:5; 5:11; 7:1; 7:2; 7:11; 8:2; 8:6; 8:13; 9:14; 9:15; 12:7; 12:7; 12:9; 14:10; 15:1; 15:6; 15:7; 15:8; 16:1; 17:1; 21:9; 21:12

Angel references in the Bible

ANGEL'S:

Revelation 8:4; 10:10

ANGELS':

Psalms 78:25

HOLY ONES: (Holy means set apart.)

Job 5:1; 15:15
Psalm 89:7
Daniel 4:13; 17, 23; 8:13
Jude 14
Acts 7:53
Galatians 3:19
Hebrews 2:2

WATCHER: (Means vigilant—on the order of reconnaissance agents.)

Many eyes references:
Daniel 4:13;
Ezekiel 1:18
Revelation 4:6, 8

HEAVENLY HOST: (God's heavenly army, military force to fulfill His will and war in His battles.)

2 Chronicles 18:18
1 Samuel 17:45
Psalm 86:6,8

SONS OF GOD: (Created beings created by Jesus Christ, the Son of God.)

Colossians 1:16
John 1:3
Hebrews 1:2,10
Job 1:6; 2:1; 38:7

MINISTERING SPIRITS: (Spirit-servants.)

Hebrews 1:14

THE LORD OF "HOSTS": ("Hosts" are His heavenly attendants, His military force and His agents that accomplish His will.)

Exodus 12:41

1 Samuel 1:3; 1:11; 4:4; 15:2; 17:45

2 Samuel 5:10; 6:2; 6:18; 7:8; 7:26; 7:27

1 Kings 18:15; 19:10; 10:14

2 Kings 3:14; 19:31

1 Chronicles 11:9; 17:7; 17:24

Psalms 24:10; 46:7; 46:11; 48:8; 59:5; 69:6; 80:4; 80:7; 80:14; 80:19; 84:1; 84:3; 84:8; 12; 89:8; 103:21; 148:2

Isaiah 1:9; 1:24; 2:12; 3:3; 3:15; 5:7; 5:9; 5:16; 5:24; 6:3; 6:5; 8:13; 9:7; 9:132; 9:19; 10:16; 10:23; 10:24; 10:26; 10:33; 13:4; 13:13; 14:22; 14:23; 14:24; 14:27; 17:3; 18:7; 18:7; 18:7; 19:4; 22:12; 19:16; 19:17; 19:18; 19:20; 19:25; 21:10; 22:5; 22:12; 22:14; 22:14; 22:15; 22:25; 23:9; 24:23; 25:6; 28:5; 28:22; 28:29; 29:6; 31:4; 31:5; 37:16; 37:32; 39:5; 44:6; 45:13; 47:4; 48:2; 51:15; 54:5

Jeremiah 2:19; 5:14; 6:6; 6:9; 7:3; 7:21; 8:3; 9:7; 9:15; 20:12; 23:15; 23:16; 23:36; 25:8; 25:27; 25:28; 25:29; 25:32; 26:18; 27:4; 27:18; 27:19; 27:21; 28:2; 28:14; 29:4; 29:8; 29:17; 29:21; 29:25; 30:8; 31:23; 31:35; 32:14; 32:15; 32:18; 43:10; 42:2; 44:7; 44:11; 44:25; 46:10; 46:18; 46:25; 48:1; 48:15; 49:5; 49:7; 49:26; 49:35; 50:18; 50:25; 50:31; 50:33; 50:34; 51:5; 51:14; 51:19; 51:33; 51:57; 51:58

Hosea 12:5

Amos 3:13; 4:13; 5:14; 5:15; 5:16; 5:27; 6:8; 6:14; 9:5

Micah 4:4

Nahum 2:13; 3:5

Habakkuk 2:13

Zephaniah 2:9; 2:10

Haggai 1:2; 1:5; 1;7; 1;9; 1;14; 2:4; 2:6; 2:7; 2:8; 2:9; 2:9; 2:11; 2:23; 2:23

Zechariah 1:3; 1:3; 1:3; 1:4; 1:6; 1:12; 1:14; 1:16; 1:17; 2:8; 2:9; 2:11; 3:7; 3:9; 3:10; 4:6; 4:9; 5:4; 6:12; 6:15; 7:3; 7:4; 7:9; 7:12; 7:13; 8:1; 8:2; 8:3; 8:4; 8:5; 8:6; 8:6; 8:7; 8:9; 8:9; 8:11; 8:14; 8:14; 8:18; 8:19; 8:20; 8:21; 8:22; 8:32; 9:15; 10:3; 12:5; 12:5; 13:2; 13:7; 14:16; 14:17; 14:21; 14:21

Malachi 1:4; 1:6; 1:8; 1:9; 1:10; 1:11; 1:13; 1:14; 2:2; 2:4; 2:4; 2:7; 2:12; 2:16; 3:1; 3:5; 3:7; 3:10; 3:11; 3:12; 3:12; 3:14; 3:17; 4:1; 4:3

HEAVENLY HOST: (Divisions of an army, heavenly armies.)

Genesis 2:1; Genesis 32:2
Joshua 5:13; 5:14; 5:15
1 Kings 22:19
2 Kings 17:6; 21:3; 21:4; 21:5
2 Chronicles 14:13; 18:18; 33:3; 33:5
Nehemiah 9:6
Isaiah 34:4
Jeremiah 8:2; 19:13; 33:22
Daniel 8:10
Zepheniah 1:5
Luke 3:13
Acts 7:42

MAN: (Angels described as in the appearance of a man.)

Ezekiel 10:8; 40:5
Daniel 5:5; 8:16

Additional copies of this book and other
book titles from DESTINY IMAGE are
available at your local bookstore.

Call toll free: 1-800-722-6774.

Send a request for a catalog to:

Destiny Image® Publishers, Inc.

P.O. Box 310
Shippensburg, PA 17257-0310

*"Speaking to the Purposes of God for this
Generation and for the Generations to Come."*

**For a complete list of our titles,
visit us at www.destinyimage.com**